Sagwitch

Shoshone Chieftain, Mormon Elder

1822–1887

"Se-go-witz and his bride in her rabbit-skin robes— Utes." Evidence
suggests that this image may actually be of Chief Sagwitch and his last wife,
Beawoachee. Photograph and caption by Salt Lake City photographer
Charles R. Savage, ca. 1875–1880. Copy of original stereographic image
courtesy LDS Church Archives, Salt Lake City, Utah.

Sagwitch

Shoshone Chieftain, Mormon Elder

1822–1887

Scott R. Christensen

Foreword by Brigham D. Madsen

UTAH STATE UNIVERSITY PRESS
LOGAN, UTAH

Utah State University Press
Logan Utah 84322-7800

Typography by WolfPack

Cover design by Barbara Yale-Read

10 9 8 7 6 5 4 3 2   01 02 03 04 05 06 07 08 09 10

Library of Congress Cataloging-in-Publication Data

Christensen, Scott R., 1963–
  Sagwitch : Shoshone chieftain, Mormon elder, 1822–1887 / Scott
R. Christensen ; foreword by Brigham D. Madsen.
    p. cm.
  Includes bibliographical references and index.
  ISBN 0-87421-270-7 (pbk.)
  ISBN 0-87421-271-5 (cloth)
  1. Sagwitch, 1822–1887. 2. Shoshoni Indians—Kings and rulers
Biography. 3. Mormons—Utah—History—19th century. I. Title.
  E99.S4S243 1999
  979.2004'9745—dc21
    [B]
                                        99-6663
                                        CIP

To my parents

For instilling in me
the love of learning and a sense of integrity

To my grandparents

For engendering in me
an appreciation for the past

To Megan

For her love, faith, patience,
encouragement, and support

To A. J. Simmonds

For introducing me
to Sagwitch and to my profession

To Sagwitch

Although I never met you,
you taught me a great deal

Contents

Illustrations

Foreword

Brigham D. Madsen

For too long, Utah writers and others interested in the history of Native Americans in the state have emphasized Indian-white relationships in the central and southern regions south of Salt Lake City. The story of the numerous Northwestern Shoshone who inhabited northern Utah has been strangely neglected. Only in the past twenty years, with the publication of a few relevant books and articles, has attention been directed to these forgotten people and the tragic slaughter of almost three hundred of their men, women, and children at the hands of Colonel Patrick Edward Connor's California Volunteers on the bloody day of January 29, 1863.

Sagwitch, one of the surviving chiefs of that unforgettable massacre, is at last finding his rightful place in Utah history. Author Scott R Christensen begins his narrative by describing the various bands of Northwestern Shoshone, whose almost two thousand members populated the northern and eastern shores of Great Salt Lake and the river valleys of this region. The largest group lived in Cache Valley under war chief Bear Hunter; Little Soldier's band occupied the lower reaches of Weber River and the area near present Ogden, Utah; Sagwitch directed his people to winter camps on the lower Bear River just above its entry into the Salt Lake; Sanpitch also led his group to camps along Bear River below Bear River Gorge; and, finally, Chief Pocatello supervised the hunting and gathering activities of his band along the northern shores of Great Salt Lake from Grouse Creek in present northwestern Utah to the eastern shores of the Salt Lake.

There was, of course, much mingling of these closely related people as they traveled on their annual hunts for wild game and, especially, native grass seeds. The cattle herds of Mormon settlers would destroy much of that grass cover by 1861. The loss of this basic food source led to starving periods, demands for food from the settlers of northern Utah, and, eventually, attacks by young Northwestern Shoshone men on travelers through their homelands. The resulting calls for troops to secure the emigrant roads led directly to the massacre at Bear River near the Utah-Idaho line and west of Franklin, Idaho. The author describes this defining moment in the life of Sagwitch, who escaped the butchery with a wound to his hand.

During the years immediately following the Bear River Massacre, the chief and his band came to know the Mormon residents of Brigham City, near the Indians' winter camping grounds, and eventually joined the Church of Jesus Christ of Latter-day Saints under the tutelage of Mormon missionary George Washington Hill. These were trying times for Sagwitch and his people, as they tried to adapt their lifestyle to the new white civilization, knowing that they would have to cease their roving habits and learn to be settled farmers. Hill worked hard to find farms for his Indian charges, finally settling on some acreage near present Bear River City, Utah, close to the traditional winter camps of Sagwitch's people.

The Indian agents at the Fort Hall Reservation in southeastern Idaho did their best to persuade the Sagwitch band to join other Northwestern Shoshone who by 1870 had settled on the reserve established for the Shoshone. But Sagwitch and his followers refused to leave their traditional homeland and preferred the help offered by Hill to establish them on farms along Bear River as committed members of the Mormon Church.

Unfortunately for Hill and his Indian followers, the farm was located just a few miles from the gentile (non-Mormon) town of Corinne, which was a freight transfer station on the Central Pacific Railroad. The Corinnethians (as they liked to call themselves) were virulent opponents of anything Mormon. Frightened by their local newspaper editor, who saw the Mormons and their Indian converts as a real menace to their town, they called on the territorial governor to dispatch troops from Camp Douglas in Salt Lake City to evict the Shoshone from their farms and send them to Fort Hall. Eventually, three companies of troops arrived. The frightened Indians abandoned their farms and tipis and were able to save only a meager harvest of wheat and of peas. Everything else was lost.

The "Corinne Indian Scare" temporarily alienated Sagwitch and his Mormon followers from missionary Hill, who had been caught in the same Corinne trap as his converts. But Sagwitch reconciled with his Mormon friends and, with the other Mormon converts in his band, finally settled at the small Shoshone colony of Washakie, located in southern Malad Valley just north of the Utah-Idaho border. For the rest of his life, Sagwitch, now an elder in his church, remained faithful to Mormonism. With his followers, he farmed at Washakie on several thousand acres purchased in 1880 by the LDS Church for its Shoshone adherents. The author paints a detailed and comprehensive picture of life at Washakie and the efforts of its Indian leaders to maintain a branch of the church there. Sagwitch died in 1887, but his descendants and other members continued farming at the Malad Valley settlement until economic opportunities in World War II enticed nearly all the congregation to relocate at such nearby communities as Brigham City and Ogden. Most of the descendants of the Washakie Mormon branch live in these communities today, where they do their best to maintain their original culture, language, and history so that it will not be forgotten.

Sagwitch: Shoshone Chieftain, Mormon Elder, 1822–1887, is an excellent contribution to the history of Utah's Native Americans and is especially significant in reminding Utahns that the Northwestern Shoshone were a vital part of the Great Salt Lake region before the coming of Mormon settlers and that they are still a vibrant part of our culture today.

Preface

Chief Sagwitch remained hidden from my world for many years. I knew nothing of the Shoshone leader or of his significant legacy, even though I was born and raised in a portion of his homeland—Cache Valley, Utah. Some years ago, as I was searching for a meaningful topic for a graduate thesis, Utah State University Archivist A. J. Simmonds suggested that I consider writing a historical biography of one of Cache Valley's most significant men. He then rehearsed for me bits and pieces of Sagwitch's story learned through many years of his research as a historian. Captivated by what he shared, I yearned to know more. I was hooked.

I soon learned that nineteenth century Mormon pioneers had named two mountain peaks and a basin, located between the Cache and Ogden valleys in northern Utah, for Sagwitch and that the Daughters of Utah Pioneers in nearby Paradise called their local branch the Sagwitch Camp in his honor. Clearly he had been well known and important to Cache Valley's early Anglo population.

Then I read Brigham Madsen's *The Shoshoni Frontier and the Bear River Massacre* and was horrified by the accounts of brutal killings and rapes of Sagwitch's people by Colonel Patrick Connor's federal troops.[1] About three hundred Indians—and, in a sense, the Northwestern Shoshone as a nation—perished on that bloody field near present-day Preston, Idaho, in January 1863. In the history of the trans-Mississippi West, the Bear River Massacre, as the event has come to be known, has the ignominious reputation of representing the single greatest loss of Indian lives in battle with whites.[2]

The soldiers wounded Sagwitch at the massacre and killed many in his family, but the story did not end there. As I continued to sift through historical sources, I discovered evidence that he had homesteaded on land near Portage, Utah. Other sources documented

Sagwitch's activities at Washakie, a small Mormon-sponsored Indian community in Box Elder County, Utah, and his service in helping to build the Mormon Temple in Logan, Utah. His descendants included Moroni Timbimboo, the first Native American bishop in the Church of Jesus Christ of Latter-day Saints, and Bruce Parry, for many years the director of Utah's Bureau of Indian Affairs.

It became clear that Sagwitch's life had been replete with sorrow, triumph, and, most of all, change. In addition, his story was far more complex and his decisions farther reaching than I had ever supposed. I came to see Sagwitch as a visionary leader at a time when forced change and acculturation demanded that the Shoshone make significant, life-altering choices. The opportunity to learn more about the man who made many of those decisions for his people became irresistable.

At his birth Sagwitch's life was encompassed by the traditional patterns of a hunting and gathering society, but the advent of fur-trapping mountain men and, after 1847, of hosts of EuroAmerican settlers forever altered that world. Sagwitch adapted successfully. He witnessed the near annihilation of his people at the Bear River Massacre and ended his life as a devoted, temple-attending Mormon elder. In studying Sagwitch, I not only learned about one of Utah's most significant native sons but also had the opportunity to view, as experienced in one man's life and survival, all of the forces of accommodation and acculturation that came during this pivotal time in Northwestern Shoshone history.

Finding Sagwitch was made easier by the significant support of his own descendants—especially his granddaughter-in-law Amy Hootchew Timbimboo and great-granddaughter Mae Timbimboo Parry. I sincerely thank them and other Sagwitch descendants for allowing me to research and write about their ancestor. I consider it an honor to have had that opportunity. I thank them for the documents, information, and photographs they shared with me and for the many other kindnesses they extended.

I am grateful to Clyde A. Milner II, Charles S. Peterson, and former Utah State University archivist A. J. Simmonds for their knowledge and insight, for their enthusiasm for this project, and for their genuine and constant interest in my success as a historian. I consider them to be mentors and dear friends.

I am also grateful for the support of my colleagues in the Archives of the Historical Department of the Church of Jesus Christ of Latter-day Saints. I thank the Historical Department for allowing me access to many documents I needed for this biography. I thank my friends and former colleagues at Utah State University's Merrill Library Special Collections and University Archives for their support and interest in my research and for access to numerous sources. I am also grateful to the staffs of the Utah State Historical Society, University of Utah Marriott Library Special Collections Department, and National Archives and Records Administration. Each institution had carefully preserved pieces of Sagwitch's life and graciously made them available to me.

I appreciate the staff at USU Press for their help and patience with this project, especially editor John Alley. His insights and suggestions were absolutely critical as the book came together.

Finally, I am grateful to my family for nurturing my youthful interests in history and for always encouraging me in my pursuits. I especially thank my dear wife, Megan, for her love and faith in me. I also thank Megan and my little son Jacob for enduring many lonely evenings and weekends while I pursued Sagwitch through the nineteenth century.

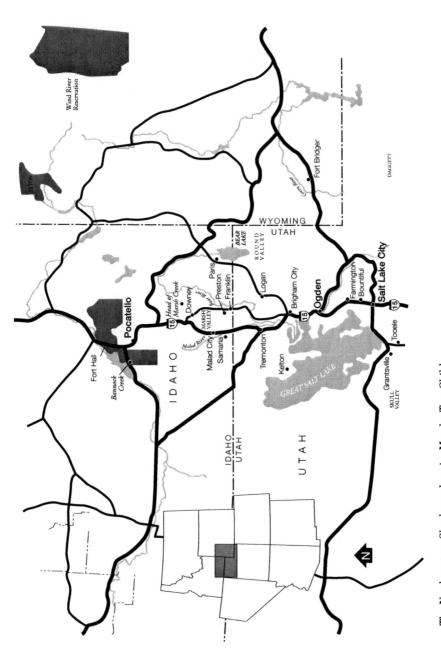

The Northwestern Shoshone domain. Map by Tom Childs.

I have been intimately acquainted with the white man from my childhood, and I appeal to any white man, when have I played false with him? Whom have I killed or even threatened to kill? I have ever been an advocate for peace. I abhor war to-day. I want peace. I sue for peace to-day. I want to be at peace with all men . . . The white man roams the mountains all over, hunting for the gold and silver that belong to the Indian until he sells the land. When have I interfered with him? The railroads pass through my country and have scared the game all away. Still I have made no objection to this, nor do I want to. I want all men to have the privelage of doing as they like, undisturbed, and make all the money they can, and all I want is peace and to be allowed to make a farm in a small, very small, portion of the country I have always lived in and still want to live in.

Sagwitch, August 31, 1875

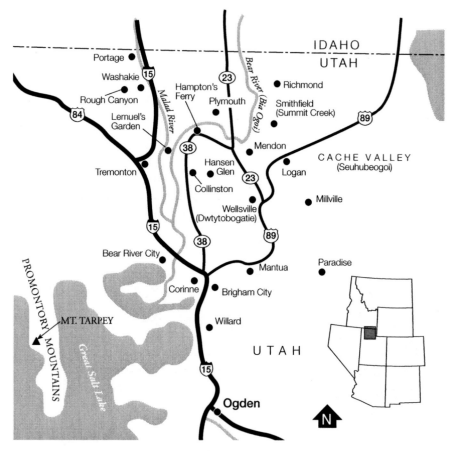

Northwestern Shoshone homelands in northern Utah. Map by Tom Childs.

Introduction

Newe, "The People"

For activities concerning the entire band—trips to Wyoming for bison, antelope hunts, and festivals— Segwitc, assisted somewhat by Kwudawuatsi, was chief.
Julian Steward, ethnographer, 1938

Sagwitch's people experienced great historical and cultural changes during his lifetime. In fact, by the time of his death in 1887, they had incorporated into their culture many elements from neighboring Anglo societies. Much of Shoshone society remained distinctive, however, and the history of Sagwitch and his people cannot be understood without knowing something of his people's traditional way of life and prehistoric origins in the intermountian region.

We now know more than ever about the history of Numic-speaking peoples—including the Shoshone, Ute, and Paiute—in the Great Basin and Colorado Plateau. Yet many questions remain. Linguists have documented relationships between Numic tongues and a number of other Indian languages, including Nahuatl, which was spoken by the Aztecs. They have classified these languages as the Uto-Aztecan language phylum.[1] It now seems likely that, over several hundred years, Numic-speaking people first migrated from northern Mexico to parts of southern California and Nevada, and then, centuries later, beginning in about A.D. 1000, expanded into the eastern Great Basin.[2]

Some scholars have postulated that the Fremont, an agriculture-based people who lived throughout much of present-day Utah between A.D. 400 and A.D. 1300, are ancestors of the Shoshone. Recent archeological and anthropological studies dispute that connection by showing that the Fremont and Numic peoples had separate and

1

distinct cultures, although their occupation of parts of Utah appears to have overlapped for a few hundred years. Evidence at a few Utah sites suggests that these two very different groups may have interracted.[3]

As Numic-speaking people settled throughout the intermountain region, their common language began to diversify into related yet distinct tongues. Those who settled in central and northeastern Nevada, northern Utah, western Wyoming, and southern Idaho came to speak Shoshone, while others in southern Nevada, southern and eastern Utah, and Colorado became speakers of the closely related Ute and Southern Paiute languages. A third branch of Numic was spoken by the Northern Paiute of western Nevada and southern and eastern Oregon and the Bannock, who associated with the Shoshone in southern Idaho.

The Shoshone followed an age-old nomadic lifestyle that included annual cycles of travel; families resided somewhat consistently in the same region throughout the year, returning to specific resource areas during particular months or seasons. They came to be identified as different groups based upon where they lived and traveled. Nothing except blood relations, however, bound them to live in a particular place or to associate with any specific group. Lines of social demarcation beyond the family were of little importance to the Shoshone. Political divisions were, however, of importance to government agents, who eventually classified several Shoshone groups as distinct tribes or bands. These included Sagwitch's Northwestern Shoshone, at home in parts of southern Idaho and in northern Utah's Bear River, Cache, and Bear Lake valleys; the Northern Shoshone, frequenting northern Utah and south and central Idaho; the Eastern Shoshone, centered in western Wyoming; the Lemhi, living along the Salmon River in central Idaho; and the Gosiute, or Western Shoshone, residing in western Utah and along Utah's northwestern boundary line.[4]

Anthropologists in the twentieth century have grouped Shoshone speakers differently, placing them within three larger groups, namely, the Western Shoshone, residing in eastern and central Nevada and northwestern Utah and including the Panamint Shoshone, the Gosiute, and the Weber Ute; the Northern Shoshone, occupying most of south and central Idaho and parts of northern Utah and including the Lemhi; and the Eastern Shoshone, in western Wyoming.[5]

Scholars generally consider the Northwestern bands, including Sagwitch's people, to be part of the larger Northern Shoshone subdivision, although they lived near and shared many traits and relationships with Western Shoshone groups.[6] For this study, it is helpful to understand that most nineteenth-century writers referred to Sagwitch's people as the Northwestern Shoshone and, prior to the 1863 Bear River Massacre, further divided them into bands led by Pocatello, Sanpitch, Little Soldier, Bear Hunter, and Sagwitch. While the Northwestern Shoshone shared many common ties with the Western Shoshone, they also associated significantly with the Northern and Eastern Shoshone. That meant that Sagwitch's people enjoyed a greater range of travel due to full utilization of the horse and the adoption of some plains culture lifeways. Nowhere is this mixing of Shoshone traits more evident than in the hunting and gathering cycle pursued by Sagwitch's people.

All Shoshone groups followed an annual cycle that placed them in prime food-gathering areas at the most opportune times. Traveling from spring through fall, extended-family groups returned to established areas within the core of their domain to pass the winter with relatives and others with whom they shared the region. Sagwitch's people had a rather distinctive annual pattern, partly because of the mobility the horse gave them and partly because their homelands in the Cache and Bear River valleys were more fruitful food-gathering areas than those most other Shoshone groups utilized.

That Sagwitch's family traveled extensively is evidenced by the fact that Sagwitch was born at Bear River, Utah, while his father was born at Goose Creek, Idaho, and died on the Promontory peninsula that juts into the northern Great Salt Lake. Sagwitch's brother Sewahoochew and nephew Quash-i-wat-titsi-say were also born at Goose Creek, Idaho, but another brother, Anga-poon-moot-say, was born in Park Valley and died in Bountiful, Utah. Sagwitch's first son, Soquitch, was born at Blue Creek, Utah, and his second son, Yeager, at Green River, Wyoming.[7]

Sagwitch's band often began their food-collecting cycle in early spring in Cache Valley, or Seuhubeogoi, "Willow River," where they could harvest edible greens, roots, and wild strawberries. Leaves and stems of edible plants that grew along streams and lakes and on low foothills, where snow disappeared and warmth came first, could be boiled or eaten raw. The many mountain streams that flowed into the valley carried *tsapankwi*, "good fish" (mountain trout), which could be caught by individuals with hook and line or by larger communal effort with net wiers. The valley of the Bear River immediately west of Cache Valley also provided a wealth of roots, bulbs, and seeds. Its streams carried trout as well as *auwok*, or sucker fish. Sagwitch's people also utilized the rich fish and waterfowl resources of Bear River Bay on the Great Salt Lake, and Sagwitch was known to have conducted communal duck drives there. In the valley east of Cache, the Bear River and Bear Lake provided dependable sources of trout and white fish.[8] The Cache and Bear River valleys also supported buffalo herds, which were an important resource to the Shoshone until their extinction in Cache Valley by about 1826 and in northern Utah generally by 1832.[9]

Descendants of Sagwitch say that their people occasionally traveled to the Salmon River region in springtime to share in the harvest of running salmon, which they would dry and prepare for later use.[10] Sagwitch's people also sometimes joined Chief Washakie's Eastern Shoshone for bison hunts on the western plains.[11] A return to Cache Valley in the summer allowed the Shoshone to harvest abundant seeds from the luxuriant grasses that grew there. They threshed and roasted the seeds, often grinding them into meal for winter use. The Shoshone often set fire to the grasses in Cache Valley after the seed harvest was completed in order to encourage new growth of grasses and to discourage infiltration of sage and other brush. They also harvested a carrot-like vegetable called *yampah* and some types of berries, including wild raspberries, which matured in Utah's northern valleys in mid-summer.[12]

The people often hunted woodchuck and ground squirrel near present-day Franklin, Idaho, in northern Cache Valley at a place they called Mosotokani, "House of the Lungs," because the lava rock outcroppings at that place reminded them of the texture of lung tissue. Like Western Shoshone groups, they probably captured squirrels and other burrowing rodents, including pocket gophers, by digging them out with rodent skewers or by flooding or smoking them out of their burrows. Clever hunters also utilized traps and deadfalls where practical.[13] Abundant grasses in Utah's northern mountains and valleys provided a dependable source of feed for elk and deer.

Sagwitch's descendants recall that his band successfully hunted both animals in northern Utah and in the Malad Valley of present-day southern Idaho. Deer and elk were less common and thus less utilized in other parts of the region.[14]

Toward autumn, the Shoshone watched for changes in the wild roses and rabbit brush. When the rose petals dried up and exposed reddening rose hips and when the rabbit brush turned deep yellow, they knew that the piñon nuts in western Utah and eastern Nevada were ready to harvest. On their way toward the piñon groves, Sagwitch's people usually stopped to harvest serviceberries and chokecherries in Cache Valley. They utilized a site near present-day Paradise that produced the "biggest, the blackest, and the sweetest" chokecherries. This site continued to be visited by Sagwitch's descendants well into the twentieth century. The resourceful Shoshone would mash the berries into patties and then arrange them on a bed of wheat grass, where they would dry without molding. They also made fermented drinks from the bark of chokecherry bushes.[15]

On their way west, the Shoshone sometimes stopped in the Malad Valley to harvest thistle roots, serviceberries, and *kooyah* tobacco. The Shoshone would not stay there long, however, as they needed to get to the piñon stands by early fall. Family traditions say that Sagwitch's people harvested pine nuts in the Yost and Clear Creek areas of northwestern Utah and sometimes went as far as present-day Wells, in northeastern Nevada. Because pine nuts were such a critically important food source for the lean winter months, the Shoshone would remain in the area for about a month, long enough for a typical family of four to gather about twelve hundred pounds of nuts, a supply which would last that family about four months.[16]

While in western Utah for the piñon nut harvest, Sagwitch's people also participated in communal rabbit drives in an area near Kelton, Utah, that they called Beacamogapa, "Big Rabbit's Bed." Shoshone of both sexes would chase black-tailed jackrabbits into a series of loops suspended from horizontal cords, which functioned somewhat like a net. Another method simply involved surrounding the rabbits and clubbing them with sticks. Sagwitch's people would dry the meat for winter consumption and use the fur for clothing, shoes, and housing.[17]

The Shoshone sometimes held communal antelope drives both on the Promontory and east of there on the Bear River flats. Often, they would build a corral with rocks and sticks to which was attached a woven sagebrush hedge. The people would drive the herd into a V-shaped corridor which ended in the corral. The opening would be secured by the people or "closed" by fire, after which archers could easily kill the animals. Because a local antelope population could be decimated in this way, similar antelope drives were not conducted in that area for a "considerable time" while the herd recovered its numbers.[18]

The Shoshone also utilized other foods throughout the year as needed. A variety of birds, such as ducks and geese, were of value to them; particularly important were doves, mockingbirds, sage hens, and quail. In times of extreme need, owls, hawks, and crows were also eaten. In addition, the Shoshone harvested several varieties of insects, including grasshoppers, crickets, insect larvae, and bee eggs.[19]

When winter began to enclose the intermountain area, the Shoshone, who traveled most of the year in nuclear or extended family groups, would gather to wintering sites, where they would spend the long, cold season in the company of relatives and friends, some of whom they probably saw only during the winter encampment. The best sites were those centrally located between food sources, easily defensible, and offering some protection against the elements. Two of the most important wintering sites for Sagwitch's people were along the lower Bear River, near the later site of Bear River City, Utah, and in a protected ravine near a bend of the Bear River in southern Idaho, north and west of present-day Preston, Idaho. At the first site, Sagwitch was born, and at the second, troops led by Colonel Connor attacked and killed many of the Northwestern Shoshone during the Bear River Massacre in 1863.[20]

If the Shoshone had cached sufficient foods to last through winter, the encampment could be a pleasant time filled with socializing, athletic competitions, dancing, games, and courting. At other times in the year, food-gathering activities that required communal cooperation, including rabbit and antelope drives and the piñon harvest, also brought larger groups of Shoshone together and provided opportunities for socializing and traditional dances. The Shoshone also enjoyed playing and competing in athletic games. Foot races were apparently open to both sexes, and a family oral history says that Sagwitch's mother-in-law Quehegup and her daughter could outrun men in long-distance races. Other games included a hoop and pole game, four-stick guessing games, juggling stones, and target shooting with bow and arrow.[21]

The Shoshone believed in supernatural spirits or powers centered in nature, including the sun, thunder and lightning, geographical features such as rocks and mountains, and the four winds, or which drew from the mythological figures of the coyote, wolf, and cottontail rabbit. Some mythological stories appear to have been told strictly for entertainment, while others, including stories about monster beings and water giants, were serious or instructive. When Mormon pioneers settled the Bear Lake valley in the 1860s, Shoshone told them about monsters that lived in Bear Lake. An 1868 editorial written from Logan, Utah, and published in the *Deseret News* stated that it was "well known that the Indians will not camp near the Lake, and they have never been known to bathe in its waters. They have persisted in stating that there were terrible monsters in the Lake, of which they were in fear, two of their tribe having, within the memory of some of their number, been carried off by them."[22]

Shoshone religion did not include a formal priesthood, but people could become empowered as healers, or shamans, by having "visionary and dream experiences." There were three categories of shamans: specialists known for curing specific ailments, those who used otherwordly powers for personal benefit only, and others who had "general curing ability." As part of the healing ritual, the shaman would place his or her hands on the patient's body and exorcise the illness. The Shoshone treated illnesses and injuries that were not considered to have been caused by supernatural intervention through the application of an impressive array of herbal remedies. Shamans were also important in some communal hunts, including antelope drives, wherein the shaman would "capture antelopes' souls through dreams, songs, and other ritual activities, charming the animals into the center of the corral," where they were killed.[23]

Contemporary sources do not tell us much about the role shamans played among Sagwitch's group, though it is apparent that shamans did function among them and that Mormon leaders at least for a time tolerated shaman-directed rituals at the Washakie settlement in Box Elder County.[24]

After Sagwitch's band of Northwestern Shoshone converted to Mormonism, they began to mix elements of Native American beliefs with Mormon doctrines. In one example from the turn of the century, a Shoshone Mormon from Washakie named Ammon Pubigee related how his wife died, had a visionary experience, and then returned to life again. Her death vision included an expression of her people's fairly recently instilled belief in God and Christ, "instructed her how to live on earth," and caused her to have additional dreams and visions. The people at Washakie made her a beaded dress and saddle and would lead her on horseback around in a circle, asking for the story to be told over and over again. Apparently they considered her to have gained special spiritual powers as a result of the experience.[25]

The power shamans possessed had specific applications. A person so empowered could not automatically claim a leadership role among the people. Such leadership came in other ways and was often temporary in nature. Before contact with European populations, Shoshone societies were not organized in ways that required an encompassing political system, but leaders were important in directing communal projects such as rabbit and antelope drives and piñon harvests. During these events, headmen, "variously referred to as chiefs or directors (tekwahni)," were selected. Similarly, the Shoshone would elect a *tonihunt* from their ranks to conduct the round dance. The leader of a round dance would "stand in the center of the camp half-circle, face the east and pray to the sun." He might pray for rain and abundant wildlife. In the evening, between performances of the round dance, he would admonish the people to "be industrious, the men to provide abundant game and fish, the women to gather seeds and roots." At the conclusion of either a hunt or a dance, the leader's authority dissolved, and the people "resumed foraging for food as individual camp units."[26]

Unlike temporary summer and fall gatherings, the winter camp provided a longer period of relatively stable residency for the Shoshone. It was common to elect a headman to direct affairs at such camps through the cold months. Anthropologist Julian Steward documented that for an unspecified number of years, "Segwitc"

(Sagwitch) functioned as "village headman and band chief" at Tongicavo, a Shoshone settlement near Mount Tarpey on the western side of the Promontory Mountains. Such a position generally lasted through the winter until camp broke in early spring and would not neccesarily be reinstated the following autumn.[27]

Sagwitch's leadership seems to have been more constant than was traditional among the Shoshone, probably because he could offer his people consistently sound counsel, which ensured success in communal hunts, but also because he could speak for them with outsiders in a powerful way, a role that became far more important after non-Indians became a regular presence in Shoshone territory. Julian Steward interviewed several informants that had known Sagwitch personally and had lived in his band. The information they gave him caused Steward to conclude that "for activities concerning the entire band—trips to Wyoming for bison, antelope hunts, and festivals—Segwitc, assisted somewhat by Kwudawuatsi, was chief, dagwani." A family oral history says that Sagwitch was an exceptional hunter whose skills on one occasion even saved his people from starvation. Family traditions also hold that Sagwitch's name, which means "orator," was given to him because of his significant speaking and negotiating skills. A great-granddaughter commented that "He had a way of speaking to his people that made them listen and obey. He knew the power of words; he probably became their leader because of his use of words. He could reason with Indians and also tried to make the white man understand the Indian way."[28]

It seems that even in an uncomplicated Shoshone society which had little call for leadership, Sagwitch often functioned as a leader or chieftain and his role expanded greatly after the 1840s as increasing numbers of non-Indians passed through and settled in Northwestern Shoshone territory. Surviving documents show that government agents and Mormon settlers who interracted with Sagwitch considered him to be a chief of the Shoshone and negotiated with him on behalf of his people, apparently with their full sanction.

Although many EuroAmerican observers in the nineteenth century judged Shoshone lifeways as "uncivilized" and "wretched," it is clear that those bearing such ethnocentric biases did not understand the wonderfully ingenious ways that Native Americans had

Soquitch's tepee, Washakie, Utah, 1884. Although many of the Northwestern
Shoshone at Washakie lived in houses made of logs or lumber, some
continued to live in traditional Shoshone wickiups and tepees. Photograph
courtesy Mae T. Parry.

learned to live very comfortably in a marginal ecosystem. Sagwitch's
people enjoyed a generally full and happy existence until incursions
by outsiders cut them off from many of the resources which made
that life possible. The history of Sagwitch and his people can only be
understood in this fuller context.

1

The Shoshone Orator

*A second chief, whose name we understand is Tsi-
Gwitch—to catch or grab—was the speaker in the powwow. A dark, heavy set, greasy-looking son of the
mountains about sixty years old, and five feet eight inches
in his moccasins. Of course, we who do not understand the
language were not much edified by the speech, but the old
man grew quite eloquent judging from his gestures, and
action, by the way, is about all there is of oratory.*

Reporter, *Salt Lake Daily Herald,* August 9, 1874

In the early autumn of 1822, Pin-in-netse, Woo-roats-rats-in-gwipe,
and their extended family made a temporary camp at one of their
people's traditional campsites along the lower Bear River in Box
Elder Valley. They wished to move on quickly west to the
Promontory and Kelton regions to harvest enough pine nuts and rabbit meat to last through the long winter close at hand. Inside a
quickly erected woven enclosure, Woo-roats-rats-in-gwipe began the
travail of childbirth, probably attended by one of the other women in
camp. The couple's family already included seven-year-old son
Sewahoochew, or Síhípihuiccuu (Tree Bird); five-year-old daughter
Bowjanapumpychee, or Poca-na-pampicci (Buffalo Head); and a
toddler, Duabowjanapumpychee, or Tía-poca-na-pampicci (Little
Buffalo Head). Pin-in-netse likely kept them busy with simple but
important tasks while waiting for the birth. In due time, the cries of a
newborn infant announced the birth of another son. After a short
period of recovery and rest, Woo-roats-rats-in-gwipe swaddled the
baby on a cradleboard and the family resumed its travel in quest of

food. Without pageantry, a great leader of the Shoshone Nation, Sagwitch, had been born.[1]

Sagwitch's parents called their new son Sagwip (Sakkwippíh), roughly translated as "Mud Puddle," or "In the Mud."[2] Family traditions are mute as to the origin or purpose of that name. The Shoshone often assigned a name to a child to acknowledge a physical characteristic or attribute or to note an event or an environmental feature significant to the parents or extended family. Even so, a name like Sagwip is difficult to understand.

Fur trapper Warren Angus Ferris visited an encampment of Shoshone in Cache Valley on July 16, 1830. He noted that "crowds of dirty, naked children followed us from lodge to lodge, at each of which were seen more or less filthy but industrious women."[3] Sagwip would have been about eight years of age when Ferris made his observation and well might have been present at the gathering. Although Ferris's statement must be understood in the context of his own subjective judgement, it might be argued that perhaps Sagwitch, even as a small child, was distinctively more active or inquisitive—and hence more dirty—than the typical children that Ferris saw. It is also possible that his name could reflect something as simple as rainy, and thus muddy, weather conditions at the time of his birth.

In keeping with Shoshone tradition, Sagwip received his first test, or rite of passage, while very young. His descendants say that his father stripped the little boy naked and rolled him in the snow. Tradition held that if a male child complained or cried during such a ritual, he would likely be cowardly throughout life. If he endured the test well and without complaint, his future as a great hunter was assured. Family traditions say that Sagwip did not cry or complain.[4] Ferris witnessed this rite performed on a newborn baby while he was staying with the Shoshone. He recorded that "infants, when they first appear on life's stage, are immediately immersed in a snow-bank in a state of perfect nudity, a few moments, for the purpose of familiarizing them to the endurance of cold." This initiation continued among Sagwitch's people until at least the beginning of the twentieth century.[5]

Descendants say that Sagwip excelled at making the weapons needed for hunting. At a very early age, he could select appropriate roots and sticks for the construction of bows and arrows. He mastered the techniques involved in heating and bending certain roots to produce flexible, accurate bows. As part of the process, he learned to turn obsidian chips into arrowheads. Sagwip was equally adept in using his tools on the hunt. Family tradition records an occasion when the people were starving. Sagwip volunteered to go on a dangerous hunt for big game in order to supply them with meat. He succeeded in the quest, and his people credited him with saving them from death.[6] Sagwip also exhibited significant athletic abilities and competed in sports and games the Shoshone played.[7]

Sagwip was born at the beginning of the fur trade era in the Rocky Mountains. He likely attended the four rendezvous held in the Cache and Bear Lake valleys between 1826 and 1831 and probably never knew a time without white contact. Family tradition says that the trappers considered him to be a friend and taught him how to trap game, especially beaver. He learned to negotiate shrewd trades of pelts to the mountain men for pots, pans, axes, and knives. A tradition also says that Sagwip willingly shared "his knowledge of the wilds" with the trappers.[8]

As he reached young adulthood, Sagwip stood a scant five feet eight inches "in his mocassins" and was lightly built. In fact, he was so light that when he was wounded in the spring of 1863, one of his sisters was able to carry him on her back from Mantua to Brigham City in order to get help.[9] In spite of his smaller size, Sagwip soon distinguished himself as a leader of his people through the "power of words." He had a way of speaking to, and reasoning with, his people that made them heed and trust him. Even more than his hunting prowess, this ability to speak well elevated Sagwip quickly to a position of leadership and importance. It was because of his persuasive oratorical style that Sagwip soon came to be called Tagwitch, and then Sagwitch, terms meaning "Speaker" or "Orator."[10]

Several historical references show that the Northwestern Shoshone considered Sagwitch to be one of their leaders and viewed him as their spokesman. Unfortunately, very few of his powerful orations are recorded. Those that have survived serve to confirm that his oratorical techniques included the use of logic to build a case or establish a fact. To skillfully crafted sentences, Sagwitch added effective gestures and actions that showed his audiences the importance of the things he told them. A newspaper reporter who witnessed Sagwitch speak at a powwow in 1874 noted that "the old man grew quite eloquent judging from his gestures—and action, by the way, is about all there is of oratory."[11] The reporter did not speak Shoshone and could not grasp the full significance of Sagwitch's oratorical style, though he could not deny the power of an effectively delivered address.

Sagwitch married his first wife, Egyptitcheeadaday (Icappíh-tí-cciattattai), "Coyote's Niece," sometime in the late 1830s while still in his teens. In about 1840, at age eighteen, he married Hewechee (Haai-wicci), meaning "Mourning Dove."[12] Sagwitch must have already acquired much personal property to be able to support two families. In early Shoshone culture, having more than one wife could be viewed as a symbol of prominence, a fact that hints at the possibility that the youthful Sagwitch had already earned a position of importance among his people by 1840.[13] It is likely that Sagwitch fathered at least a few children during the early 1840s, though if he did, none lived long enough to be known to his descendants. In 1846, Sagwitch's first wife, Egyptitcheeadaday, gave birth to a baby boy whom they named Tuinipucci (Tua-na-ppucci), roughly translated as "Young Man." Before long, the boy was also known as Soquitch (Soo-kuiccih), meaning "Many Buffaloes."[14] Soquitch, who was said to resemble his father both in general size and facial features, was also Sagwitch's first known child to live to adulthood.[15]

Family traditions say that, in early July 1847, Sagwitch's people got word through a Shoshone network that extended well into Wyoming that another group of white people had been sighted traveling through the mountains from the east. The Indians relayed that the group appeared to be friendly. Family traditions say that when the wagon train including Brigham Young and the first Mormon settlers came into the Salt Lake Valley, Sagwitch and other chiefs greeted and welcomed them.[16] Though no early Mormon records list the names of the Indians visiting their campsite that first month, they do record that on July 31, 1847, a delegation of about twenty Shoshone men, along with several Shoshone women, came into camp to trade with the company. While exhibiting an air of friendship and accommodation, the Shoshone leaders asserted the claim that "they were the owners of the land" and wanted it clearly understood that the Utes who had visited the camp that day did not own the land but had "come over the line" to interfere with Shoshone rights.[17]

Soquitch, "Many Buffaloes" (ca. 1846–1927), son of Sagwitch and Egyptitcheeadaday, in about 1920. Photograph courtesy Mae T. Parry.

The Shoshone delegation likely included Sagwitch, and it is possible that he acted as spokesman for the group. John Moemberg—or Ejupitchee (Ica-ppí-cci), meaning "Wolf"—a cousin of Sagwitch who acted for many years as his translator, told of visiting the Mormons soon after they entered the Salt Lake Valley in 1847, when he was twenty years old. The presence of Ejupitchee confirms that the delegation included Northwestern Shoshone from Sagwitch's band. It is unlikely that such representation would not have included the band's leader and orator, Sagwitch.[18]

The next day, Heber C. Kimball preached to the small Mormon congregation and discouraged the Latter-day Saints from paying any Indians for the land, arguing that if they paid the Shoshone, the Ute and other tribes would also make claims on the same property. He then declared, "The land belongs to our father in heaven, and we calculate to plow and plant it; and no man will have power to sell his inheritance, for he can not remove it; it belongs to the Lord."[19] By late August 1847, some complaints were raised that the Indians were "in the habit of taking a share of the grain for the use of the land."[20] Thus, within the first month of Shoshone-Mormon interraction, disputes over both property ownership and the payment of "rent" for the use of Indian lands had begun. These problems would continue to create friction in what was generally an amiable cross-cultural relationship until the Bear River Massacre sixteen years later crushed the Northwestern Shoshone and removed them from the bargaining table altogether.

As Sagwitch's people began to accommodate a population increase in the region due to emigrating Mormons, the chief's own family also grew. In 1848 Sagwitch and second wife Hewechee welcomed the birth of a son. They named him Taputsi, meaning "Little Cottontail"; later, they renamed him Yeager.[21] It was probably during this time that Sagwitch's extended family wintered with about three other families at a place called Tongicavo (Toona-kki-kkapa), "Chokeberry Tree Water," on the western side of the Promontory Range near Mount Tarpey. Sagwitch was considered the "village headman and band chief" at Tongicavo.

When not wintering at Tongicavo, along the lower Bear River, or at Beaver Creek, Sagwitch sometimes camped with his band at Nanavadzi, near Little Mountain, east of the Promontory. This was a

Yeager (ca. 1848–1937), son of Sagwitch and Hewechee, in about 1930.
Photograph courtesy Mae T. Parry.

large campsite where approximately twenty-three families wintered each year.[22] When larger communities of Shoshone gathered for social activities or communal hunts, they benefited from Sagwitch's presence because he possessed leadership and hunting skills that made such activities successful. Ethnologist Julian Steward noted in 1938 that "for activities concerning the entire band—trips to Wyoming for bison, antelope hunts, and festivals—Segwitc, assisted somewhat by Kwudawuatsi, was chief."[23] Sagwitch also directed communal duck drives in the marshes around Bear River Bay.[24] He clearly played a vital role in his tribe's economy.

The Mormons and Shoshone generally maintained friendly relations early on. Family tradition reports that Sagwitch aided the Mormons by showing them which plants and berries were good to eat and that members of his band occasionally sewed mocassins or made shoes from bark and other natural materials for the settlers.[25] Several recorded instances document the kindness of the Shoshone in bringing ducks, geese, and fish as gifts to their Mormon neighbors. The Shoshone also enjoyed bartering with the settlers, often trading currants or serviceberries for flour or other needed staples and furs for corn.[26]

Shoshone leaders enjoyed broad access to Brigham Young (or at least to his appointed Indian agents) in the early years of settlement. This was significant. Young was more than just the leader of the Mormons. In 1851, federal officals had appointed him governor and superintendent of Indian affairs for Utah Territory, a position he held until 1857. Not only was it Young's religious duty to attempt the conversion and "salvation" of the Indians, but it was also his administrative duty to negotiate with them and maintain peaceful relations between Native Americans and everyone else living in or traveling through the territory.

It is likely that Sagwitch had at least a few audiences with Young in the early years of Mormon settlement. One gathering of Shoshone and Bannock leaders met with Brigham Young in May 1852 and might well have included Sagwitch.[27] He might also have attended a meeting of Mormon and Shoshone leaders held in the Council House in Salt Lake City on September 5, 1853.[28] Sagwitch likely attended another gathering held five miles north of Ogden City on September 4, 1854. At that meeting, Governor Young had a "mutually gratifying talk" with the leaders and members of seven Shoshone bands who lived in that region. The Shoshone leaders, who had requested the meeting, "desired a continuation of peace, and professed to be perfectly friendly."[29] Governor Young must have been grateful to hear of their desire for peace, especially considering the lasting effects of an 1849 incident in which emigrants in a wagon train headed for California killed at least two Shoshone women and then stole several horses from the Indians. The result had been a reprisal upon two other wagon trains by the "hitherto peaceful tribe" and a resultingly very different "disposition" toward the whites from the friendly attitude that had before existed.[30] Young decried such actions against the Indians by "desperadoes and murderers," whose actions, he said, tended to excite the natives "to retaliation and revenge on our people, and thousands of honourable men from the States."[31]

But it was not only injustices on the immigrant trails that angered the Shoshone and encouraged retaliatory "eye for an eye" justice. The Mormon settlers in northern Utah engaged in occasional skirmishes with the Shoshone, and some of the disagreements ended with the deaths of Native Americans. In September 1850, Ogden settler Urban Van Stewart noticed a Shoshone leader named Terikee shucking corn in his garden. The settler ordered the Indian out of the garden and, after waiting only a short time, shot and killed him, reportedly because he "did not walk as fast as Brother Stewart wanted."[32] That same year, at the Bear River ferry, a settler stole a horse from a Shoshone band and then fled to the mountains. Other Mormons caught the thief and returned the horse to the band. An old chief represented the band in a discussion with the Mormons who had returned the stolen animal and declared that his people never stole from the whites "and felt bad that the white men should steal from him."[33] In a skirmish the next year, a group of Indians stole six horses from a settlement on the Weber River. When a Mormon posse went in pursuit of their property, they caught up with those responsible. One Indian pulled a knife and was immediately shot.[34] Similar events occurred periodically during the early years of settlement.

In spite of occasional episodes of violence, whether caused by Anglos or Native Americans, relations between the Mormons and the Shoshone generally remained amicable through the 1850s.

Brigham Young (1801-1877). It is likely that Sagwitch first met Young in 1847. The two conducted business on several occasions over the next thirty years. Charles W. Carter, photographer, Salt Lake City, ca. 1866. Photograph made from original glass plate negative courtesy LDS Church Archives, Salt Lake City, Utah.

Brigham Young helped maintain peace at home by preaching a practical policy of offering foodstuffs to Indians, whom the Mormons had displaced and thus placed in a position of jeopardy and potential privation, rather than expending the resources necesary to fight them. In several settings, he also reminded his followers of the Mormon belief which ascribed to Native Americans a noble biblical heritage. In an April 1853 address delivered at the old Tabernacle in Salt Lake City, Young was very direct. He told his audience that the Mormons were "here in the mountains, with these Lamanites for our neighbors," and declared, "These Indians are the seed of Israel through the loins of Joseph who was sold into Egypt, they are the children of Abraham and belong to the chosen seed."[35]

That philosophy was reiterated the following year when Young and his counselors published the "Eleventh General Epistle of the Presidency." In the document, they suggested that Latter-day Saints assume a defensive posture against the Indians but also urged them to "treat them civilly, friendly; endeavor to get speech with, and treat with them in a friendly manner." They also counseled, "Let us also exert ourselves to save Israel, not destroy them, for the promises concerning them will be fulfilled."[36]

Perhaps to help the Saints develop the friendly and civil relationships with Native Americans that the First Presidency advocated, the Church's press in 1853 printed a pamphlet on the Shoshone and Ute languages authored by Dimick Huntington, and another on the Piede (Southern Paiute) language compiled by George and Nephi Johnson. That winter, Huntington lectured at "Common Schools" sponsored by various wards and at evening schools, teaching the Saints words and phrases from those languages.[37]

President Young did not stop with speeches from the pulpit. In May 1855 he selected twenty-seven men as missionaries to the Lamanites, as Mormons referred to Native Americans. Young instructed the party to "settle among the Flathead, Bannock, or Shoshoni Indians, or anywhere that the tribes would receive them . . . teach them to cease their savage customs . . . to cease their roving habits and to settle down; also to teach them how to build houses and homes; in fact, to do all that they could to better the conditions of these fallen people."[38]

The missionary corps settled among the Lemhi Shoshone, near the Salmon River in Idaho, anxious to share Mormonism with them and reclaim them to Israel. The zeal of the missionaries as they began their service is captured in a poem written by one of the elders, Richard B. Margetts.

> Awake, Awake, the camp from sleeping!
> Watchman, watchman, what's the hour?
> Four o'clock and twenty minutes.
> Rise up, camp, and say your prayer.
> For we are going to the land of Laman
>   To plant the Gospel standard there,
> To bring them out from degredation
>   To a people, white and fair.[39]

After three years of moderate success and numerous Indian baptisms, the Lemhi Mission failed and was abandoned March 28, 1858. Missionaries at the settlement had attempted to retain friendships with warring Indian groups. Hospitality toward one group, however, came to be "interpreted as an act of hostility toward the other," and Native Americans began a series of raids on Fort Lemhi, murdering two of the missionaries. Even so, many of the Mormons who worked at the mission gained a knowledge of, and appreciation for, the Shoshone. Some, including George Washington Hill, who later played a most significant role in Sagwitch's life, also learned to speak Shoshone while at Lemhi.[40]

While relations between Mormons and the Shoshone in the Lemhi area deteriorated, connections remained strong with most Native American groups in northern Utah, including Sagwitch and his band. Community celebrations for the Mormon July 24 holiday in 1856 included Native Americans and indicated the positive relations between the two peoples. Not only did Native Americans attend, they took an active role in the festivities. At Ogden, Shoshone chieftain Little Soldier marched with eleven braves in a parade, jubilantly carrying a banner he most likely did not understand. It declared them to be "The Thousands of Manassah," a title suggesting the Mormon belief that the Indians were literal descendants of the Old Testament Joseph through his eldest son. At Fort

Supply, twenty-four young Native Americans dressed in buckskin pants, blue shirts, and mocassins carried a poster declaring Mormonism's ethnocentric scriptural goal for them—"We shall yet become a white and delightsome people"—while at North Willow Creek, Latter-day Saints seated fifty Indians for a holiday dinner, "much to their satisfaction and delight."[41]

Church leaders were pleased to have amicable relations with the Indians, perhaps especially so after learning in July 1857 that United States military forces under Colonel Albert Sydney Johnston were enroute to Utah. One month after that ominous July 24 announcement, Mormon officials directed a detachment from the Weber Military District of the Nauvoo Legion militia under Captain Marcellus Monroe to patrol Cache Valley. In the course of their reconnaissance, they came upon Sagwitch and his band somewhere in the southern part of the valley. At the meeting that followed, held on August 19, 1857, Sagwitch smoked with them and received a gift of some tobacco. He also discussed the approaching army. Through interpreter James Brown, Monroe gave the Shoshone "instructions," probably soliciting their support of the Mormons if a shooting war broke out. Sagwitch must have been supportive of the Mormons in their struggle with the U.S. Army, because he took the message "with a good spirit," and his band shared with the Nauvoo Legion what little they knew about the soldiers.[42]

The friendly relations between Mormons and Indians in northern Utah were to be tried greatly in the years that followed. One development that increasingly became an irritation was the settlement of Cache Valley by the Mormons, beginning at Wellsville in 1856. Brigham Young had learned about Cache Valley through a report filed by scouts he had sent to explore the region in August 1847. Their report had been overwhelmingly positive, recording that "It was beautiful and had more timber than any place . . . explored." The report also commented on twelve streams which fed the lush valley. At that time, much high quality land remained unsettled and available along the western side of the Wasatch range, so Cache Valley with its colder climate and relative distance from the Mormon center was allowed to remain relatively undisturbed for several years.[43]

Still, the valley was too resource rich to ignore for long. As early as July 1851 a contingent of Mormon militia had ridden into

Cache Valley on the trail of Indians who had stolen horses along the
Weber River. The animals were not recovered, but Colonel Canfield,
who led the expedition, was quite taken by the valley. According to
Isaac Clark, who penned a report to Brigham Young, Canfield had
declared "Cash is the best valley of land timber and water he has
seen in the mountains beautiful and rich."[44]

By the mid-1850s, an ever-increasing Mormon population had
reduced available grazing lands dramatically in the settled regions,
as houses and fenced farms replaced open plains. In looking for a
solution, Brigham Young remembered Cache Valley with its rich
grasses and thick timber stands and felt that it would be an ideal
land for ranching. He petitioned the Utah Territorial Legislative
Assembly in 1855 for herding rights and was granted exclusive priv-
ileges to Cache Valley. Young organized a company to drive his stock
and the church's cattle herd into the valley. The company arrived in
July 1855 and quickly established a small settlement near present-day Millville that they called Elkhorn Ranch.[45]

The Latter-day Saints were not the first whites to use Cache
Valley in this way. In 1849, at the recommendation of government
explorer Howard Stansbury, the federal government drove its mules
and cattle herd from Fort Hall into Cache Valley. The ensuing winter
had been so severe that half of the animals perished, forcing the government to abandon its plans there. Like the government, the church
had also chosen a bad year to begin their ranching experiment as the
1855–1856 winter proved to be one of the worst ever experienced.
By spring, only 420 animals survived of the 2,000 driven there the
previous summer.[46]

In the end, however, it was not just the rich soils of Cache
Valley that encouraged settlement, despite a sometimes forbidding
climate. It was the repeated failure of crops in Tooele County west of
Salt Lake City that created sufficient impetus for a permanent
Mormon residential presence in Cache Valley. The Tooele saints had
struggled since 1849 to build a prosperous farming community in
the desert. While they met with modest success in the early years of
settlement, they also experienced devastating crop failures in 1855
and 1856 due to grasshoppers and saleratus. The saints under Peter
Maughan petitioned Brigham Young for assistance. Young suggested
that the community send a delegation into Cache Valley to assess it

as a possible location for settlement. The delegation returned enthusiastic about the prospects there and most of the population of E. T. City relocated to Cache Valley in September 1856.[47]

Native Americans had always valued Cache Valley highly. The Shoshone called the area Seuhubeogoi, meaning "Willow River," and considered it a critical hunting and gathering stop in their yearly food-gathering circuit. The valley was rich in animal and plant life, waterfowl and fish. Most importantly, the valley's rich soils supported a great variety of seed-bearing grasses so critical as a food source. The north end of the valley at the confluence of Beaver Creek and the Bear River was also one of the most popular wintering sites for several Shoshone bands. Until this time, the Shoshone had been able to adjust to the loss of the rest of northern Utah to Mormon settlement largely because Cache Valley had been left virtually untouched and retained resources for them.[48]

Jacob Forney, Brigham Young's replacement as superintendent of Indian affairs for the territory, worried that the rapid settlement of Utah's valleys would leave the various tribes without homes or options. In a letter to the commissioner of Indian affairs dated February 15, 1859, he noted that "The Indians . . . have become impoverished by the introduction of a white population. The valleys occupied and cultivated at present, were formerly their chief dependence for game." Forney added that "most of the valleys susceptible of succesful cultivation are already occupied by industrious farmers, and the game, roots, &c, the Indians only salvation, has given place to a thriving population." Forney correctly assessed that the Indians were thus forced to starve or steal and suggested that Cache Valley be set aside as a reservation for the Shoshone since the tribe claimed it as part of their domain. More importantly, it was the only valley left that was yet relatively unsettled, and the government would not have to buy out homesteaders' improvements. Water-rich Cache Valley was also ideal for a reservation, he argued, because it would not be neccesary for the government to construct expensive irrigation systems. He encouraged quick action "as the valleys are fast filling up."[49]

Forney was right but largely unheeded by his superiors. In the meantime, efficient Mormon farmers, beginning with their small foothold at Wellsville, soon effected a wholesale transformation of Cache Valley to European farming methods and crops and to animal husbandry. Large parcels of land fell under the plow, other acreages became enclosed within wooden fences, and large herds of cattle were set out to graze on the valley's luxuriant grasses, greatly depleting seed resources. Settlers also overhunted meat animals and purposely killed off other species that they did not consider valuable. By the end of 1859, six small communities had found firm root in Cache Valley: Wellsville, Providence, Mendon, Logan, Smithfield, and Richmond, with a combined total of about 150 families. By 1860 Cache Valley's virtues were becoming so widely praised that a rush of Mormon converts from abroad chose to settle there. Many settlers from established Mormon communities, the *Deseret News* wrote, were people "in search of new homes and better locations" who chose to relocate to Cache Valley.[50]

Tensions grew. Native Americans had not sold or treated away any part of Cache Valley. As the settler population increased, especially after 1857, Indians more and more frequently demanded beeves, flour, potatoes, and other staples from the settlers as compensation for the use of the land and as a stopgap to starvation. In the early years of Cache Valley settlement, the Mormon settlers could scarcely scratch out a living for themselves, let alone develop surpluses. Complying with Indian demands depleted supplies that they desperately needed themselves and greatly increased tensions and Mormon resentment toward Native Americans.

An occurrence in early June 1857 is typical of those tensions. Peter Maughan reported to Brigham Young that a group of fifty Indians had come into the Mormon settlement in Cache Valley "all stripped naked and rode round and yelled like as many fiends . . . they ground their knives and charged their guns." The chief of the band told Maughan that his people were very hungry, "and that we was living on their land." He demanded shirts, flour, powder, and two oxen as compensation. Maughan negotiated a reduced offer of a single cow, which satisfied their immediate hunger and ended the confrontation. Future conflicts were assured, however, as Maughan reported in the same letter the efforts of the twenty-six Mormon families to raise diverse crops and his desire for more settlers to come because "there is plenty of room for more."[51]

The Cache and Box Elder valleys shared a close proximity to the Oregon and California trails, and that closeness became an additional source of difficulties for white-Indian relations by the late 1850s. The trail itself slashed through the heart of the Shoshone homeland, assuring frequent contact between the over-landers and the Indians. In a significant number of instances, ruth-less or inexperienced travelers shot and killed Shoshone people whose friendly intentions they could not or did not care to under-stand. In a September 1857 report to the commissioner of Indian affairs, Brigham Young declared that the Shoshone were not hostile generally but a company of "returning Californians" the previous spring had shot at every Indian they encountered. In retaliation, he reported, many Indians had begun to kill and plunder with impunity. Young argued that it was hard to build trust and friend-ship with the Indians "when perhaps the very next party which crosses their path shoots them down like wolves." He encouraged kinder treatment and more liberal government appropriations.[52]

Utah Territory's new Indian superintendent, Jacob Forney, was anxious to investigate the causes of trouble on the emigrant roads. In September 1858 he began a several weeks-long tour of the region by visiting Shoshone bands in northern Utah, then proceeding on to other Indian groups in the Humbolt region. He visited many bands that he knew had been accused of committing "sundry depreda-tions" against emigrants on the trails. While he concluded that they were responsible for at least some of the offenses, he also found cause to blame the Bannocks from Oregon for some of the thefts. Forney felt compelled to excuse the Indians' actions to some degree because "They knew nothing of our Government, were entirely and completely ignorant of it, and its laws," and thus "never knew their duty towards white men." He was also moved towards compassion for them because many of their number had been "shot down for triv-ial causes." He added that they had been robbed and "have received other ill treatment from the whites." Depredation on the emigrant road was clearly a more complex issue than Forney had originally believed.[53]

Although sporadic attacks on immigrant trains occurred throughout the 1850s, none had a direct impact on Sagwitch's Northwestern Shoshone band until 1859. In the latter part of July of that year, two Flathead Indians entered an emigrant camp hoping to trade with the whites. The travelers shot both to death without provocation. In retaliation, other Flatheads, in league with Shoshone warriors, on July 24 ambushed the Ferguson-Shepherd emigrant train in a canyon on the Sublette Cutoff about eighty miles northwest of Salt Lake City. Five men died and a woman and her baby received serious, though not fatal, wounds.[54]

On July 30, Shoshone men rode into Brigham City from the north in possession of a number of horses, mules, and oxen "which they seemed very anxious to dispose of." Suspicious Mormon settlers refused to purchase them. The Indians reportedly had in their possession "very neatly executed dagueretype likenesses of a man, woman, and two young ladies." Joseph Tippetts purchased the image and gave it to Samuel Smith, who sent it with a report of his preliminary findings to Indian Superintendent Jacob Forney. Forney was convinced that a massacre had occurred and asked Governor Alfred Cumming to call troops from Camp Floyd to locate the guilty Indians and "execute swift and terrible punishment on them."[55]

Cumming responded on August 3, requesting that General Albert Sydney Johnston "detach a suitable command . . . with a view of arresting the murderers and furnishing protection upon the road." Johnston dispatched Company G under command of Lieutenant Ebenezer Gay to a position west of the Bear River on the California Road, with orders to investigate the massacre, protect emigrants, and recover the stolen property. If his company came upon the Indians guilty of perpetrating the massacre, they were to "inflict upon them exemplary and decided punishment." At the same time, Johnston sent word to 7th Infantry commander Major Isaac Lynde, then patrolling in the Humboldt region, ordering those troops to the Bear River crossing to "keep the road under observation" and to "arrest or punish the murderers" if they could be found.[56]

By August 10, Agent Forney felt confident that the massacre had been perpetrated by a combined force of Bannocks from the Oregon country and Northwestern Shoshone from Utah's northern valleys. He wrote to the Indian commissioner that the Shoshone must have been involved because they were the Indians who had brought horses, mules, and cattle, as well as Colt revolvers, watches, jewelry, and gold coin believed to have belonged to the emigrant train into the Brigham City area within days after the killings on the trail. Forney issued a notice that, under "the severest penalty of the law,"

persons should not purchase any goods from Indians in the vicinity
of Willow Creek or Brigham City, or in the Cache, Malad, or Bear
River valleys, underscoring his belief that Shoshone from these valleys were responsible for the massacre.[57]

When Lieutenant Gay and his troops reached Brigham City on
August 14, he was informed that the Indians responsible for the
Ferguson-Shepherd killings had encamped at Devil's Gate in the
canyon between Brigham City and Cache Valley. Gay felt that the
evidence, though largely circumstantial, constituted a compelling
link from the Indians in the canyon to the massacre and "immediately resolved to attack them." In the pre-dawn hours of August 15,
Gay's company charged the Shoshone encampment as they slept
and engaged them in battle for a few hours before returning to
Brigham City. He felt vindicated when one of the twenty horses captured was found to be from the unfortunate emigrant company. The
troops killed one man and reportedly wounded a woman, though
Gay's report noted twenty dead among the Shoshone. Six of his men
received wounds. Brigham City area pioneer Joseph Packer later
reminisced about the engagement and noted that "one of Sagwitch's
squaws was killed in this encounter." Family traditions do not confirm that Sagwitch's band was involved or that a wife died in this
way. But it is true that the encounter took place in a section of the
country frequented by Sagwitch's people, and the event aroused
concerns about the nature of the Northwestern Shoshone bands in
that vicinity.[58]

By August 15, Gay had led his troops to a position on the
Bear River, from whence he began to send troops on reconnai-
sances looking for Indians who were supposed to have been
encamped in Malad Valley. On the seventeenth, his infantry
engaged in gunfire, sparring with twenty-five Indians for the better
part of an hour "without any damage on either side." Gay was
joined on August 19 by Major Lynde, who authorized additional
reinforcements from Camp Floyd to prepare for an anticipated
engagement that never materialized. In fact the soldiers could not
find any Indians in the region, forcing Major Lynde to report on
September 2 that "I have had Cache valley and the adjacent country thoroughly examined, and no trace of Indians could be found."
He reported that he would send a command to Bear Lake the next

day, and if that guard found no Indians, he would assume that they
had gone north into the mountains "out of our reach from this
point."⁵⁹

Meanwhile, the Northwestern Shoshone began a series of
depredations on Mormon communities in Box Elder, Weber, and
Cache valleys to display their anger over the fact that Box Elder
County sheriff Sheldon B. Cutler, a Mormon, had helped Gay's
attacking troops by guiding them to the Shoshone camp. Most of the
attacks that followed involved the theft of cattle and the theft or poi-
soning of horses, but some included direct confrontations with the
settlers. Cache Valley pioneer Walter Walters experienced the
Indians' rage when they rode into Brigham City in 1859. He
recorded, "During the summer the first hostile Indians came upon
us. we thought it was the end. They Praded around and Danced and
Sang they were all Painted ready for war." Walter's community was
spared after giving flour and a beef to the visitors.⁶⁰

Just slightly more than two weeks after the Devil's Gate skirmish, Indians attacked Edward Miltimore's emigrant train
twenty-five miles west of Fort Hall. They tortured and killed five
men, one woman, and two children. Although the incident had no
apparent connection with Sagwitch and his people, it ultimately
affected them by establishing in the minds of government officials
and federal troops the belief that Indians made the emigrant trails
unsafe and that the Shoshone living in northern Utah shared guilt for
the offenses against the travelers.⁶¹

It was during this period that Sagwitch married his third wife,
Dadabaychee (Tan-tapai-cii), meaning "the Sun." In so doing, he
accepted responsibility for three new family members rather than
just one, because Dadabaychee brought to the union two sons from a
previous marriage: Hinnah, born around 1855, and Potton, meaning
"Mano" or "Grinding Stone," born about 1858. Sagwitch now
boasted a family of four sons. It is not known when Sagwitch's first
wife, Egyptitcheeadaday, died. She may have still been alive in
1860, giving Sagwitch three wives and four children—an extremely
large family for a hunting and gathering society—with the attendant
challenge of keeping them fed, clothed, and protected. The challenge only became greater as settlers continued to compete with the
Shoshone for resources.⁶²

The year 1860 began quietly enough for the Northwestern Shoshone bands wintering in Cache Valley. That changed by late April when several men, apparently under the direction of Weber Tom, stole fifteen hundred dollars worth of horses from the settlements at Wellsville and Mendon and reportedly planned other thefts as well. To Mormon Church representatives this seemed like the ultimate insult after they had fed those very Indians through the winter. While companies of minute men were organized in Logan and Wellsville to protect the settlements and their stock from further raids, Peter Maughan sent word to the offenders via some friendly Indians that the Mormons would "positively" not feed the Shoshone again unless the horses were returned and that any further depredations would force the community to "use them up if it took us all summer to do it." The combined response must have been effective, because Ezra T. Benson noted on May 22 that the Shoshone had returned all but two of the horses and that many of the Indians "manifest a spirit of repentance."[63]

Brigham Young had been kept informed of the difficulties with the Shoshone in the area. He responded by penning a letter of instruction on June 18, 1860, to be read in all the settlements of Cache Valley. Young urged his saints to a high level of caution "in your settlements, on your ranges, in your fields, and in the kanyons" and warned the settlers to continue to refrain from hunting and fishing and "thus deprive the Indians of a plausible pretext for killing or driving off your animals." He also encouraged the organization of mounted patrols that could be quickly assembled as needed.[64]

The summer's most serious problems began with the arrest of Shoshone leader Pagunap on July 23 in Smithfield, in Cache Valley, on charges of having stolen a horse and a mule from the nearby Richmond settlement. While detained at Smithfield, Pagunap's followers, about ten in number, approached the makeshift jail intending to free him. As he tried to join his liberators, he was shot dead. The Shoshone retaliated by opening fire on the Mormons there, hitting and seriously wounding Samuel Cousins. They quickly retreated northeast towards Smithfield Canyon, where they came upon Franklin settlers John Reed, James Cowan, and Thomas Slater. They shot Reed through the neck, killing him instantly. Cowan was less seriously wounded. As the Shoshone continued up the canyon they came upon Smithfield settlers Ira and Solyman Merrill. They shot Ira dead, but his brother survived bullet wounds to his stomach and arm. The Smithfield Minute Men mobilized quickly and pursued the Indians five miles into the canyon, at times exchanging fire, before returning to the valley.[65]

That evening at Smithfield, the militia discovered and arrested an Indian and his wife. They were placed under guard in Logan, and it was hoped that they could be exchanged for the Indian murderers. In response, Chief Bear Hunter gathered about twenty men and made a charge on the schoolhouse where the Indian couple was being held, "yelling like fiends." They were met by a well-organized militia with over one hundred guns. Bear Hunter and his men reconsidered the attack and, according to Peter Maughan, "cooled right down." Maughan reported the events of the previous day to Brigham Young, who responded by letter, reasoning that "It only remains that their death profits the living by prompting [them] to increased and unrelaxing vigilence and wariness." The events of the previous few days made the Saints very willing to be vigilant and wary. The *Deseret News* noted on September 5 that Smithfield's residents had dragged their houses into a makeshift fort "so that they will be more secure from attack than in their former scattered condition." The Mormons in every other Cache Valley community soon did the same. Events in the summer of 1860 had shown the residents of Cache Valley that they could no longer be fully at ease with their Shoshone neighbors.[66]

Surviving records do not document Sagwitch's movements in 1860. It seems likely that diarists or news reporters would have mentioned him had he been involved in a substantial way in any of that year's Cache Valley skirmishes. At least by year's end, Sagwitch and his band had established their camp in Box Elder County. Brigham City bishop Alvin Nichols stated in a letter penned January 11, 1861, that a band of seven to ten lodges of Shoshone Indians had encamped near the city. He noted that it was "commonly known as Sagwich's band, he being the chief and a well disposed Indian, friendly to the whites." Interestingly, Nichols suggested that while Sagwitch was a valuable friend to the settlers in the area, four or five Indians from his band "make a practice of plundering and stealing" from Indians and whites alike "to the great annoyance of both."[67]

Indian-white relations proved to be relatively quiet for Sagwitch's people in 1861. Even Sagwitch's fellow chief, Bear Hunter, who had led a charge on the Logan schoolhouse in 1860 and had been involved in other skirmishes that year, sued for peace. Indian agent Colonel Benjamin Davies met Bear Hunter in Salt Lake City and dressed him in a complete suit of "citizens clothing," including boots and hat, which reportedly made him appear "much like an 'American.'" Bear Hunter was very pleased and promised to go hunting and not return again to Cache Valley until the wheat harvest, a promise that the reporter suggested would be a great blessing to the whites in the valley.[68]

In mid-July 1861, at least fifteen hundred Shoshone gathered at Blacksmith Fork in Cache Valley. The presence of such a large contingent of Indians intimidated Mormon leaders Ezra T. Benson and Peter Maughan to the extent that they cancelled a planned meeting with President Young because they considered it unwise, on account of the "movement of the Indians," to leave their homes. Maughan noted that the Indians "feel a little more stuborn than we would like to see" due to losing a battle with the Cheyenne. On July 14, 1861, Benson, Seth Blair, and other Mormons met with selected Indian leaders "to councill on general matters." Chiefs Pe-Ads Wicks, Sagwitch, Bear Hunter, and others represented the Native Americans, who requested a peace gift that would include a wagonload of blankets, shirts, and other goods. Mormon leaders replied that they could not give them much in the way of clothing. Benson then proposed a gift of twenty-four hundred pounds of flour, several beef cattle, and new shirts for the five chiefs represented, including Sagwitch. The Indian delegation accepted the offer and promised "to leave us to follow our business" after they had eaten up their provisions. By July 22, many of the Indians remained in Cache Valley, and one of the chiefs threatened to winter in the valley, telling Benson that "the land, water, grass &c are his and [he] wants to sell it to us." As a precaution, Benson and Maughan assembled fifty minute men at the church's farm and instructed the Mormons in all Cache Valley settlements to be ready for an emergency. Beyond some minor thefts later in the summer, however, no further problems occurred.[69]

In a gesture of friendship to the Mormons, Bear Hunter and his band returned twenty-one stolen horses to the settlement at Logan on

September 17, 1861. Other Indians returned horses to settlements at Franklin and Richmond. Through the remainder of the year, few altercations between the Indians and the settlers occurred. Conditions of peace must have been welcome to Sagwitch, who became a father once again in 1861. His wife, Dadabaychee, gave birth to a strong and healthy boy whom they named Beshup (Pisappíh), meaning "Red Oquirrh." He also became known by another name, Timbimboo (Tímpin-poo), translated as "Rock Writer," or "One Who Writes on Rocks," a name that eventually became the surname for many of Sagwitch's descendants.[70]

As a new year dawned, an old and very familiar problem arose once again. A band of Indians under Pine began in January 1862 to make forays against the settlers' communal cattle herd in Cache Valley. The Indians, characterized by the whites as hostile and threatening, had already shot a number of cattle. It was soon learned that the natives intended to drive as many of the animals as possible to the Fort Hall area and that they had already sent word to the Whiteknife Shoshone of Nevada to come and help them in carrying out their plans. Peter Maughan immediately sent twenty armed men to reinforce the seventeen herdsmen and reported to Brigham Young that he would send 150 men if necessary to protect the cattle from being stolen by "a parcel of vagabonds." The thefts seemed especially surprising considering that Pine had been well treated by the Latter-day Saints during the previous two years.[71]

Maughan instructed Dudley J. Merrill, the "captain" of the herd, to call a council of the friendly Indians in order to obtain all the information he could concerning the matter. Maughan specifically asked that "Sige-watch" (Sagwitch) and his band be consulted in council because "they are the friendly ones, they have always been so since the settlement of this valley and we hope they will continue their friendship." Maughan asked Merrill to avoid a "collision" with the Indians if possible, but if Pine's forces attacked, the herdsmen were to "chastise [them] in a way that will make them remember for years to come."[72] The increased forces standing guard on the herd, aided by the information from Sagwitch, proved sufficient to protect the herd, because Pine was not able to carry out his plans in the spring as he had hoped.

Frank Warner (ca. 1861–1919), in about 1880. Warner, originally known as Beshup Timbimboo, was the son of Sagwitch and Dadabaychee. He was adopted by the Amos Warner family some time after the Bear River Massacre and raised in Willard, Box Elder County, Utah. Photograph courtesy LDS Church Archives, Salt Lake City, Utah.

Frank Warner, ca. 1915. Photograph courtesy Mae T. Parry.

Sagwitch experienced a significant loss in 1862 when his second wife, Hewechee, died. The cause of her death is not known, but family traditions say that it was due to natural causes. Sagwitch buried her on a knoll near Mantua and placed her *poto*, or grinding stone, on the grave as a marker. It was probably of some comfort to him that during the same year, his third wife, Dadabaychee, gave birth to a baby daughter. Her given name has been lost to history.[73]

Through the spring and early summer of 1862, several Indian bands came into Cache Valley to visit with Mormon leaders. They had watched U.S. Army detatchments patrolling the northern borders of the region and were undoubtedly well aware of Lieutenant Gay's attack on the Shoshone camp at Devil's Gate a few years earlier. Many feared a possible union of Mormons and U.S. soldiers against them. Even the Salmon River Shoshone sent a delegation to ask the Mormons if they were "willing to overlook the outbreak at that place in 1858." They were speaking of events surrounding the Shoshone-sponsored expulsion of Mormon missionaries from the Lemhi area and the subsequent closing of the Salmon River mission in 1858. Maughan responded that the Indians would have to stop stealing the settlers' horses if they expected to retain the friendship of the Mormons. With or without Maughan's threat, the summer of 1862 passed without any further Indian problems. A *Deseret News* correspondent reported on July 16 that the Indians were not "troublesome" since most had left for their summer hunting grounds.[74]

Toward autumn, problems with the Indians began again. On the California Trail, raids, thefts, and murders marked a bloody year for emigrant travel. Newspapers sketched the often-exaggerated gruesome details of human mutilations and scalpings, and some reports concluded with demands to make the trails safe once more. The *Idaho Enterprise* called for action against the Indians along the Humboldt responsible for the "Gravelly Ford Massacre." The editor's suggestion proved to be chillingly prophetic in describing what would happen to Sagwitch and the Northwestern Shoshone at Beaver Creek three months later. "It is quite time that something was done to teach the savages a severe lesson" the editor argued, suggesting that a winter campaign against the Indian perpetrators would be the most succesful course of action and then noting "Colonel Connor's boys have been spoiling for action, [it] would be a wise plan to let them vent a little of their pent up fighting spirit."[75]

Colonel Patrick Edward Connor, senior officer of a regiment of U.S. troops called the California Volunteers, was in fact in Ruby Valley, Nevada, at the time the editor offered his thoughts. Connor did not wait until winter, in the case of the Humboldt Indians, but immediately assigned Major Edward McGarry to find and execute those Indians responsible for the Gravelly Ford killings on the California Trail. Twenty-four Western Shoshone supposedly guilty of the crime were soon gathered and executed. The Shoshone had experienced their first taste of Colonel Connor's style of justice.[76]

It is important to understand why Connor was in Nevada and where he was headed at the time his troops made their short detour to the Humboldt region. In 1862, with the Civil War under way, leaders of the Union worried that resource-rich California might fall into the hands of the Confederacy and were anxious to keep emigrant, telegraph, and mail lines to the west coast protected and operational. Marauding Indian parties along the trail threatened those connections. California governor John G. Downey appointed Connor to lead an enlisted body of volunteers to Utah to maintain the communication routes and keep the Indians and Mormons, whose loyalty the federal government doubted, in check. After stopping in Nevada to build a fort in Ruby Valley and to punish those responsible for the Gravelly Ford deaths, Connor continued on. His troops arrived in Utah on October 20, 1862. Six days later, he founded Camp Douglas a few miles east of Salt Lake City.[77]

As autumn approached, troublesome Indians again returned to Cache Valley, where it was noted that they had become "saucy and belligerent in their deportment, and have committed some depredations, and threaten to do more." Raids on cattle herds resumed, and one herdsman narrowly escaped death when an Indian's bullet passed through his hat, barely missing his skull. Horse stealing also resumed on a major scale. Peter Maughan noted in a September 29, 1862, letter to Brigham Young that a hundred horses had been stolen in the previous three weeks and unsuccessful attempts had been made to steal many others. Even more troublesome, however, was the new attitude of the thieving bands. Maughan noted, "I have never seen them so bold and daring in the Brethrens houses, insulting the

women &c." What most alarmed Maughan was that some of the
Indians who still professed to be friendly "will harbour those scamps
about their wickeups untill they get their plans laid for stealing, at
the same time we have been given them tons of flour and Beef, hoping for peace."[78]

By early October, the Northwestern bands under Sagwitch,
Bear Hunter, and Lehi were encamped on the Bear River west of
Smithfield. They were nervous. Bear Hunter had informed Sagwitch
that the Mormons in Box Elder County planned to "kill all the
Indians" there. On the basis of that story, the bands had immediately
moved their camp to a more defensible position. Sagwitch must have
doubted the veracity of the report, however, because he asked
Mormon settler I. J. Merrill to inquire of Peter Maughan if it was
true. Maughan in response invited Sagwitch to come in for a visit,
ensuring him "that the report[s] were false." Sagwitch must have
been satisfied with Maughan's assurances, as the three bands
decided to remain in Cache Valley for the time being.[79]

The situation generally remained very tense and unsettled
though, as various Indian groups continued to participate in thefts
and confrontations with settlers through the remainder of autumn.
Perhaps the chaotic events of late autumn 1862 can be better understood when realizing how desperate the situation for the Shoshone
had become. The offerings from the Mormon communities were not
sufficient to sustain the Shoshone, whose needs increased each year
as their food-gathering options became more limited, and the government had never provided any level of assistance to the
Northwestern bands, with whom they had no treaty. James Duane
Doty, now superintendent of Indian affairs for Utah Territory, made
an official visit to northern Utah and Cache Valley in March and
April 1862. He reported that he had found the Indians there to be
"in a starving and destitute condition." He lamented that no clothing
or provisions had ever been given to them by his predecessors and
that they were "enduring great suffering." Doty purchased and distributed some wheat and a modest amount of clothing and flour to the
Shoshone, predicting that in their destitute condition, they otherwise
"would rob the Mail Stations to sustain life."[80]

Superintendent Doty and his agents understood the potential
value of a treaty between the government and the Northwestern

bands, not only to extinguish Shoshone title to lands already occupied by whites, but also to establish a system for the orderly distribution of goods to them and thus to avoid the kinds of violence brought on by privation. On July 22, the commissioner of Indian affairs instructed Doty to use a congressional appropriation of $20,000 to secure a treaty with the Shoshone. In responding to the commissioner on November 26, 1862, Doty argued against treating with the Shoshone until around May 1863. He felt that negotiations should wait until the government could also appropriate funds to treat with the Bannocks and Utes, who he felt were so "mixed" with the Shoshone as to be almost impossible to separate. Further, he argued that to enter into negotiations with the Shoshone alone would send the message to the other tribes that the Shoshone had received presents "for 'killing' the white men." His arguments made sense and successfully derailed treaty negotiations until the next year. Ironically, a generous distribution of goods to the Shoshone bands in November or December 1862, while problematic in some respects, likely would have averted the final desperate acts of Shoshone violence in late 1862 and January 1863 that brought on the Bear River Massacre.[81]

Meanwhile, Mormon leaders in Logan did what they could to satiate the needs of the Indians by dispersing to them hundreds of dollars worth of produce from the Logan Tithing Office, apparently several hundred dollars worth more than in 1861. Some of those goods made their way to Sagwitch and his people, including a gift of forty bushels of wheat to "Sagwich, Bear Hunter, & Lehighs Band" on the last day of October 1862.[82]

2

Massacre at Bear River

Two of the Brethren visited the Battle field and counted
235 Indians laying Dead, besides Squaws and Papooses
that are badly wounded, laying upon the field, and left
their to perish by Col Connor who has rendered them no
assistance whatever, besides he has Destroyed all there
wheat, Burned up all there wickeups[,] taken all their
Ponies and in fact he has left them nothing.
Apostle Ezra T. Benson, January 31, 1863

Just think, at the tender age of two years receiving seven
wounds which I carry today as a souvenir of that merciless
battle, when women and sucking babes met their death at
the hands of civilization.
Frank Warner (Beshup Timbimboo), June 9, 1918

A series of events in the late fall of 1862 set the stage for an ultimate confrontation between the Northwestern Shoshone and
Colonel Patrick Connor's California Volunteers. In November 1862,
Zachias Van Orman requested Connor's help in rescuing his
ten-year-old nephew, Reuben Van Orman, from the Shoshone in
Cache Valley. The child had been taken by Indians in the fall of
1860 after his family was killed in the Otter Massacre on the lower
Snake River. Van Orman had learned from a relative who traveled
through Cache Valley on his way to Oregon in 1862 that a white boy
approximately the same age as Reuben was living with a band of
Indians there. Van Orman was certain that the child was his nephew
and convinced Colonel Connor to intervene and retrieve the boy, by

force if neccesary. Connor assigned Major Edward McGarry to the task.[1]

Arriving in Cache Valley on November 22, 1862, Major McGarry learned that the Indians were encamped near Providence. By early morning of the twenty-third, he had, with military precision, located, surrounded, and overtaken the camp. Unfortunately for him, the Shoshone had fled their wickiups in the night and only two frightened Indian women could be found. At 8:00 A.M. Bear Hunter and about forty men appeared on the benchland about one mile from the settlement, in clear view of the major and his men. According to McGarry, they initiated a "warlike display" that included shouting, riding in a circle, and "all sorts of antics known only to their race." McGarry divided his forces into three groups and drove the Shoshone to the mouth of the nearby canyon. After the Indians opened fire, McGarry gave the order "to kill every Indian they could see." The skirmishing continued for about two hours. According to the military report filed by McGarry, three Shoshone were killed and one wounded while his troops emerged "without the loss or scratch of man or horse."[2]

Finally Bear Hunter appeared on a knoll waving a flag of truce. McGarry allowed Bear Hunter and his men to surrender, and he interviewed them at length regarding the whereabouts of the Van Orman boy. The chief said that the child had been "sent away" a few days earlier. McGarry held Bear Hunter and four of his men hostage for a day until the child was retrieved and delivered to the troops. The boy hardly looked to be an Anglo, "and acted like a regular little savage" when he was turned over to the troops, who felt it neccesary to wash the paint from his face to determine "his white decent." Satisfied that they had the Van Orman boy, the troops departed victoriously for Camp Douglas. Bear Hunter was furious about his loss to McGarry's troops. On November 25, he gathered warriors to a position near Providence and "made hostile demonstrations" against the Mormons, who Bear Hunter accused of having fed the troops. Seventy men from the Logan militia were quickly dispatched to Providence to aid in the defense. Leaders Ezra T. Benson and Peter Maughan were able to negotiate peace by complying with Bear Hunter's demands for two beeves and a large supply of flour.[3]

Reuben Van Orman (front row, center) with members of Major Edward McGarry's detachment who on November 24, 1862, rescued him from Bear Hunter's band in Cache Valley. Photograph courtesy Special Collections and Archives, Merrill Library, Utah State University, Logan, Utah.

In November 1862, as the Van Orman incident unfolded in southern Cache Valley, traders opened a new road at Cache Valley's north end, which effectively linked Utah's mercantile supply houses to the lucrative mining camp markets in Montana and Idaho. Although the road offered many advantages over other routes, including an abundance of feed and water, it had one distinct disadvantage. The new Montana road passed within a half mile of the age-old Shoshone winter camp at Beaver Creek, north of Franklin, Idaho.[4] George Clayton and Henry Bean, both Montana miners and part-time contract mail carriers, were among the first to use it. The two left Bannack City, Montana, on November 25 headed for Salt Lake City. At a narrow part of the road known as "Robbers Roost," Indians ambushed and killed them. The Shoshone in the area declared that the killings had avenged those who died at the hands of McGarry's troops in the Van Orman incident. Furthermore, it was reported that the Indians intended "to kill every white man they should meet with on the north side of Bear River, till they should be fully avenged for the Indian blood which had been shed by the soldiers in the recent fight."[5]

On December 4, 1862, Major Edward McGarry once again led a detachment of cavalry from Camp Douglas north. This time they intended to recover some of the stock allegedly stolen from emigrants the previous summer and fall and, as the editor of the *Deseret News* summarized, to "give them [the Shoshone] a little taste of the fighting qualities of the Volunteers, should opportunity present."[6] McGarry's troops traveled to Empey's Ferry on the Bear River, where they planned to cross. Anticipating the approaching force, the Indians cut the lines of the ferry. With some difficulty, part of McGarry's soldiers crossed the river, leaving their horses on the south side.

In the next two days, the soldiers captured four Shoshone. They then sent an Indian boy to the Shoshone camp to announce that the four prisoners would be executed the next day at noon unless the stolen stock was returned.[7] On Monday, December 8, at the appointed hour, the Shoshone failed to return the stock. Keeping his awful promise, McGarry ordered the four prisoners tied by their hands to the ferry ropes, after which the soldiers riddled their bodies with fifty-one bullets. Then the soldiers cut the ropes and the dead bodies tumbled into the river. The *Deseret News* editor "feared that it will tend to make them [the Indians] more hostile and vindictive."[8] He was correct.

The executions incensed the Shoshone, who afterwards became "very hostile in their demeanor." Another correspondent noted that the Indian code demanded "blood for blood" and predicted that they would not be satisfied until some of the whites had paid the ultimate price in exchange for the deaths of the executed captives. By the end of January, a large contingent of Shoshone had camped near Bear Lake, where they began holding "frequent councils . . . relative to their future movements and operations." A reporter summarized, "The Indians in the vicinity of the northern settlements are mad, and determined to do as much injury as possible to the white race."[9]

A company of eight miners traveling from the Grasshopper gold mines in Dakota Territory were among the few whites to travel the new route in the weeks immediately following the execution of the four Indian hostages at Bear River. As the men, each with a team and wagon, continued down the road, they missed the path that would have taken them to a ford of the Bear River near Franklin and instead ended up mired and lost. Three men from the party crossed the river and sought provisions and a guide at Richmond. When they returned, they found that the Shoshone had visited their impromptu camp, taken valuables from their wagons, and driven off their stock, apparently acting "very uncourteously" to the five men left behind, who could only watch as their goods were stolen.

Somehow, the men induced the Indians to return some, though not all, of the stock. While some of the miners began ferrying their wagons across the river, one of them obtained the services of an interpreter at Franklin and visited the Shoshone camp on the Bear River. There he attempted to negotiate the return of the other goods, an effort that proved fruitless. By the time he returned, his comrades had nearly completed the transfer of their wagons and supplies across the river. As the miners stood on the banks of the Bear, Shoshone warriors appeared on the other side and began shooting. John Henry Smith was killed, and the other miners fled to Richmond. The Indians then retook the livestock they had returned. The next day a small delegation from the Mormon settlement visited the Indian camp and had an interview with some of the Shoshone chiefs and principal warriors, probably including Sagwitch. Twelve mules and one horse were recovered "with great difficulty" from the Indians, who informed the delegation that the attack was a retaliatory move "to avenge the killings of their friends" by the soldiers.[10]

Within the week, on January 19, 1863, one of the eight assaulted miners, William Bevins, appeared before Chief Justice John F. Kinney in Salt Lake City and swore out an affidavit of facts concerning the attack and the death of Smith. Judge Kinney issued a warrant for the arrest of chiefs Bear Hunter, Sanpitch, and Sagwitch and placed it in the hands of Marshal Issac L. Gibbs. The extremely dangerous nature of the situation made Gibbs unwilling to attempt the arrests without the aid of military escort. With Kinney's approval, Gibbs presented the issue to Colonel Connor at Camp Douglas.[11] Connor had become convinced that the Indians responsible for the late attacks in Cache Valley were the same Indians responsible for depredations on the emigrant trails. In a report Connor noted that he

Brigadier General Patrick Edward Connor (1820–1891). Connor was
promoted from captain to brigadier general on March 29, 1863, after his military victory over the Shoshone at the Bear River Massacre. Charles W.
Carter, photographer, Salt Lake City, ca. 1865. Photograph made from
original glass plate negative courtesy LDS Church Archives, Salt Lake City,
Utah.

was "satisfied that they were a part of the same band who had been murdering Emigrants on the overland Mail Route for the last fifteen years and the principle actors and leaders in the horrid massacres of the past Summer." He already had made preliminary plans for an attack on their winter camp. Connor agreed to allow Gibbs to join him in a march against the Shoshone, but as for the arrest of the chiefs, Connor made it clear to Gibbs that "it was not my intention to take any prisoners."[12]

Colonel Connor's position seemed aggressive and excessive, born of his displeasure about the military appointment that isolated him in the Great Basin. He yearned for the glory and adventure of leading charges in Virginia and proving himself on the active battlefields of the Civil War. Connor anticipated that a major fight with the Indians would give his bored troops an opportunity to exhibit their fighting prowess and might gain him new and more exciting appointments.[13] He must have wanted the opportunity badly. By accepting the responsibility of "arresting" Sagwitch and the other Indian chiefs, Connor agreed to deploy his forces in an area where he had no jurisdiction; the Indian camp on Beaver Creek was still part of Washington Territory and therefore out of his district.

On January 22, Connor sent 69 infantrymen with thirteen baggage wagons and two howitzers toward Cache Valley. He cleverly waited until January 24 to personally lead an additional 220 cavalry soldiers, hoping that if Indian spies saw the first detatchment, they would inacurately assume that only a modest force with limited goals had been dispatched. The two groups rendezvoused under cover of darkness and began the final march to the Indian camp. Mormon frontiersman Orrin Porter Rockwell hired on as Connor's guide for the sum of five dollars per day.[14] He directed the troops to Franklin, and as they left that small Mormon town at 3:00 A.M. on January 29, he guided them directly to the Shoshone camp located along the Bear River.[15]

At the break of day, Connor and his troops approached the Indian camp from a small ridge to the west. Sagwitch reportedly rose early on that horrifically cold morning. He looked in the direction of the approaching troops and, as his grandson Moroni later related, said, "Look like there is something up on the ridge up there. Look like a cloud. Maybe it is a steam come from a horse. Maybe that's them soldiers they were talking about."[16] It did not take long for Sagwitch to see that it was indeed the contingent of soldiers whose arrival had been rumored in camp. The Indians initially anticipated that they would meet with representatives from the government and discuss the recent murders and thefts in northern Cache Valley.[17]

Unfortunately, diplomacy was not part of Connor's agenda, and the California Volunteers lunged forward in a headlong charge against the village. They found that the Indians had a well-protected campsite in a deep ravine on the north side of the Bear River. The Shoshone reportedly had accentuated the protective nature of the site by digging footholds into the riverbanks, which allowed them to duck down for protection and then spring up to fire at the troops as opportunity allowed. Colonel Connor reported that the Shoshone benefited from a terrain that offered "strong natural defenses . . . almost inaccessible to the troops." He also noted that the Indians had woven willows together tightly to create screens from which they could shoot without being detected.[18] One Mormon witness later recalled that the Indians had fortified their position by building rifle pits along the east bank of the creek and along part of the bank of the river.[19]

As the troops began their charge with a frontal offensive, the Shoshone shot several of them without endangering themselves. Connor reported that as the Indians fought "with the ferocity of demons, my men fell fast and thick around me." Casualties were high, and the soldiers were forced to pull back and regroup. Connor sent Major Edward McGarry and a number of troops in a flanking action around and behind the village in an effort to pry the Shoshone from their stronghold in the ravine. Other companies approached the village from its sides.[20]

The temperature that morning felt unseasonably cold, even for southern Idaho. Franklin pioneer William G. Nelson called it a "fearful cold morning." Connor reported the weather had been "intensly cold." Huge chunks of floating ice choked the Bear. As soldiers forded the river, they became so cold that some could scarcely fight, and the wet uniforms immediately froze to their skin.[21] The situation was no better for the wounded Shoshone, who would soon freeze to death in subzero weather.

The implementation of Connor's surround-and-confront tactics proved very succesful in routing the Indians from the ravine. Connor

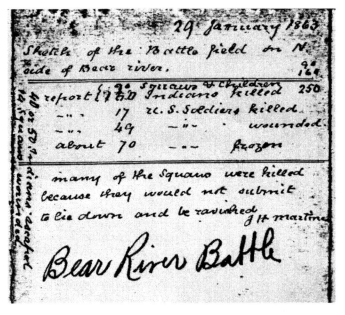

Verso of a detailed drawing of the Bear River Massacre prepared by Cache County surveyor James H. Martineau on January 29 or 30, 1863, just hours after the massacre. The drawing is printed on the following page, and facing it is a transcription of the commentary Martineau wrote on it. Copy of drawing courtesy LDS Church Archives, Salt Lake City, Utah.

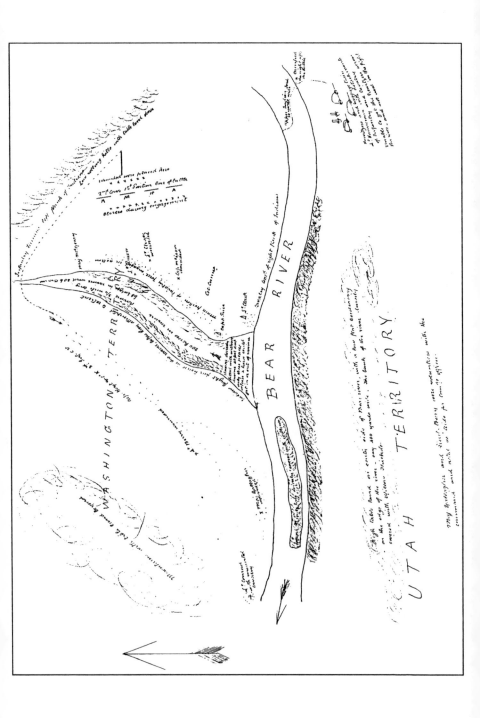

Transcription of Written Comments on Martineau Map of the Bear River Massacre

[Above the river and ravine, west to east, reading clockwise:]

- L⁺. Conrad with mounted cavalry
- Mountains with table land beyond
- Maj. Gallagher wounded
- L⁺. Berry wounded
- Cap. Hoyt & C⁰ K 3ʳᵈ Inf. CV
- Infantry turning left flank of Indians
- Low rolling hills with table land above
- Wounded were placed here
- 2ⁿᵈ Cav. 1ˢᵗ Position line of battle
  - K   M   H   A
- Horses during engagement

[Ravine area, west to east, reading from bottom to top:]

- Indians fought four hours in this ravine, before they attempted to retreat
- Ravine densely filled with willows Ravine 40 feet deep only three places where a horse could get in or out of ravine

- 200 horses in ravine
- Ravine ¾ miles long
- 68 Lodges in ravine and 306 Braves
- Capt. Price
- L⁺. Queen

- Maj. M⁰Geary
- Main portion of Cavalry force engaged in action
  - L⁺. Clark
  - Col. Conner
  - Cap. M⁰Lean wounded
  - L⁺. Chase wounded
  - Cavalry Com⁰. of right flank of Indians

[River and below, north to south, reading left to right]

- Island ¾ mile long densely covered with willows
- Upper Indian Ford 70 yards wide
- camped the night after the battle
- High table land on south side of Bear river, with a low flat bordering on the edge of the river—say 400 yards wide. The bank of the river densely covered with Willow Thickets.

- Howitzers and baggage train
- L⁺. Hanneman with detachments of Infantry and Cavalry unable to get the howitzers across the river—and not used in the fight.

- Maj. Gallagher and Lieut. Berry were volunteers with the comand and acted as aids for Com⁴ᵍ. Officer reported with great satisfaction that as the Shoshone were pushed from behind and attempted escape from the ravine, a company of soldiers at his command shot them. He boasted that most of those who made it out of the ravine alive were shot as they attempted to swim the Bear River. The soldiers' superior guns and larger quantities of ammunition overmatched the inferior weaponry of the Shoshone, which included outdated rifles, bows and arrows, and tomahawks. The large number of mothers, children, and aged adults who needed protection but could not help in the battle also handicapped the Shoshone. Very quickly, the lopsided battle became a wholesale slaughter. The soldiers massacred Shoshone men, women, and children, and held infants by their heels while they "beat their brains out on any hard substance they could find."[22] McGarry's soldiers swarmed the village from behind while other divisions attacked from the front and sides. Local Mormon resident Alexander Stalker noted that once the Indians had been routed, the soldiers pulled their pistols and shot many of them directly in the face from arm's length. Soldiers began burning the wickiups and tepees and killing any who they found still living.[23]

Connor allowed a handful of Mormon settlers to walk over the village turned massacre ground. They observed as the soldiers "mopped up" afterwards. James H. Martineau was sickened by what he saw, including the rape of Indian women. He noted that "many of the squaws were killed because they would not submit to lie down and be ravished." An Indian named Matigan also saw numerous occurrences of rape and declared "the way the 'Soldiers' used the squaws after the battle was 'shameful.'"[24]

Martineau and Shoshone interpreter Israel J. Clark reported to Peter Maughan "sickening accounts of the inhuman acts of the soldiers, as related to him by the squaws that still remain on the ground, after they had routed the Indians, they killed the wounded by knocking them in the head with an axe and then commenced to ravish the Squaws which was done to the very height of brutality, they affirm that some were used in the act of dying from their wounds. The above reports are substantiated by others that were present at the time."[25]

Early reports placed the number of Indians killed at between 210 and 300, with at least 90 Shoshone women and children among the dead.[26] A reporter on the scene at the end of the battle reported that "in one pile forty-eight bodies were counted, and a great many more were killed in attempting to get into the river and after they reached it."[27] Colonel Connor's official report documented 224 Indian casualties and suggested that several others likely remained uncounted in the soldiers' haste to remove their own wounded to safety. Connor also noted the capture of 175 horses and destruction of over seventy lodges and most of the Indians' wheat and other provisions. He wrote that he left "a small quantity of wheat" for the benefit of "160 captive squaws and children." Apostle Ezra T. Benson, who characterized the incident as a "slaughter," disagreed. He had been briefed by Mormon settlers Martineau and Clark about the massacre after they returned from visiting the site. Based on their findings, Benson noted that at least 235 Indians had been killed and a number of Indian women and children "that are badly wounded" remained on the field, "left their to perish by Col Connor who has rendered them no assistance whatever, besides he has Destroyed all their wheat Burned up all there wickeups taken all there Ponies and in fact he has left them nothing." A reporter for the *Deseret News* estimated that most of the Indians had been killed in battle and the rest were "left to take care of themselves as best they could."[28] Seventeen soldiers had been killed. Serious wounds and badly frozen feet and hands affected another seventy. Several of the wounded soldiers died within the week.[29]

Only a part of Sagwitch's family survived the massacre. His eldest son, Soquitch, fought as long as possible and then corralled a horse, which he and a Shoshone woman mounted to attempt their escape. A well-placed bullet killed the woman. He mounted the horse again and bolted from the battlefield. Soquitch hid under an old cedar tree on a nearby hillside, where he watched with horror as his nation was destroyed.[30]

A younger son, Yeager, somehow located Quehegup, his grandmother, who told the boy to follow her out of the wickiup. She instructed him to lie down at her side among the dead and pretend that he was dead. As the two lay motionless, the soldiers began a systematic walk-through of the village, using their bayonets to determine whether the fallen Indians had died, shooting others, or using axes to split the heads of those yet alive. As Yeager heard the screams and commotion of the massacre, he could not stand the tension and finally opened his eyes. He saw a soldier towering over him with gun raised. The soldier lowered his rifle, raised it again, then lowered it. After raising the gun a third time, Yeager was certain that the soldier would shoot him. The soldier finally put the gun down and moved on. Later in life, Yeager commented that he felt he had been saved from death so that he could tell the true story of the massacre. His grandmother was not as fortunate and perished on the field.[31]

Sagwitch's wife, Dadabaychee, attempted to protect her family by hiding them in a small woven grass wickiup, which she attempted to inch off the battlefield and to safety. In spite of all she did, soldiers killed her and her sons Hinnah and Potton.[32] At least one of her two children by Sagwitch fared slightly better. The troops shot two-year-old Beshup Timbimboo numerous times but the boy somehow lived long enough to be rescued by family members, who discovered the child wandering over the battlefield in a dazed condition, still clutching a bowl of frozen pinenut gravy. He recovered from his wounds. Many years later Beshup, by then known as Frank Timbimboo Warner, recounted scenes from the battle, which he claimed to remember in some detail despite his young age at the time it took place. He said, "Just think, at the tender age of two years receiving seven wounds which I carry today as a souvenir of that merciless battle, when women and sucking babes met their death at the hands of civilization."[33]

As troops closed in and the situation became hopeless, Sagwitch jumped on a horse and attempted to escape. He saw another Indian running just ahead, and yelled at him to grab the horse's tail and he would pull him along. His horse lost traction, however, and fell to the ground. A second attempt met with the same results. As Sagwitch raised up, he received two balls in his hand. An Indian named Matigan reported that Sagwitch then ran down the ravine and tumbled into the river, floating under some brush, where he hid until nightfall.[34]

The soldiers set up temporary camp away from the ruins of the Indian village. Their absence from the battlefield allowed Sagwitch and other survivors to quietly return and care for their wounded. The Indians built a fire and called out to those who were still alive to

Frank Warner, also known as Beshup Timbimboo. Caption on verso of photograph reads: "This was taken at Battle Creek (Preston) July 24-1918. Frank stands on the spot where he last saw his mother alive in 1863." Photograph courtesy Mae T. Parry.

Yeager Timbimboo (ca. 1848-1937) and Ray Diamond
Womenup (ca. 1830-1940), who were among the last living
survivors of the Bear River Massacre when the photograph was
taken, ca.1935, near the Washakie Ward meetinghouse.
Photograph courtesy Mae T. Parry.

come and warm themselves. Sagwitch anxiously looked for his family. He reportedly went to what was left of his wickiup and found his baby daughter lying yet alive next to her dead mother. Having no one to suckle the infant, Sagwitch wrapped her in a blanket and placed her in a cradleboard that he hung on a tree, hoping that Mormon settlers would find the baby and save her.[35]

Sagwitch and a few others then rounded up two of the soldiers' horses and a handful of their own ponies and rode off quickly.[36] As one of the leaders specifically targeted by the soldiers, Sagwitch could not risk capture. One source suggests that he made his way to the Franklin home of John Comish, a Mormon settler who had developed a friendship with the chief after Comish's 1862 move to the area. Perhaps he remained hidden there for a few days while his hand healed.[37] Sagwitch had survived the massacre and had also succeeded in his escape. Meanwhile, Colonel Connor, Superintendent Doty, and newspaper reporters agreed in their initial reports, which concluded that Sagwitch, like Bear Hunter and Lehi, had been found dead among the corpses at Bear River.[38]

After the massacre, local Mormon settlers welcomed the wounded and frostbitten soldiers into their homes and public buildings, where they fed them and doctored their injuries. Margaret McNiel Ballard sent bread, butter, and eggs to the soldiers temporarily camped at "Tabernacle Square," while Sarah Earl Harris cooked dinner at her home for several others.[39] Meanwhile, Connor hired area residents who owned sleds to carry the wounded soldiers back to Camp Douglas. The government paid each man with team $42 plus provisions for the round trip.[40] The morning after the battle, local Mormons William Head, William Nelson, and William Hull traveled to the battlefield looking for survivors among the Indians. Hull later wrote:

> We drove our sleigh as far as the river and rode our horses through the river. The first sight to greet us was an old Indian walking, slowly with arms folded, his head bowed in grief, lamenting the dead; he didn't speak to us, and soon left, going toward the north. Never will I forget the scene, dead bodies were everywhere. I counted eight deep in one place and in several places they were three to

five deep; all in all we counted nearly four hundred;
two-thirds of this number being women and children. We
found two Indian women alive whose thighs had been
broken by the bullets. Two little boys and one little girl
about three years of age were still living. The little girl
was badly wounded, having eight flesh wounds in her
body. They were very willing to go with us. We took them
on our horses to the sleigh, and made them as comfortable as possible.[41]

The Hull family adopted the little girl and named her Jane. Some
have speculated that they adopted Sagwitch's infant daughter.[42]

Most Mormons viewed the massacre as a gruesome, but necessary action. Some went further. Franklin-area settler Ralph Smith
called the work of the soldiers nothing less than the "intervention of
our heavenly Father."[43] Mary Ann Weston Maughan, wife of Bishop
Peter Maughan, wrote that the residents of Cache Valley regarded
Connor's efforts as "an interposition of providence in their behalf"
and commented that the Indians had caused so much trouble that
"patience had ceased to be a virtue" in dealing with them.[44] Henry
Ballard, bishop of the Logan second ecclesiastical ward, mentioned
the massacre in his journal, then commented "This put a quietus
upon the Indians, the Lord raised up this foe [Colonel Connor] to
punish them without us having to do it. We had bore a great deal
from them and still had been feeding them, yet some of the wicked
spirits amongst them would stir up trouble against us."[45] George L.
Farrell, secretary of the Logan first ward, recorded in the official
minutes that "We, the people of Cache Valley, looked upon the
movement of Colonel Connor as an intervention of the Almighty, as
the Indians had been a source of great annoyance to us for a long
time, causing us to stand guard over our stock and other property the
most of the time since our first settlement."[46]

Peter Maughan, in a letter to Brigham Young on February 4,
soberly tabulated the number of Indians killed at the massacre and
then added, "I feel my skirts clear of their blood. They rejected the
way of life and salvation which have been pointed out to them from
time to time (especially for the last two years) and thus have perished relying in their own strength and wisdom."[47]

Colonel Connor was quick to characterize the massacre as a complete military success, though he still hoped to kill or capture Pocatello and Sanpitch with their bands, after which, he felt, "the Overland route west of the Rocky Mountains will be rid of the Bedouins who have harassed and murdered Emigrants on that road for a series of years."[48]

Connor reported that his men had suffered "beyond description" in their march from Camp Douglas to the Shoshone village and that they had performed their duties heroically. The United States government agreed, heavily decorating Connor's troops for their valor. To Colonel Patrick Edward Connor went the greatest prize, however. On March 29, 1863, General-in-Chief H. W. Halleck advanced him to the rank of brigadier general as a reward for his leadership in the Indian slaughter.[49]

The Indians had witnessed the annihilation of the greater part of the Shoshone bands headed by Sagwitch, Lehi, Sanpitch, and Bear Hunter, a loss from which they would never really recover. Sagwitch, who had always been mild mannered, now sought revenge. Franklin settler Alexander Stalker was among the first to learn of Sagwitch's intentions, and he reported them in a letter written to local church leaders on February 8, a little over a week after the massacre. Stalker said that an Indian named Noah-a-anger had just informed him that "Sagwitch was not killed, but shot through the hand, and that he is very mad at the Mormons." The Indian informant further noted that Sagwitch had told him that he had seen Mormons helping the soldiers in the fight and promised that he "will use all the influence he has with other Indians to steal from us" in retaliation for that cooperation.[50]

At the same time, Samuel Roskelley, another Franklin settler, learned from the Indian Matigan that Sagwitch and about twenty warriors had escaped and were camped at the head of Marsh Creek, "this side of the California Road."[51] Perhaps Sagwitch knew of Orrin Porter Rockwell's involvement as Connor's guide, or possibly he recognized familiar faces among the small handful of Mormons who watched the battle from a hillside a safe distance away. Perhaps he was angry that the Mormon settlers had taken an active role in feeding the troops after the battle and in nursing wounded soldiers. Whatever the case, Sagwitch was determined to avenge the wrongs that had come to his people. Although Connor's soldiers had earned Sagwitch's anger, it appeared that the Mormons in northern Utah would bear the brunt of it.

On March 22, a Logan correspondent writing to the *Deseret News* noted that the Indians continued to be troublesome and had engaged in stealing horses from various Cache Valley settlements. He further elaborated that "Sagwitch, the chief who was reported killed at Bear river battle, says he will steal every horse he can from settlers or travelers, as does San Pitch also." The reporter added that Indians who had just arrived from the north had declared that they would fight the troops should any dare to return to that country.[52]

Sagwitch's wrenching losses at the Bear River explain his intense anger over what occurred there and his efforts to avenge those wrongs. But he was not alone. Reports through early spring suggested that Indians continued to appear threatening along the road to the northern mines, and as one reporter predicted, they "intend to make good the losses they sustained at the battle of Bear River before the end of the year."[53] Perhaps such reports, as well as continued concerns for the safety of immigrating citizens, were strong factors in General Connor's decision in April 1863 to found a military post near Soda Springs.[54] The actions of Sagwitch's band and other Shoshone groups soon seemed to validate Connor's precautionary move.

Within a short time after the massacre, Sagwitch took to wife a woman known as Wongosoff's Mother and accepted her young son Hyrum Wongosoff as his own.[55] The union meant that Sagwitch once again had a companion and wife and his three sons and stepson had both a mother and a father. The marriage was to be short lived, however.

Trouble with the Shoshone continued into May 1863. On May 1, three Indians attacked Andrew Morrison and William Howell as they gathered wood in Cub River Canyon northeast of Franklin. The Indians reportedly told the men that, because whites had killed the Indians at Battle Creek, "now they were going to kill every white man they could." With that, they shot Morrison twice in the chest with arrows. Howell escaped and ran to Franklin for help. The Indians cut the harnesses and stole both span of horses, soon putting enough distance between them and the local militia to make a clean escape with their booty. Peter Maughan and Ezra T. Benson reported the incident to General Daniel H. Wells, commander of the Nauvoo Legion, adding, "they now threaten to steal some of the Mormon women."[56]

The next day, May 2, men from Sagwitch's band raided the herds at Millville, escaping with several horses. A "friendly Indian" told the Mormons that the Shoshone were responsible for the thefts and that the guilty band could be found in the mountains above Paradise. Captain Franklin Weaver quickly organized a posse to retrieve the animals, and in a half-hour, he with fifteen armed men rode up the canyon. As the group neared the head of the canyon, they saw movement among the aspens. It proved to be men from Sagwitch's band. As John Fish Wright and Lee Dees acted as decoys to draw the Indians out, the other men surrounded and captured them, then marched them back to the Indian camp. John Fish Wright recorded, "The women and children had run off but we took all of the men we found, including the old Chief Segwitch. We told him we were after horses which the Indians had stolen, but he said that he didn't have them, that Bear Hunter, and Pocatello, and one hundred and seventy five warriors had them, they were camped where we had seen the smoke."[57]

Captain Weaver asked Sagwitch to surrender an Indian to be held as a hostage until the chief could go to the big camp and reclaim the horses. After Sagwitch agreed, his son—probably Soquitch—"accused his father of being a coward" and, with bow and arrow, tried to shoot Weaver. Wright, who was standing next to the younger Indian, "grabbed the arrow as he was letting it fly." The other men drew their pistols and prepared to shoot Sagwitch's son. Weaver ordered them not to fire.[58]

Weaver and his men returned to Paradise with their Shoshone prisoner to await Sagwitch's return with the animals. During his absence, as Wright recorded, "We feared an attack from the large camp. We sent out a call for help and by sunset the next day we had several hundred men gathered from various points. We maintained a strong guard there for several weeks but the Indians did not attack the town." On May 8, Sagwitch and his band returned to Paradise without the horses and told the Mormons that they refused to do anything more about the issue. As a result, on May 9, the settlers

arrested Sagwitch, his wife Wongosoff's Mother, his sons Soquitch
and Yeager, and a brother-in-law and placed them under guard in the
Paradise meetinghouse. In reporting the action to General Wells of
the Nauvoo Legion, Peter Maughan and Ezra T. Benson justified
holding Sagwitch because "he has shed so much blood in years that
is past it seems he intends to continue it among us." They also told
Wells that they would hold the Indians as long as he thought it advis-
able to do so.[59]

They apparently kept Sagwitch for only a few days, though his
family remained imprisoned. Peter Maughan noted, in a report to
Brigham Young penned May 23, "We sent Sige-a-watch [Sagwitch]
after some horses about two weeks since. he has returned with four
and had to steal them to get them away. he reports a great many of
our horses at Sanpitches Camp East of Bear River Lake and says
that those are the Indians that are doing us the damage as a retaliation for the Mormons helping the soldiers at Bear River last winter."[60] Commenting on the Shoshone's vengeful justifications for the
thefts, Maughan added, "I am compelled to admit that they have reason to feel bad."[61]

Family accounts record that during her captivity, Sagwitch's
wife, Wongosoff's Mother, felt insulted and shamed while being held
by the guards. Her son, Hyrum Wongosoff, later recalled that in
addition to the generally distasteful circumstances of her confine-
ment, his mother was not even given a moment of privacy when she
needed to *sú*, or relieve herself. During even those times, an armed
guard stood over her. Protesting her situation, Wongosoff's Mother
began a fast, refusing to take any food or water. Within a matter of
days, Sagwitch was again widowed. Shortly thereafter, the settlers
agreed to release him and the others, provided they promised never
to steal horses from the people of Paradise again.[62]

During the time that Sagwitch and his family were held hostage
in Paradise, men from his band continued their involvement in various raids on nearby settlements. On May 8, a handful of them happened upon two Mormon boys just outside of Mantua. The Indians
initially exhibited a friendly attitude and asked the boys if they knew
where the soldiers were. The young men said that they did not know
but assumed that the soldiers could be found at their camp east of
Salt Lake City. One of the Shoshone then said, "You lie, you do

know; the soldiers camped near Ogden last night and you know it, and you know they are coming to fight us again." One of the Indians then leaped from his horse, snatched one of the boys' hats, and rode off with the others all the while "exhibiting a great deal of impudence and madness."[63] The Indians then stole nine head of horses and an ox and attempted to drive off the Mormons' entire cattle herd. The resistance mounted by several Danish farmers foiled their efforts.

As the Indians made their escape into a nearby side canyon, they came upon William Thorp, a Brigham City resident engaged in burning coal. They shot him with arrows, split his skull with a tomahawk, and cut his throat with a large knife.[64] On the same day, perhaps the same Indians stole a large number of horses pasturing in Cache Valley. The next day, Shoshone bands in Ogden Valley stole one hundred horses from settlers in that area. Correspondent Jonathan Calkin Wright reported these incidents and said: "It is very evident that the design of the Indians is to steal as many horses and as much other property and kill as many of the men, women and children of these northern settlements as will satiate their blood-thirsty propensities and traditions of revenge for their defeat and the losses sustained by them in the battle last winter on Bear river with the California Volunteers."[65]

Wright noted that companies of men from Box Elder, Weber, and Cache counties had begun to gather as one large battalion with a goal to reclaim the stolen property and "inflict such chastisement upon the murderous thieves as the magnitude of their outrages justly demands."[66] The assembled battalion overtook the Indians in a canyon near Bear Lake, recovering most of the stolen stock and sending the Shoshone in quick retreat to the north. The reporter for the *Deseret News* suggested that if the Indians continued their "flight" and did not stop "This side of the Cariboo, it would be a great blessing to the people in the northern counties."[67]

Conflicts leading to the Bear River Massacre convinced western Indian agents that lasting peace with the Shoshone would not be achieved without formal treaty negotiations and the promise of yearly government annuities. Retaliatory skirmishes in northern Utah following the massacre strengthened their resolve to do something quickly.

James Duane Doty, Utah territorial governor and acting superintendent of Indian affairs, spent six weeks in May and June 1863
traveling through much of the Shoshone domain in northern Utah
and southern Idaho, meeting with Shoshone bands, and preparing
them to participate in treaty negotiations. As a result of his tour,
Doty concluded that it would be possible to meet with about one-
third of the Shoshone bands that summer and necessary for the
treaty commissioners to meet them "at several points," owing to the
scattered locations of the different bands. Doty was pleased with the
responses received in his preliminary visits. He noted in a June 20,
1863, report to the Indian commissioner that "Many of these Indians
have been hostile, and have committed depredations upon the persons & property of Emigrants & settlers, but now express a strong
desire for peace." He noted three exceptions. "The only Bands that
appear determined to continue hostilities were those of Pokatelo,
Sagowitz [Sagwitch], and Sanpitz—and with those I could obtain no
communication. They must be left to Gen'l Connor's troops."[68]

Doty scheduled first to meet with Chief Washakie's Eastern
Shoshone at Fort Bridger on July 2. Over one thousand people of the
estimated three or four thousand members of the tribe attended the
treaty negotiations. Strangely enough, in his official report, Doty
included Sagwitch and Sanpitch's bands as members of that nation,
noting that the bands under both chiefs "were nearly exterminated"
at the Bear River battle. He added that "Sagowitz . . . and Sanpitz
endeavored to be at Ft. Bridger to unite in the treaty there, but did
not arrive in time."[69]

The commissioners next scheduled to meet the Northwestern
bands at Brigham City on July 30. Doty also listed Sagwitch and
Sanpitch as chieftains of this nation and invited them to represent
their bands at the meeting. On July 26, Sagwitch traveled through
Box Elder Canyon en route to Brigham City for the treaty talks. His
young son, Yeager, and a white man named David Lindsey who had
been "up the creek on a a fishing excursion, with whom Segwitch
had fallen in on his way down the Kanyon," accompanied him.
When the chief neared Mantua, a small detatchment of Connor's
California Volunteers escorting a government train from Fort Connor
at Soda Springs to Camp Douglas misunderstood Sagwitch's intentions and arrested him and the others. Governor Doty soon learned of

the arrests and sent an express message from his temporary quarters at Brigham City to the officer camped near Mantua informing him of the scheduled treaty negotations and "expressing a hope that no violence would be done to the chief by the Volunteers."[70]

Unfortunately, Doty's request was not enough to protect the old chief. The following night, an unknown assassin approached the makeshift prison where Sagwitch was yet held and shot him. The ball reportedly entered his left breast and exited through his right shoulder, "inflicting a fearful, but it is believed not a mortal wound." Family stories say that Sagwitch was shot in the hip, rather than in the upper torso, with the injury being so severe, that Sagwitch walked with a limp for the remainder of his life.[71] After the shooting, the California Volunteers released Sagwitch. His sister Payhaywaikip Payhaywoomenup then loaded her wounded brother on her back and with much effort carried him from Mantua to the Brigham City home of David Rees, who the Shoshone called Quepkachee. Rees, a fluent Shoshone speaker and a longtime friend of Sagwitch, willingly took the injured leader into his home, where he cared for him until his wounds healed.[72]

The gunshot wound rendered Sagwitch unable to attend the treaty negotiations and the signing on July 30 of a document that came to be known as the Treaty of Box Elder. Governor Doty and General Connor presented the terms of the document, which included a call for the restoration of "friendly and amicable relations" between the Shoshone and the people of the United States; acceptance by the assembled natives of the terms of the Fort Bridger treaty with Chief Washakie, including provisions for continued use of government and emigrant roads through Shoshone lands and the safety of those traveling on them; and the allotment of a $5,000 annuity to the Northwestern Shoshone as compensation for the loss of game along the routes traveled by the whites.[73]

Chieftains and leading men including Pocatello, Toomontso, Sanpitch, Tosowitz, Yahnoway, Weerahsoop, Pahragoosohd, Tahkwetoonah, and Omrshee signed the document as the representatives of their bands. Superintendent Doty noted in his official report that Chief Sagwitch had been unable to sign the treaty because he had been "shot by a white man a few days before the treaty and could not come from his Weekeeup to the Treaty ground." Doty added "but he assented to all of its provisions." Bear Hunter's band was apparently not represented at the meeting since, as Doty recorded, "All but 7 of this Band were killed at Bear River battle."[74]

A writer for the *Deseret News* applauded the signing of the document at Brigham City and hoped it would "prevent a reccurrence of the robbing, plundering and tragic scenes which have been enacted in the vicinity of the northern border of Utah within the last eight or ten years."[75] Peace, it seemed, had finally been secured between the Shoshone and the settlers of the area.

Mormons were quick to take advantage of the newly struck peace created by treaty and ensured by the considerable reduction of the Shoshone population. On September 18, 1863, a company of Mormons under direction of Apostle Charles C. Rich crept into Bear Lake Valley with intentions to found a permanent settlement there. Ezra T. Benson reported to Brigham Young that they had selected fifty families for the experiment and that they would need to get established quickly or "they will have cold fingers before they get fixed for winter." The Shoshone were about to lose their last mountain valley to the Mormons.[76]

By the spring of 1864, Sagwitch's band was destitute. The small amount of government goods distributed the previous summer had not been nearly enough to meet even basic needs. On April 15, Sagwitch applied for, and received, 104 pounds of flour from the Mormon tithing office at Logan. In October his band returned to the tithing office for 116 pounds of beef. Through November, Sagwitch took delivery of five bushels of wheat, six bushels of corn, fifteen bushels of potatoes, and fifteen bushels of carrots.[77] In 1864 the Mormons in Cache Valley also hosted Chief Washakie and two hundred members of his tribe at a "public dinner," then sent them on their way with eight sacks of flour, one beef ox, and some tobacco. Chief Pocatello ventured into Logan in July 1864; he was provided with a nice meal at Peter Maughan's home and sent off with a sack of flour.[78] It was apparent that Brigham Young's often-quoted dictum about feeding the Indians rather than fighting them continued to be followed, even though the massacre of the previous year considerably reduced the chances of a war with what remained of the Northwestern Shoshone.

Such distributions from Mormon tithing houses to Sagwitch on behalf of his people, and to other Shoshone, Gosiute, and Bannock bands, continued throughout the 1860s. Occasionally, newspaper writers accused Logan bishop Peter Maughan of authorizing the distribution of tithing goods to the Indians out of fear. In an 1869 letter to the *Deseret News,* Maughan sought to disabuse the public of that assumption and declared: "We have fed them [the Indians] thousands and thousands of dollars in wheat, beef, flour, vegetables, &c., &c., not through fear but through a sense of humanity, realising that they look upon the very lands we occupy as a portion of their inheritance, bequeathed to them by their forefathers, consequently our policy has thus far secured to us, through the blessings of God, that peace which enables our boys to roam over these mountains and kanyons, and our women to travel from place to place unmolested."[79]

In Cache Valley at least, Mormon policies regarding the Indians would continue to be pacific and generous, a situation that Sagwitch must have appreciated. Surviving documents suggest that after 1863, he never again took action against the Mormons but in fact remained friendly to them to his death.

At some point in one of the years immediately following the massacre, Sagwitch and his translator Ejupitchee left for a meeting with Mormon leaders, where the chief would ask for a gift of food for his band. He trusted his young son Beshup Timbimboo to the care of a brother-in-law named Tom. Tom reportedly lost patience with the child and traded him to Mormon settler Salmon Warner for a bag of beans, a sheep, a sack of flour, and a Mormon quilt. Family traditions record that Sagwitch was furious with the transaction. After some thought, however, he decided to leave the boy with the Mormon family. Sagwitch's wife Dadabaychee had been killed at the massacre, and his wife Wongosoff's Mother had died as a result of a protest fast. He had no one to care for Beshup. Family traditions say that he felt that the whites could give Beshup better opportunities than he and his people could hope to provide. A short time later, Salmon Warner traded Beshup to his brother Amos Warner of Willard, Utah. The Warners raised the boy, whom they renamed Frank Warner, as one of their own children. He graduated from Brigham Young College in Logan and enjoyed a distinguished career as an educator. He also served three Mormon proselytizing missions.[80]

Sagwitch continued to wield influence among his people after the massacre. In an interesting case in October 1865, Utah Indian

superintendent Colonel O. H. Irish questioned Sagwitch concerning
the missing wife of a Native American named Indian Tom. The case
came to Irish after the residents of Box Elder County got tired of
hearing Tom's "loud and long . . . lamentations throughout the city."
Sagwitch openly admitted that he had taken the woman away from
Tom but stated that he had done so only because she was happier
with her Shoshone kin than with her husband. Nevertheless,
Sagwitch, who was clearly in control, agreed to visitation rights
that allowed Tom to winter that year with his wife and Sagwitch's
Shoshone band in Cache Valley.[81] Surviving records do not say
if Indian Tom was able to reconcile with his estranged wife. At
around the same time, Sagwitch married Bear Hunter's widow,
Beawoachee. Unlike his four previous wives, Beawoachee would
outlive him by several years.[82]

Situations remained calm through the remainder of 1865, but
in May 1866 Indians from the Salt Lake area rushed into Cache
Valley to warn the Shoshone that "the Mormons were killing the various tribes off in the south by wholesale." They were referring to
Native American casualties of the Black Hawk War, which had
begun in 1865 in central Utah as a series of skirmishes pitting various Ute, Paiute, and Navajo bands against resident Mormon settlers.
The Indian informants implied that the Shoshone residing in the
northern valleys would be the next victims and urged them to flee to
the mountains for their lives. Most of the Indians in Cache Valley
were motivated to do just that. Sagwitch, however, was more cautious. As Peter Maughan recorded, "Sige-watch and his tribe refused
to go untill he had talked with me, he told them I had been his true
friend ever since I came to Cache and I would tell him if the
Mormons were mad." Maughan explained to Sagwitch the nature of
the war in the south and assured him that the Indians in Cache
Valley would be safe as long as they lived at peace with the
Mormons. The explanation satisfied Sagwitch, who immediately sent
runners out to the other bands scattered around the valley with the
news that they were not in danger. For the most part, Sagwitch's message resolved the situation, though Ezra T. Benson implied that the
Shoshone were still nervous when he reported in June 1866 that the
Cache Valley Indians were peaceful, "although sometimes they act a
little strange."[83]

In situations such as the scare caused by the Black Hawk War, Sagwitch exhibited his friendship with, and apparent trust of, the white settlers in Cache Valley. Another instance involved the disappearance on April 7, 1868, of Rosie Thurston, the two-year-old daughter of G. W. Thurston of Mendon Mill in Cache Valley. After the settlers' exhaustive search failed to locate the child, they concluded that Indians must have taken her. While the Mormons questioned many Native Americans, none had information or they were unwilling to tell what they did know. Sagwitch, however, talked to Peter Maughan within a month of the child's disappearance. Maughan reported that "Sige-Witch informed me that he had heard through other Indians that Po-ka-tel-lo's second mother (stepmother) stole the child."[84] Maughan followed the lead Sagwitch gave him and gathered additional corroborative evidence that seemed to confirm his story. Sadly, the little girl was never recovered, but Sagwitch's information at least allowed Maughan to console her grieving parents with news that the child was alive and reportedly well cared for.

Correspondence from the late 1860s and early 1870s from Mormon leaders in Cache Valley contains a handful of reports involving purported Indian alliances. In some cases, the stories detail threatened attacks by an amalgamated Indian force on the Mormon settlements in Cache and Box Elder valleys. Other cases involve Indians banding together for protection from anticipated attacks by Mormons or federal troops. The stories illustrate how unsettled, desperate, and frightening life had become for Native Americans. They also show the role played by Sagwitch in investigating such threats, then negotiating peaceful solutions.

One such case was reported by Peter Maughan to Daniel H. Wells, head of the Nauvoo Legion, on March 29, 1870. Earlier that same month, a large meeting of various Indian groups, including several Shoshone from Cache Valley, had been held at Battle Mountain near Elko, Nevada. A large number of the Shoshone from Fort Hall had reportedly attempted to induce Indians from the Northwestern bands to become part of a large force that planned to attack the northern Mormon settlements on April 10. For their participation, the Cache Valley bands would be given all of the houses, lands, and cattle north of Box Elder. When the plan was reported to Sagwitch, he immediately opposed it and openly spoke against the alliance. He also reported the information to Peter Maughan who wrote:

> I consider Sigewatch the most reliable Indian in this region, he has been with us from our first settlement of this valley and has prevented a collision between us and the Indians several times, he positively refuses to join any party against the Mormons, and often he made his noble speech to the other Indians[.] a few days ago in this office he said, if the Indians should help the soldiers to either kill or drive off the Mormons, they would next kill the Indians on purpose to get their squaws to—then when they got tired of the squaws, they would kill them which would make a final end of the Indian race."[85]

Nothing became of the anticipated April attack, though the plan had many enthusiasts. Sagwitch's spirited oratory against it had been effective in greatly reducing the interest of the Northwestern bands.

A few months later, however, Sagwitch was to be pressed into service again. During June 1870, Brigham Young and other church officials traveled by wagon on a tour of the church's northern settlements. After leaving Soda Springs they intended to visit the Mormon towns surrounding Bear Lake. Little did they know the peril they potentially faced at the hands of a combined force of two thousand Shoshone and Ute Indians. However, Sagwitch understood the gravity of the situation, and rushed to the Round Valley home of Lewis L. Polmanteer on June 16. As Polmanteer reported, Sagwitch "earnestly begged me to accompany him to the camp . . . to explain to them the object of President Young and party's visit to Rich County."[86]

Sagwitch ushered Polmanteer into a council with twenty-five Shoshone leaders. He explained to them that Brigham Young simply intended to lead a small party of the church's leaders on a tour of the settlements. After what was described as a sullen pause of a few minutes, one of the chiefs then exclaimed "What the hell does all this talk mean?" When Polmanteer asked to what he was referring, the chief continued, "The talk about Brigham Young coming here with two thousand men to use us up." Polmanteer assured them that

Young and his small entourage, which included nine women, had absolutely no such intentions.[87]

The Shoshone then explained that they had been told by government employees at Fort Bridger that Young intended to kill them, that they should take the offensive by plundering the Mormons, and that they could be assured of assistance from the soldiers in their efforts. Lewis Polmanteer reminded the gathered natives of the many times the Mormons had fed and helped the Indians and of the long-standing Mormon policy of peaceful coexistence with them. Some among the council then spoke in support of Polmanteer's comments. Eventually the leaders agreed to "stick to the Mormons who had always been their friends" and not attempt an attack on Young's party. Only because of Sagwitch's visit had Polmanteer been given the opportunity to defuse a potentially explosive situation.[88]

Through the 1860s, the Northwestern bands continued to follow, as much as possible, a pattern of travel that placed them at prime food gathering sites at the appropriate times in the year. Of course they were forced to alter that age-old circuit significantly to compensate for resources lost to Anglo settlement.

The completion of the transcontinental railroad in May 1869 made matters even worse. Large numbers of emigrants could now easily reach Utah and compete with the Shoshone and other Indian groups for land and resources. The new railroad also spawned the birth of Corinne in the heartland of the Shoshone domain, a development that from its beginning proved to be problematic to the Indians.

Another important development affecting the Shoshone was the establishment of the Fort Hall Reservation as the permanent home of the Northern Shoshone and Bannock tribes. Fort Hall had been set apart, via executive order, by President Andrew Johnson on June 14, 1867, as a reserve for the Shoshone. A series of agreements including the Treaty of Fort Bridger in July 1868 and a treaty with the Bannock in February 1869 complicated those plans. On July 30, 1869, Ulysses S. Grant signed an executive order placing the Bannock at Fort Hall. It was clear that the Northern Shoshone and the Bannock would share the single reservation. Around the same time, Colonel De Lancey Floyd-Jones was appointed Idaho superintendent of Indian affairs and Lieutenant W. H. Danilson as Fort Hall agent to administer the Indian commissioner's programs for the two tribes. Although the Northwestern bands were recognized as an independent group from the Fort Hall and Boise and Bruneau Shoshone settling on the reservation, they too fit under the larger umbrella of the Northern Shoshone and were allowed, even encouraged, to settle at Fort Hall. Many of the Northwestern Shoshone chose to do just that in the years that followed.[89]

The Northwestern bands did have an agreement with the United States independent of those with other Shoshone groups. The Treaty of Box Elder, preceding the establishment of Fort Hall by several years, assumed that the Northwestern bands would continue to roam northern Utah and southern Idaho freely. Interaction with federal representatives was required only once during the year, during the annual autumn distribution of goods valued at $5,000. That amount of money could hardly purchase enough foodstuffs and household goods to supply the estimated twelve hundred remaining Northwestern Shoshone through a typical year. After the initial distribution in 1863, however, the government seldom, if ever, again funded even that amount. Records documenting a total expenditure for the 1870 distribution of $1,039 are probably representative of most of the years after 1863.[90]

Utah superintendent J. E. Tourtellotte noted in his 1869 report that most Northwestern Shoshone of the time still made their livelihood through hunting and fishing but that some had begun to work occasionally as "laborers or herdsmen" for area residents. Sagwitch apparently was one of those who did some herding for Mormon settlers. During a particularly bad grasshopper year in Cache Valley, cattle herds were suffering from a lack of feed. Sagwitch reportedly offered to herd cattle owned by residents of Paradise to the Promontory Mountains, where he said he would graze them until the effects of the insect infestation had passed. A few residents, including Henry Shaw, accepted his offer and were rewarded for trusting Sagwitch and his band with the return of healthy and plump animals a few months later. Shaw paid Sagwitch three dollars per head for his services. Sagwitch then divided the money equally among his group.[91] Members of Sagwitch's band also augmented their livelihood at times by selling chokecherries, serviceberries, and "Indian potatoes" to the residents of Cache Valley, and by "breaking" wild horses for the settlers in exchange for wheat or corn.[92]

Sometimes they were even more creative. On August 13, 1869, Sagwitch and members of his band came to Ogden, where they provided the evening's entertainment for a large group of citizens. The party capped off a series of events involving the reorganization of the Weber County Militia and the enlistment of a number of new recruits. As a newspaper correspondent reported, the Indians "commenced a grand 'pow wow' and serenade of the citizens. They danced lustily to their own native music, both vocal and instrumental, while Sag-Wich acted as floor manager and master of the ceremonies." The reporter noted that the appreciative audience contributed generously to Sagwitch and the others with money, dry goods, and groceries.[93]

The Shoshone often stopped at the houses of white settlers to ask for a meal and some supplies. Shoshone culture dictated that they share resources equally among their group. They likely assumed that other cultures were similarly generous. It also must have seemed appropriate to them to ask the white settlers for gifts as reimbursement for the use of their lands. Emma Liljenquist, who, as a child, settled at Hyrum, Utah, with her parents in 1863, remembered that kind of a relationship with Sagwitch. She reminisced that "An Indian named Sacquich and his squaw often came to my fathers home. They would visit with us, eat our food, and ask for provisions to take with them." She also remembered that Sagwitch would bring sacks of dried chokecherries and serviceberries and store them in her father's cellar, returning in early spring for them.[94]

The traditional homeland of the Northwestern bands straddled the boundary line between Utah and Idaho territories, leaving Indian agents in both districts somewhat unclear about their responsibilities to them. The distribution of annuity goods to the Northwestern bands in autumn 1870 is telling. The event, held near Corinne in Utah Territory, was nevertheless attended by agents from both the Idaho and Utah agencies.[95] Similarly, Idaho agent M. P. Berry traveled to Corinne in October 1871 to force the return to Fort Hall of those Shoshone belonging to that reservation. He found "two loades of Pocatellahs people" who he ordered to return to Idaho. Another 250 Shoshone were found to have never been registered at Fort Hall, and "therefore they were not disturbed." As a result of his visit to northern Utah, several lodges of Shoshone who had never resided at

Fort Hall chose to move there. Many, however, seemed happy to remain in northern Utah.[96]

Agent Berry even delayed distribution of rations to the Fort Hall Shoshone in 1871 until he could ascertain which Indians belonged to the reserve to "guard against supplying wandering families who belong to other agencies, and who being near here, come in and claim this one as their residence for the purpose of receiving goods."[97] Berry noted that around forty lodges of "Cache Valley" Shoshone "have no Agent, neither have they any Reserve or fixed place of habitation. The majority of them habitate near such places as Corinne or Ogden, and live on the offal of Slaughter Houses and by acting as general scavengers for such places—The Mormon Bishop at Brigham City occassionally issues from their private stores wheat or flour to such as live near that place—so I have been led to believe by the Indians."[98] Utah superintendent J. E. Tourtellotte in his annual report for 1870 expressed his hope that a government farm could be established for the Northwestern bands, who, he said, had "no permanent place of abode, but rove among the mountains and valleys wherever they find the best hunting and fishing."[99]

It was clear that the unattached Shoshone bands were a cause of confusion and concern for agents from both territories. It was also clear that the modest annuity goods received each fall did not satisfy the needs of these people through the year. Occasionally, Utah Indian agents utilized the services of local Mormon leaders, including Bishop Alvin Nichols in Brigham City and Bishop Peter Maughan in Cache Valley as government representatives to distribute gifts of food to these bands. In the years following the Bear River Massacre, Maughan was typically furnished with a supply of flour, beef, tobacco, ammunition, and other goods for distribution. The federal agent would personally distribute blankets and clothing on his occasional visits to Cache. Maughan felt that it had been a good arrangement, reporting to the Utah superintendant that "this worked very well."[100] It was a less successful arrangement by the end of the decade, due to the increased needs of the Indians and the decreasing supplies furnished by the government.

During the 1868–69 winter, Maughan received eighty sacks of flour from the Utah agent for distribution to several bands wintering in Cache Valley. Maughan complained that the supplies were "a mere pittance to be divided among so many in a year."[101] The agent also supplied Maughan with one hundred sacks of flour in August 1869 but not, as Maughan wrote, "one dimes worth of anything" else through October 1870.[102] The Cache Valley Mormons had to make up the difference with gifts of beef, potatoes, and additional flour.[103] Maughan told Indian Superintendent J. J. Critchlow that he found Agent Tourtellotte "so small in his notions about Indians." Maughan complained that Tourtellotte's stinginess had created a "very burdensome" situation for the settlers. He added, "Last Summer Such a host of Indians came into this valley on theire annual Summer visit, all friendly, but had nothing to Eat, that humanity required me after inducing the Citizens here to donate freely which the[y] did, to borrow Sixty four (64) sks flour to find the Indians a Scanty Subsistance while here, we have been giving to those who reside here ever since."[104] Maughan closed his letter to Critchlow with a plea for relief from the burden of feeding the Indians.

Just three days after Maughan penned his letter to Critchlow, Lorenzo H. Hatch, the mayor of Franklin in northernmost Cache Valley, also wrote to the agent. Hatch described the financial burdens his small town had endured while feeding a band of Indians who had contracted smallpox. The mayor had ordered the Indians away from town where they had already begun to spread the disease to the settlers. In order to get the Indians to leave, the community was forced to provide for all of their needs in a temporary camp. In addition, Hatch noted that his community had found it neccesary, from the commencement of settlement, to care for "quite a number of half starved Indians who are continually in our midst." Like Maughan, Hatch asked for an appropriation of supplies to support the Indians, adding, "We consider it is the place of the Government to assist the Indians & not to leave the responsibility on a poor frontier people."[105]

Critchlow forwarded Hatch's letter to the commissioner of Indian affairs. In an accompanying note, he wrote that he felt it was "bad policy" to furnish supplies to Indians at any place other than the reservation, but acknowledged that due to the government's "inability to supply and provide for them there," it was unavoidable that situations like those at Franklin would arise. Critchlow noted that a number of similar requests had come to his attention by letter and in person. So many so, in fact, that he suggested that the Indian commissioner consider hiring someone who could look into all such cases.[106]

The commissioner of Indian affairs must have agreed with Critchlow and other agents who had long complained about the unassigned bands. In October 1871, Secretary of Interior C. Delano and Commissioner H. R. Clum appointed Reverend George W. Dodge as special agent to the Western, Northwestern and Gosiute tribes.[107] The scattered Shoshone bands of northern Utah and southern Idaho were about to enter a new era.

3

The Shoshone Mormons

The day before yesterday i baptized one hundred and two[,] to day i am calld on to baptize another band of about twenty and still they come[,] and the work is extending like fire in the dry grass.

George Washington Hill, May 7, 1873

The Reverend George W. Dodge was thrilled with his appointment as special agent to the Western, Northwestern, and Gosiute tribes of Utah and Nevada and anxious to begin work as quickly as possible. Immediately after his December 10, 1871, arrival in Salt Lake City he began to make inquiries about the condition and locations of his scattered Shoshone charges. By January 6, 1872, he had become well acquainted with the "great destitution" so prevalent among the Gosiute and Northwestern Shoshone bands in the region and felt compelled to purchase and distribute provisions to a starving Shoshone group he discovered near Ogden. On January 26, Dodge submitted a request for first-quarter funds for his agency. In consideration of the "entire destitution of provisions" that he found among the Indians, he felt justified in placing all such Indians he encountered on one-half ration of flour and two rations of beef per week. He requested an appropriation of $1,850 for the Northwestern bands.[1]

By January 30, Dodge was authorizing the distribution of four pounds of fresh beef per person per week to the Gosiute at Skull Valley, the Northwestern Shoshone near Corinne, and the Western Shoshone at Camp Floyd and had signed a contract with Charles Popper to supply the meat as specified. He justified his actions to the commissioner, saying, "There are just so many Indians. They are just so needy." Dodge seemed genuinely overwhelmed by the incredible poverty and suffering that he found to be commonplace among the displaced Shoshone bands and seemed committed to single handedly fixing those problems via his agency. He rented a large warehouse and office to hold the generous provisions he hoped to soon distribute and hired a clerk to help him with his rapidly increasing "business." Dodge asked for an additional $14,709, encouraging Washington to "Try libberal things with the Indians of my charge and see if the fruits do not justify the experiment."[2]

Dodge's soft heart and generous attitude seemed to know no bounds when he estimated in a February report to the commissioner that he would need $125,000 to adequately cover the costs of his office and the needs of his charges through the remainder of the year. The Shoshone undoubtedly rejoiced to have an advocate concerned with their very real and immediate needs. Commissioner F. A. Walker, however, was not amused. He quickly fired off a response demanding that Dodge fire his clerk, move his office out of the spacious facility in Salt Lake City to a site accessible to the Shoshone, and cancel all contracts to supply provisions to the Indians.

Dodge replied on March 18 that he would comply as directed, though he felt it to be "the most painfull step I have ever been called upon to take in a business line."[3] He continued his lament to the commissioner, saying, "How Indians are to live without food, I know not. You may be able to inform me. If they can, they have different stomachs, and different systems generally from mine. I know from positive and critical inspection, that those I have been feeding have nothing to subsist upon."[4]

Dodge reported to the commissioner that the Mormons had begun to withhold supplies from the Indians and had stopped employing them in order to embarrass the government and find fault with its officials for the resulting Indian problem. He stated that the hungry and unemployed natives had flocked to him for assistance. They had no other options. Even hunting had become a worthless endeavor, Dodge argued, because northern Utah had become "more destitute of game than Maryland or Virginia," examples familiar to the commissioner in Washington, D.C. Reverend Dodge expressed a burning "shame" as he reported to the commissioner that many starving Shoshone women had turned to prostitution for their very survival.

When he tried to dissuade them from it, they replied, "We must have some food. White man no give it any other way." Dodge added, "I know not how to civilize these degraded beings if we neglect their stomachs and backs."[5] Dodge had no alternative but to greatly scale back his program of temporal salvation among his Shoshone charges.

By April Dodge was again visiting the various bands of his agency. He was delighted to note that some Gosiutes had begun to farm and had planted forty-five bushels of wheat, some potatoes, and vegetables from seeds he had provided. The Northwestern bands, however, had no need for seeds as none of them were engaged in agriculture. He reported that "They roam here and there, through the northern part of this territory, and give me more trouble by their incessant begging, gambling away, or selling of their goods than all others." Dodge was especially concerned that he often found Shoshone from the Northwestern bands mingling with the Mormons, including the church's Indian interpreter, Dimick B. Huntington, whom he judged to be a very unsavory character.[6]

Reverend Dodge was very concerned about the friendships that seemed to exist between many of the Shoshone he interviewed and the resident Mormons. In an April 1872 report he decried the Mormons' view of Indians as "'Noble Red men' the 'Desendents of Joseph,' who are 'Prophetically delivered over to the Latter Day Saints to be defended and enlightened.'" By July Dodge seemed beside himself as he reported that a "mysterious movement" that seemed steeped with Mormon doctrinal overtones and involved a "Great White Prophet" had created great excitement among diverse Indian groups and was causing Indians to flock to Utah in large numbers.[7]

Dodge learned that many Indians expected the "prophet" to announce that they were descendants of biblical Joseph through his son Manasseh and that they were to be "taken under the supervision of the Mormon Church." Dodge added, "They say that the Mormons have always treated the Indians with kindness, which is true in the maine, no doubt. They say the Indians have great confidence in Brigham Young, the Bishops, and Mormon people generally. They say that the Indians have not any confidence in the agents that Govt. appoints from a distance."[8]

More pressing issues in July and August—including a serious disagreement with Agent J. J. Critchlow concerning the Uintah

Valley Reservation and troubles with the Ute Indians in central Utah—distracted Dodge from pursuing further what he probably viewed as a treasonous relationship between the Mormons and the Indians. Through the remainder of the year he could only toss occasional barbs at the Mormons, whom he continued to view with great mistrust and contempt.[9]

In an August 1872 report, Agent Dodge noted that the Northwestern bands, undoubtedly including Sagwitch and his people, would not farm but preferred to beg for provisions from the settlers. He noted that six hundred of them had camped near Logan, that they claimed "proprietorship in the soil," and that they were in the habit of levying contributions from the settlers as their "rentage."[10] Over time, Dodge became convinced that these kinds of problems could only be solved if the various Ute and Shoshone tribes in the territory were gathered to a large reservation. He also felt that the Gosiutes and Northwestern bands could successfully be relocated out of the territory and settled at Fort Hall in Idaho or at Camp Brown in Wyoming.[11]

Agent M. P. Berry at Fort Hall agreed. He had become increasingly frustrated with Shoshone from the Northwestern bands who drew provisions at Fort Hall but did not remain there. Rather, they "scattered along the Rail Road and among the Mormon settlements." Berry recommended that they all be sent to Fort Hall permanently.[12]

In his annual report to the secretary of the interior, penned in October 1872, Reverend Dodge expressed the difficulties of administering any kind of program with a people so geographically scattered. He noted that not even half of his charges who had treaty agreements with the government could be reached to receive their annuity gifts. Dodge also complained that the monies allotted for the special agency had only been one-fourth or one-fifth of the $100,000 that had been needed. He encouraged the government to settle the Indians on reservations where they could receive comprehensive training in industrial arts, hygiene, and Christianity.[13]

Dodge must have been pleased to note in his December 7 report that the Northwestern Shoshone bands which had previously disdained farming "are now pleading for the privilege of going to work" and had requested removal to Fort Hall. Agent Dodge asked them to consider moving to the Indian Territory instead, where they would be given "good land." He reported to the commissioner that the Shoshone were willing to go to either reserve if the government furnished them with the necessary tools needed to succeed at farming. Dodge felt that the Indian Territory would be ideal because the Comanche residing there also spoke Shoshone and perhaps Utah's bands could be placed in a single agency with them.[14] It was George W. Dodge's final official recommendation. He received word on December 5 that his special agency had been discontinued, likely due to the perceived excesses of his administration. In a letter of response, Dodge defended his record of service and expressed concern for the Shoshone thus affected by the agency's closure.[15]

It was appropriate that he do so. Dodge's reports of "great destitution" among the Shoshone bands had not been exaggerated, and the closure of the only office concerned with their welfare placed them in a perilous position. Without governmental sponsorship or representation, the scattered Shoshone bands would have to continue to scratch out an existence in a region that became more heavily populated with whites every year. Even Cache Valley, where Mormon settlement of the old Northwestern Shoshone homeland's epicenter had begun just sixteen years earlier, boasted an impressive 9,798 white settlers by 1872.[16]

Faced with almost insurmountable odds and few options, the Shoshone from Dodge's agency, including Sagwitch's people, sought otherworldly help. In this action they were not alone. Agent Dodge had been greatly concerned in 1872 by reports of a "mysterious movement" affecting Indians from several tribes in the region. That movement, which included the belief that a Nevada Paiute had been selected by the "Great Spirit" to "foretell the future of all the Indians in America," continued strong throughout 1873. Many Native Americans felt that this "Voice From the West," as they called their Paiute prophet, would reveal to them their "origin and destiny" and tell them what they must do to once again have the good life they had lost. Dodge reported that the Indians had already been told they were Israelites and that they would be "taken under the supervision of the Mormon Church." That is why, according to Dodge, so many Indians had been flocking into the Mormon settlements from outlying areas through the summer of 1872.[17]

The Mormons enjoyed an interesting and unique relationship with Native Americans. They managed to maintain generally peaceable and friendly relations with Indian groups even as their European-style settlements displaced them, forcing the Indians to find new homes and adopt new lifeways. It was a gradual process, but the results were no less dramatic than if a conquering army had abruptly and forcibly taken the region from them. Many Native Americans resented the white settlers for these losses, though a general Mormon policy of kindness and relative generosity toward them seemed to soften that impact considerably. Even Dodge grudgingly noted that Indians he spoke with claimed that the Mormons had settled upon their lands "by their permission" and that the "most friendly relations" existed between the two peoples.[18]

The Mormons felt that they had been divinely guided to Utah where they were to establish their kingdom of God on earth. Logic followed that it was therefore God's will that the lands be utilized by Mormons for farms and villages, regardless of who had owned or used them previously. Church leaders were at least somewhat cognizant, however, that such development displaced the Indians and left them at risk. In the early 1850s, Brigham Young had declared, "When we came here, they could catch fish in great abundance in the lake in the season thereof, and live upon them pretty much through the summer. But now their game has gone and they are left to starve. It is our duty to feed . . . these poor ignorant Indians; we are living on their possessions and in their homeland."[19]

More important, however, than official statements or individual acts of benevolence towards Native Americans were the theological underpinnings for such philosophies. Pioneer Mormons shared their era's view that the Indians represented a degraded and ignorant race. However, unlike their "gentile," or non-Mormon, neighbors, Mormons claimed for the Native Americans a royal lineage as literal descendants of the biblical tribe of Joseph, making the "dusky natives" pure-blooded Israelites.

The founding text of the Church of Jesus Christ of Latter-day Saints, published in 1830 as the Book of Mormon, claimed to be no less than the history of God's dealings with ancestors of the American Indians. In fact, the title page of every edition of the Book of Mormon included the following statement of purpose: "Written to the Lamanites [Indians], who are a remnant of the house of Israel; and also to Jew and Gentile . . . which is to show unto the remnant of the house of Israel what great things the Lord hath done for their fathers; and that they may know the covenants of the Lord, that they are not cast off forever."[20] The introduction made it clear that the book, though utilized overwhelmingly by whites, had been written primarily for the Indians.

Mormonism's first prophet, Joseph Smith, emphasized the importance of missionizing the Indians by sending four men, including two of the "three witnesses" of the Mormon scripture, "into the wilderness among the Lamanites" just six months after the founding of the church.[21] The group visited several tribes, including the Catteraugua, Wyandot, Shawnee, and Delaware, and felt that they received a warm reception from the Indians, if not from Indian agents and sectarian missionaries who already had established governmental and religious programs there.[22] Brigham Young could do no less in the West. Besides continued utterances upholding the doctrinal importance of the Indian, Young's acts, as the driving force behind similar missionizing activities in the western United States, included the creation of church-run farms and reservations intended to be centers of conversion to both Mormon theology and American agrarian ways.[23]

Many tenets of Mormon gospel, as presented by its elders to native peoples, were reminiscent of the Indians' own religious beliefs. One anthropologist concluded that "the emphasis placed on Joseph Smith's visions by the missionaries attracted the natives because visions, dreams, rain dances, and other religious experiences had for centuries been part of the various Indian subcultures."[24] Mormonism shared a commonality with most Christian faiths of the era in believing in the power of good and evil, the breath of life, spirit, and soul, and in the creation of man. However, few faiths other than Mormonism emphasized the importance of dreams, visions, speaking in tongues, the raising of the dead, the laying on of hands, and the gift of prophecy, all familiar concepts in various native religions.

The Mormon ordinance of healing by the application of oil and the laying on of hands was believable to Native Americans because it resembled their own shamanistic healing rituals in which touching or rubbing a part of the body was part of curing sickness or raising the dead.[25] After Mormon leaders officially acknowledged polygamy as a church practice on August 29, 1852, the Indians, some of whom had practiced polygamy on a limited scale for centuries, had an additional point of reference with Mormons that they did not share with other Christian faiths. Further, mainstream Americans viewed both Mormons and Native Americans in a negative light for such unusual practices. This at times fostered an "us versus them" attitude that might have further allied Indians and Mormons.

It is impossible to know how such factors affected Sagwitch. He undoubtedly understood that the expansion of Anglo colonization threatened the future of his people and that the failure to choose a new course could eventually doom them. However, Sagwitch's decision in the spring of 1873 that he and his band would accept Mormon baptism from George Washington Hill seems to have gone beyond a calculated response to his circumstances. Contemporary Mormon sources imply that Sagwitch and other band chiefs experienced some kind of spiritual conversion to Mormonism through dreams or visions.

Ech-up-wy, one of Sagwitch's fellow chiefs, related one such experience from early spring 1873, a vision in which three men supposedly came to see him at his lodge in Skull Valley. One of the messengers, acting as spokesman, told him, according to missionary George Washington Hill who reported the story, "that the 'Mormons' God was the true God, and that he and the Indians' Father were one; that he must go to the 'Mormons,' and they would tell him what to do, and that he must do it; that he must be baptized, with all his Indians; that the time was at hand for the Indians to gather, and stop their Indian life, and learn to cultivate the earth and build houses, and live in them."[26]

Sagwitch and other Shoshone leaders believed Ech-up-wy's experience to be a valid expression of the Great Spirit's wishes for them. They soon broke camp and headed to Ogden to find the person shown to them in the vision. They sought out George Washington Hill.

George W. Hill seemed to be a natural contact for Indians seeking to affiliate with Mormonism. He was well known to the Shoshone, having worked with them extensively as a missionary in the Salmon River mission at Fort Lemhi between 1855 and 1859 and occassionally thereafter as a translator. Throughout 1872 he had also worked under direction of Agent George W. Dodge to distribute goods to the Northwestern bands in the Ogden area.[27]

During the earlier assignment at Salmon River, Hill mastered the Shoshone language and gained a great understanding and respect for the Shoshone people and their culture. Hill's son later wrote of that period:

> George built himself a house, one of the best in the fort, and invited the Indians in. He busied himself in learning to talk to them in their language, would visit them, and eat the food they prepared. Thus he soon gained their confidence and love, and they felt that he did not think himself above them . . . when they visited him he gave them something to eat and partook with them at the same time, and when he visited them, they returned the hospitality in the same way. It did not take [him] long to master the Shoshone language . . . He soon became a great favorite among the Indians."[28]

The Shoshone honored Hill by acknowledging one of his physical traits in a special name they gave him, Inkapompy, meaning "Man with Red Hair."[29] When Sagwitch called at Hill's house in 1873, he asked for Inkapompy, signifying that he already knew Hill personally.[30]

Hill's friendly approach made him a popular and trusted associate of the Shoshone. His reputation, however, had been greatly enhanced by the performance of Mormon healing ordinances, the results of which the Shoshone viewed as miraculous manifestations of the power of God and as indications of Hill's spiritual power. Hill's reputation as a healer went back to the summer of 1855, when the Lemhi Shoshone invited him to help them build fishing weirs for the salmon run and then invited him to be the first to use the new equipment. Hill's son George later recounted what happened next: "He [Hill] snagged a large salmon, but in attempting to hoist him out of the water the hook tore loose and the pole which George was using came back with great force, striking one of the Indians on the side of

George Washington Hill (1822-1891), ca. 1875. Known by the Shoshone as
Inkapompy, "Man with Red Hair." Copy photograph courtesy LDS Church
Archives, Salt Lake City, Utah.

the head. The Indian fell prone and seemed lifeless. Great excitement was manifested by the Indians, but George immediately administered to the stricken brave, and in a few moments he revived. Peace was restored and the Indians were deeply impressed, feeling that the stricken warrior had been healed by supernatural power."³¹

In another incident, during the fall of 1855, Hill cemented his reputation as a spiritual leader. As he later recorded,

> A band of Indians came in from their hunt, with a little girl, very sick of mountain fever. Their relatives told them that we practiced the ordinance of laying on hands for the healing of the sick. When the father came after me, I told him that we did not make a practice of administering to those that did not belong to the Church; and if we went and administered to the child, and it recovered, I should expect him to be baptized. He said it was a bargain. Accordingly I took David Moore, of Ogden, and B. F. Cummings, Sen., with me, and we anointed the child and laid our hands upon her. When we took our hands off her head, her face was literally covered with large drops of sweat; the fever was gone, and the child got well immediately.³²

The following Sunday, the father of the little child, along with dozens of others, came to Fort Lemhi and requested baptism at the hands of Inkapompy. "After explaining the seriousness of the ordinances [Hill] asked if any still desired baptism." Many replied in the affirmative, and Hill baptized fifty-six of them.³³ The Shoshone's special regard for Hill was evident during the baptismal service. Hill wrote that after he had baptized all of the adult males, the president of the mission suggested that he come out of the icy water while one of the other missionaries baptized the women. When Hill told the Shoshone that someone else would baptize the remainder of them, "They refused to come, saying if I did not baptize them they would not be baptized. At this I told them to come along and I would baptize them, which I did."³⁴

Eighteen years later, as Sagwitch contemplated embracing the Mormon faith, he sought out the Latter-day Saint who not only spoke his tongue but was also widely known for the miracles he had performed among the Shoshone. That the two men were the same age perhaps gave them an additional point of reference and respect. When Sagwitch came to seek an audience with him, Hill had just completed an all-night shift as watchman at the Union Pacific Railroad station in Ogden, and his wife, Cynthia Stewart Hill, refused to disturb him. Sagwitch waited and greeted Hill when he awoke in mid-afternoon. George's son later recalled, "Chief Tsaguitch acted as spokesman and told George that the great spirit had sent his people dreams and other manifestations, telling them that the Mormon people had the true Church. The chief then continued saying, 'We want you to come to our camp and preach to us and baptize us.'"35

Hill must have been pleased to hear Sagwitch's request, having long been committed to "reclaiming" the "Lamanites," as Mormon scriptures called the Indians. He suggested that they could be baptized at Ogden. The Indians objected, wishing him to come to their camp instead.36 Because he was not an ordained missionary at the time, Hill regretfully declined their request, explaining that there was order in the church of the "Great Spirit" and that "when the time came that He wanted a work to be done He visited His prophet and told him to send someone to do it." Hill concluded "When the Great Spirit visited his prophet and the prophet called upon him, then it would be time for him to go out and preach to them and baptize them."37

After hearing Hill's response, Sagwitch and the others went home. In a few days, however, they returned with the same request. Again, they were refused.38 A few days later, however, Hill received a letter from Brigham Young summoning him to Salt Lake City. When Hill entered the president's office, Young said to him,

> Brother Hill, there has been a load resting on my shoulders for some time. I have tried to shake it off. Now I am going to give it to you. It is going to be your load from now on. I want you to take charge of the mission to the Indians in all this northern country. You know the Indian language. You are acquainted with the Indians, with their habits and customs. You may go at the work in your own way. Seek the Lord and be guided by the inspiration of

the spirit. If you want counsel, come to this office, I always will be glad to counsel with you and advise you, but you must consider this is your load. I suggest that you find some way of getting the Indians located somewhere where you can establish a central gathering place where they can be taught the art of civilization, where they can be taught to cultivate the soil and become self-supporting. I don't know just how you should go about this, but you will find a way. Now go to it and God bless you.[39]

Hill left Young's office with a "mission to the house of Israel" and a heavy sense of responsibility.[40] He contemplated his new mission over the next few weeks. On May 1, Sagwitch and other chiefs again visited Hill at his home and requested that he come to their camp and preach to them.[41] In response, Hill boarded the Central Pacific freight train to Corinne on May 5. He then walked twelve miles to the Indian camp on the Bear River, some five miles above Bear River City. [42] After he had traveled about a mile, Hill wrote that he

met an old Indian named Tig-we-tick-er, who came up laughing, and said Ti-guitch, their chief, had told them as soon as he got up that morning that 'Ink-a-pompy,' as they call me, was coming to see them that day, and that they must clean up and all stay at home, as I was going to preach to them. He also told them that I was coming on foot, and wondered why I did not come with my mules and wagon, as he thought I was getting too old to walk so far. The old Indian . . . gave me directions to camp, and said he would hurry back, so went on. About three miles farther on I met Po-pe-ah and another young Indian going to Corinne on the same business as the old man. They came up laughing and told me the same story that the old man had told me, and also said that they would hurry back to meeting. I went on pondering these things over in my mind and asked myself how it was that the old chief could tell so correctly the time I would arrive . . . I was thinking of this when lo and behold, I met the chief coming to bring me a horse to ride to camp.[43]

Sagwitch greeted Hill and said "I was surprised to see you coming that way [on foot]. I thought when you came, you would come with your mules and wagon. But when I saw you coming on foot, I thought you would be tired, so I brought you a horse to ride."[44] To Hill, Sagwitch's foreknowledge of his visit seemed to be a spiritual evidence that his calling to preach to the Indians was from God. In his own words, "This satisfied me that Father had something to do with it; so I resigned myself into His hands and said: 'Father thy will be done.'"[45]

As Hill and Sagwitch entered the Indian camp, they found the natives "eagerly awaiting his arrival."[46] Hill spent the remainder of the day in teaching the Northwestern Shoshone the Mormon gospel. He wrote that he had "baptised one hundred and one, confirming them at the waters edge."[47] He carefully recorded the names of his converts. "Tsy guitch" and his son "So quets" were prominently listed. Sagwitch and his people had become Mormons.[48] Before Hill left the Indian camp that evening, he "held a council . . . on temporal affairs, [and] talked to them awhile in regard to their duties as the spirit seemed to direct," returning to Ogden on the evening train.[49] It is likely that this discussion touched upon the importance of being ordained to the Mormon lay priesthood, a step that Mormons usually encouraged their Indian converts to take.

The next day, Hill wrote a letter to Brigham Young detailing the previous evening's events: "[I] never felt better in my life nor never spent a happier day," he remarked, noting that his converts "feel first rate and will hold prayer meetings with the whole camp men women and children in a circle every night the circle drawn in the centre of their camp."[50] Hill reported that he "found them quite destitute for provisions with the snow yet to[o] deep for them to hunt a great deal with sucsess," and asked Young to approve an order on some of the area's bishops for a few sacks of flour to help them for at least few days more.[51] Though no letter of response survives, it is likely that Young's pacific policy towards the Indians was enough to secure the requested staples for the new Mormon congregation.

George Washington Hill had little time to sit at home and relish his missionary successes at Bear River. On May 7, 1873, he wrote to Dimick B. Huntington, a pioneer of 1847 and the LDS Church's Indian interpreter, reporting that "The day before yesterday i baptized one hundred and two[,] to day i am calld on to baptize another band of about twenty and still they come and the work is extending like fire in the dry grass." Though he was hopeful that he would be able to do a great work in the "gathering of Israel," he seemed overwhelmed by the Shoshone response to the Mormon gospel and asked Huntington to show Young the report and to "tell him i crave his assistance and instructions." He also reported that "Br [Brother] Sagwitch wants to come and see pres young before he goes on his hunt." Apparently certain that Sagwitch was headed for Salt Lake City, Hill added, "I wish you would tell them of every place where there is small pox so that they will not be expoesed to that disease while there."[52]

The day after Hill sent his letter, Sagwitch and three colleagues, Warrah, Shonop, and Ejah, along with several others from their band, arrived in Salt Lake City. Dimick Huntington greeted them.[53] Huntington had the day before been ordained by Brigham Young and several of the apostles as "patriarch to the Lamanites." With other newly ordained patriarchs, he was told that his special priesthood office gave him "the highest power to bless . . . families, wives, children, and friends, and to bless fatherless children and all mankind as far as they are worthy of blessings."[54] Patriarch Huntington ordained Sagwitch and his companions to Mormonism's higher, or Melchizedek, priesthood and set them apart to the office of elder.[55]

Surviving records do not say whether Sagwitch was ushered into Brigham Young's office for the visit he had sought, but the LDS tithing office received his party and presented them with supplies. A reporter for the local newspaper noted the arrival of Sagwitch and part of his band in Salt Lake on May 8.

> The Old Chief Segwitch and about thirty of his band, Shoshones Indians, were in town to-day, just in from the northern part of the Territory. They are more cleanly and rather better looking than most of the Indians in that part of the country. They called at the Tithing Office to-day, where they received a donation of three quarters of a ton of flour. That is the way to do the fighting with Indians, treat them well, never break faith with them, and they will then know that it is to their best interests to be

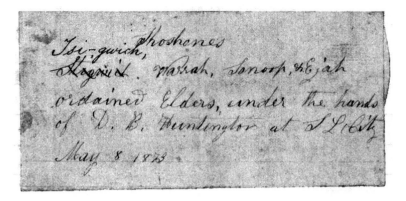

Ordination record, May 8, 1873. This manuscript fragment documents the
ordination of Sagwitch ("Tsi-gwich"), Warrah, Shonop ("Sonoop"), and Ejah
to the Mormon Melchizedek priesthood and the office of elder. Copy of original document courtesy LDS Church Archives, Salt Lake City, Utah.

peacable, and, as a general rule, they will maintain that
kind of an attitude.[56]

On the following Monday, May 12, 1873, also at Salt Lake City,
Major John Wesley Powell played host to "several principal men of
the Shoshone tribe," almost certainly including Sagwitch. Powell
dressed the Shoshone leaders in civilian clothing. One of them even
received and proudly modeled a stovepipe hat. The *Deseret News*
described the natives as having an "unusually respectable air about
them" and noted that "as they were being piloted around by Major
Powell," the Indians "desired, and had an interview with President
Young."[57] Powell expected to establish rapport with Sagwitch and
other Shoshone chiefs that would be strong enough to persuade them
to give up their homes on the Bear River near Corinne and in Cache
Valley for reservation lands in Idaho, Wyoming, or Nevada.[58]

Major Powell and colleague G. W. Ingalls had been commis-
sioned in April 1873 by the Department of the Interior to examine
the condition of several tribes in Utah, northern Arizona, southern
and eastern Nevada, southeastern California, and southeastern Idaho
and consult with them about their relocation to government reserves.
It was a high priority for this special commission to solve the problems Agent Dodge had noted in his 1872 reports by settling the

Western, Gosiute, and Northwestern Shoshone bands on reservations where they could be cared for more efficiently and no longer present an impediment to white settlement.[59] The commission arrived in early May 1873 and by May 12 had already held the meeting in Salt Lake City with Sagwitch and other Shoshone leaders. After a month filled with visits to various Ute, Gosiute, and Shoshone groups, Major Powell returned to Washington D.C. to report preliminary findings and receive approval on several recommendations concerning the different bands. G. W. Ingalls remained in the area, where he continued to meet with Indian groups and gather information.

As part of their research, Powell and Ingalls compiled a census count of the Northwestern bands. Sagwitch's band was found to contain 47 men, 64 women, and 47 children under ten years of age, representing a total of 158 people. Sanpitch's band contained 124 people, Pocatello's band, 101, and Taviwunshear, 17. Sagwitch's band was by far the largest of the four, and his cooperation was essential to the success of the commissioners' relocation plans for the four bands. Ingalls visited the Fort Hall Reservation by late May "to see if it was adapted to the Shoshones" of northern Utah and eastern Nevada. He concluded that it would be adequate for them as long as the government provided suitable provisions.[60]

By mid-June Ingalls had apparently met again with Sagwitch and other Shoshone leaders. On June 13 he sent a telegram to Major Powell, who was in Washington, reporting that he had just arranged for Sanpits (Sanpitch) and Tabashea (Taviwunshear) to meet with "Seigwits and Pacatille" (Sagwitch and Pocatello) to discuss relocation to a reservation. He noted that all four leaders "object to Fort Hall" but were willing to be placed with the Western Shoshone from Nevada on a reservation seventy-five miles southwest of Fort Hall. Ingalls must not have opposed the idea. He optimistically noted in his telegram that the designated site (probably the Raft River area) was fine country and had very few settlers.[61]

The wishes of Sagwitch, Sanpitch, and the other chieftains were little heeded. In a June 18, 1873, report to the commissioner of Indian affairs, Major Powell argued that while the Northwestern bands should, by treaty stipulations, be moved to the Wind River Reservation in Wyoming, it would be more "agreeable" to place them at Fort Hall where other Shoshone had already relocated. He therefore recommended that "The North Western Shoshones should be assembled to meet the commission at Fort Hall, and when there, their annuities should be given them, and they should be informed that the Fort Hall reservation is to be their future home, and that hereafter, no annuities will be given them at any other place."[62] Powell's recommendation represented a departure from that of Ingalls and the wishes of the Shoshone involved. Nevertheless, the commissioner of Indian affairs in a letter dated June 25 approved all of Powell's recommendations and authorized the special commission to proceed. They were also entrusted with the annuity goods for the Northwestern bands, which they were to distribute that autumn at Fort Hall.[63]

After Powell returned from Washington, he traveled to southern Utah to work with various Paiute bands. Ingalls traveled to western Nevada to negotiate with the Western Shoshone bands.[64] Through the remainder of the summer, the Northwestern bands heard nothing more from the special commissioners. They did not remain idle though. Sagwitch and his people likely attended a large powwow held on July 19 near the Logan Bridge in Cache Valley. Brigham Young Jr. noted that many of the Shoshone gathered there were "much excited" over the news of the death of several Indians at Fort Hall—rumored to have been killed by soldiers there.[65] Whether true or not, the news must have made the Shoshone people who heard it even less willing to resettle there.

Late in the fall, G. W. Ingalls was forced to make a return visit to Hamilton and Egan Canyon in Nevada Territory to conclude business and distribute annuity goods to some of the Western bands. He then proceeded to Corinne, where he was met by Major Powell. The special commissioners had intended to distribute annuity goods only at Fort Hall to the Northwestern bands. In the months since that decision had been made, however, Chief Pocatello had moved his band to Fort Hall and declared his intentions to permanently reside there. Chief Taviwunshear had similarly taken his small Northwestern band to the Wind River Reservation, "determined to cast his lot with Wash-i-ki and his men."[66]

That left just two Northwestern bands, those led by Sagwitch and Sanpitch. According to the commissioners, both "had refused to go to Fort hall, and were encamped near Corinne, and had sent a delegation to request the commission to meet them at that point." Because it was so late in the year and the cost of shipping the annuity goods to Fort Hall for distribution there would have been substantial, the commissioners decided to meet the Sagwitch and Sanpitch groups near Corinne. Word was sent out that the distribution and a general powwow would take place there.[67]

Mormon missionary George Washington Hill had been working tirelessly in his ministry among the Indians since mid-summer 1873. He had been very displeased with the work of the Powell and Ingalls special commission as it related to his converts, especially Sagwitch's band. When he learned of the planned powwow, he wrote to Dimick Huntington that: "Ingalls and powel are trying to turn all the indians from us they can by calling them to corinne to give them their goods where they can sell them for whiskey but thank god there [are] but very few there[.] They have gone to salmon river and other foreign parts and when he gets to corinne he will not find more than twenty lodges of all the north western bands of sho sho nees there to get their one blanket to a dozen indians."[68]

Hill underestimated the interest his Shoshone converts would have in the government agents' meeting. A Corinne correspondent of the *Deseret Evening News* noted that on November 7, 1873, "San Pitts, Saigroits [Sagwitch], and other chiefs" had departed for the planned fete.[69] The powwow was held on November 8, 1873. Powell, Ingalls, the U.S. Indian commissioner, and other government officers directed the meeting, which included peace talks among the Indians and instructions to the "untutored sons of the forest as to what their duty was."[70] Following the official business, a generous distribution of gifts that "were all of a highly durable quality and well adapted to the purpose" was given to the natives, including twelve suits of clothes for the chiefs and subchiefs. Sagwitch and the other chiefs expressed gratitude for the gifts but "earnestly entreated the Commission to keep the few young men who drank from being allowed any whisky."[71]

A writer for the *Corinne Reporter* present at the powwow commented on the Northwestern Shoshone: "The past of these indians is known. They fought valiantly, but were worsted, and since then have been demoralized, but are peacable. San Pits, head chief, is beloved and venerated by all the tribe. He is a fine specimen of physical humanity, prudent, potent, and friendly to the whites. Next comes the celebrated chief suiquits [Sagwitch], who in role of honor is followed by his brother John."[72]

Journalists covering the powwow were still under the impression that the Northwestern bands were to be settled on a reservation in Nevada with the Western Shoshone, rather than moved to Fort Hall. Discussing the justification for the removal of the bands to the "sage brush state," one reporter added: "The N.W. Shoshones are well behaved and quiet, and are to be taken from Utah simply because Northern Utah has settled up so fast that no stamping ground is left them. They have San Pits, Sagwits and other enlightened Chiefs who will look out for their best good."[73]

The Corinne correspondent of the *Deseret Evening News* stated that the Indians "are willing to go on the reservation, and the wise move will doubtless be made."[74] After the powwow and distribution of annuities was completed, Powell and Ingalls returned to Salt Lake to meet with other Indian groups. Despite all of their carefully laid plans, the special commissioners had not relocated the Northwestern bands to Fort Hall but had allowed them to remain in northern Utah, there to find their way through another winter without additional governmental aid. The Shoshone would need to continue to rely on their Mormon friends to survive.

George Washington Hill resigned his position as night watchman for the Union Pacific in early summer 1873 to give his full attention to missionizing the Shoshone. He had become increasingly convinced that the ordinance of baptism had to be followed by the teaching of skills that would enable the Indians to cope in white society and be self-sustaining. Hill wrote of his aspirations for the Indians, "I do not want them to always live in indian camps as they do now, but live as the whites do."[75] The natives themselves also shared his vision, including Captain George, a Shoshone from Battle Mountain who petitioned Hill for a chance to work the land and irrigate crops from a creek shared with the whites.[76] However, land was not easily found for such a purpose.

On May 26, 1874, Hill traveled to Franklin, "thinking to make a settlement there to prepare a place to gather the indians."[77] Local ecclesiastical bishop Lorenzo H. Hatch aided Hill. Together they began to lay the groundwork for an Indian settlement. The Franklin area seemed ideally suited as the location for such a community. The Northwestern Shoshone had for centuries camped in that area, which they called Mosotakani, to hunt woodchuck and squirrel.[78] A reporter from the *Salt Lake Herald* noted that the Indians "had for a long time made their home at this point, following the ordinary avocations of the noble red man, namely, hunting and fishing."[79] The availability of large tracts of unclaimed land was undoubtedly also an important consideration.

In a letter to Dimick Huntington, Hill reported that he and others had located land for the Indians "across Cub Creek, on the south side of the Little Mountain within one-half mile of Franklin."[80] Knowing how difficult it could be to protect Indian lands from white encroachment, Hill contacted the Oneida County assessor, who promised to make an official visit to the proposed Indian farm a few days later. Hill wrote, "I have instructed them to pay their taxes and prepare themselves to pre-empt land, and as soon as they can prepare themselves to file on all the land there is around there, and so prepare a home for others who will gather with them."[81]

The Mormons also had practical reasons for supporting a farm that would make the Indians self-supporting. Referring to the Indian's former "idle habits" which had "heretofore . . . imposed a very onerous tax upon the white people who have settled and improved that interesting country," a Salt Lake reporter seemed pleased to note that, "seeing how much better off the white people are who now inhabit the same country, a portion of this band seem inclined to imitate the white example."[82] Indians who had become Mormons the year before, including Sagwitch and fellow leaders with their bands, accounted for the largest portion of the natives who joined the camp. Hill "Had a good talk with . . . and baptized all there were left that had not been baptized," including Little Soldier, Sagwitch's friend and fellow chief from the Weber area, and his entire family.[83]

As Indians arrived at the farm, Hill and Hatch put them to work on communal projects or hired them out to Mormon settlers in the area. The two assigned ten Indians to dig a canal to bring water onto their proposed farmlands on the Franklin bench. Other men helped local farmer Jonathan Packer get water to his farm. Settlers employed many Shoshone to haul wood, clear land, and do general farm chores.

Others stayed at the camp planting potatoes and hauling stakes for
fencing. The Shoshone were anxious to succeed in their farming ven-
ture. Hill and Dimick Huntington noted that they "seem to be willing
to go anywhere we desire and perform any kind of labor."[84]

A Salt Lake newspaper reporter quoted Bishop Hatch as saying,
"There is plenty of work for them, and the people are willing to
employ them and pay a fair compensation for their labor."[85] In reality,
the local farmers had little money to pay their Indian help, and some
simply felt that the natives did not deserve pay for their labors.[86]
Understandably, many of the Indians became dissatisfied with their
employers' unwillingness to pay up. George W. Hill and James Hill
from Mendon met with the Indians to discuss the problem. George
Hill wrote to Dimick Huntington on June 8 that the "difficulty arose
from a misunderstanding of language intirely. We left everything all
right, and left them feeling as well as anybody you ever saw."[87]

The problem of unpaid wages was not entirely solved, however,
and the Indians decided on a plan to recoup at least a small portion
of the money owed to them. The following incident offers a delightful
window on white-Indian relationships at Franklin, as well as on the
resourcefulness of the chiefs present, who likely devised the plan.
George W. Hill's son, Joseph, recorded:

> In the latter part of the summer, the Indians worked up a
> little scheme to get even. They had two branches to their
> camp—one on the north and one on the west—both
> across the river from the town and on a hill north and
> west. Both camps gathered on the west and arranged their
> tents in a circle. They gave out the word they would put
> on an Indian dance and invited all the people of the town
> to come out and witness the performance free. They all
> came. They located in the Indian tents all with the open-
> ing[s] facing the open ground in the center. They put on
> the dance—free—but after it was over, they made the
> people pay 10 cents each to get out of the tents. It was
> taken as a huge joke, but the 10 cents was paid.[88]

In August 1874, "quite a number of ladies and gentlemen"
from outside of Franklin attended a council or powwow held at the

Indian camp. Bishop Hatch began the meeting and then turned the time to Sagwitch, who spoke for his tribe as Dimick Huntington interpreted. A reporter for the *Salt Lake Daily Herald* witnessed his oration.

> A second chief, whose name we understand is Tsi-Gwitch—to catch or grab—was the speaker in the pow-wow. A dark, heavy set, greasy-looking son of the mountains about sixty years old, and five feet eight inches in his mocassins. Of course, we who do not understand the language were not much edified by the speech, but the old man grew quite eloquent judging from his gestures—and action, by the way, is about all there is of oratory. The burthen of his discourse was love and friendship for the whites; a desire to live at peace with them; advice to the young men to work, work; but before they got ready to do so, the good old chief was very anxious to get a pass for about eight of his boys that they might go down to the city and trade a little and visit a day or two, *after* which, like obedient fellows, they will pitch in and work in the harvest and hay fields—a consummation devoutly to be hoped for. Tsi-gwitch, owing to his misfortunes, seems to be in a condition to *grab* but very little. These misfortunes consist in various wounds received at the hands of the gallant boys in blue under Connor at one time and Steptoe at another, at times we presume when Tsi gwitch and his tribe were not as friendly with the pale faces as they now are.[89]

The reporter condescendingly added, "Poor old fellow, we feel sorry for him and his race, and hope that Bishop Hatch will succeed in inducing them to go to work in a regular way and become as nearly civilized as it is possible for them to be."[90]

Sagwitch signaled in his talk a spirit of accommodation and good will toward the white people but was quick to assert his tribe's autonomy from them and his own role as chief. At one point in his discourse, Sagwitch made reference to the complaints of some white people about the Indian habit of firmly disciplining their wives. In a commanding tone, Sagwitch addressed his guests and said, "You white folks let us and our wives manage our affairs without interference, and we will not interfere between you and your wives." The reporter recoiled at Sagwitch's "liberal proposition," but conceded that he and the other guests had "no right, nor have we any inclination to interfere with anybody's wife." At the conclusion of the pow-wow, Colonel Mccallister and several of the white guests favored their Indian comrades with a rendition of the Mormon hymn "O stop and tell me, red man."[91]

Sagwitch's people worked very hard through the summer of 1874 to learn farming skills. It was their only real option since the government seemed to have completely forgotten them after the departure of Powell and Ingalls at the end of 1873. George Washington Hill wrote to the commissioner of Indian affairs in late August 1874 to ask for reimbursement of personal funds expended under direction of George W. Dodge in 1872 in feeding the Northwestern bands. He felt that Dodge had been the best agent he had known, "worth at least [one] hundred thousand of the present agent." Hill complained that in lieu of any support from the government, he had been obliged to use his own funds to buy three hundred dollars worth of flour and beef for them during the 1872–73 winter and another two hundred dollars worth of foodstuffs during 1873–74 "to keep them from starving."[92]

Hill reported to the commissioner his efforts with the Shoshone in 1874 digging ditches to irrigate the Indians' crops and hauling logs that would be used to build houses for them. Hill stated that he intended "to learn them to raise their own living and stop their begging and make good citizens of them." He added, "if government would assist me a little i could colonize all the indians in these mountains in a short time and learn them to sustain themselves and stop the Agencies expenses."[93] Hill's letter apparently failed to elicit support for Sagwitch's people from the commissioner.

In spite of the initially optimistic assessments of the success of the Franklin farm, Mormon leaders decided to close it and look for a better place to begin again in the spring of 1875. George W. Hill's official reports offer little explanation for such a decision. In one he concluded that the leaders had spent "a good deal of time runing backward and forward and everything not being satisfactory, the settlement was droped in the fall."[94] In another report, Hill simply

stated that things had not worked out "satisfactory" despite "spend-
ing a good deal of time and means."[95] The natives would have to wait
another season to realize their dreams of becoming self-sustaining
farmers.

By mid-December it seemed clear that the government was not
planning to distribute annuity goods to the Indians residing in the
Franklin area. They asked George Hill to write a letter on their
behalf. On December 14, Hill wrote to the commissioner of Indian
affairs:

> by request of the North western Sho Sho nee indians I
> send you this They want to know whether there is a going
> to be anybody to issue annuities and rations to them this
> winter or not They complain that government is not doing
> according to treaty stipulations with them . . . They would
> like to have a small reservation laid out for them here in
> their own country that they could have a chance to learn
> to work and learn to sestain themselves they think they
> should have five thousand dollars issued to them every
> year and they are getting almost nothing . . . they are in a
> suffering condition and should have help from some
> source please answer that I may know what to say to
> them[.] [96]

No letter of response survives. It seems fairly certain that if the
annuities for the Northwestern bands were placed for distribution at
Fort Hall, as Powell and Ingalls desired, no effort was made to
inform Sagwitch's people of that fact. The foodstuffs and supplies
that could have helped Sagwitch's people, if supplied at all by the
government, likely were distributed to other Shoshone residing at
Fort Hall. Sagwitch's band could not rely on the government for help
through the coming starving time of winter.

After harvest was completed at the Mormon-sponsored farm
near Franklin, the missionaries, including George W. Hill, returned
to their homes for the winter. Some of the Northwestern Shoshone
remained at the farm. Others broke camp and traveled to Brigham
City where, on November 12, 1874, Bishop Alvin Nichols authorized
the distribution to them of beef and general produce "on a liberal

scale." A. C. Worthington, one of the missionaries assigned to work with the Shoshone, met them there and noted that they were "exceedingly joyful" at receiving the foodstuffs. Before departing for the Promontory region, they pledged to "kill rabbits and bring their skins to our hattery to make hats of."[97] By accepting foodstuffs from Brigham City officials and agreeing to contribute raw goods to the hattery, Sagwitch and his band, perhaps without realizing it, ended a very eventful year by becoming agents of the Brigham City Cooperative.

4

The Corinne Scare

The white man is roaming all over my country and killing my game. Still I make no objection to his doing so, and all I want is to be let alone, with the privelage of making a small farm for the benefit of my people, and to be allowed to live on it in peace. I have not gone into the white man's country and intruded on him, and I do not think it is fair for him to come into mine and drive me from my own lands without any cause, and I ask the government to take the matter in hand and reinstate me and mine on our own lands, that we may live there in peace and friendship with all men.

Sagwitch, August 31, 1875

As Brigham Young announced new missionary assignments at the Mormon Church's general conference in April 1875, he signaled his resounding support of George Washington Hill's work among the Indians by calling fifteen men for a season of work among the "Lamanites" of northern Utah—eight more men than he called to labor in all the rest of the United States and Canada.[1] Young was willing to dedicate so much manpower to the Indian cause because he anticipated a large return in Indian converts. He had been greatly impressed by the positive reports forwarded to his office in 1873 and 1874 concerning Native American converts to Mormonism. Now he wanted to see them transformed from nomadic hunters to sedentary and self-supporting farmers. As Mormonism's prophet, he was undoubtedly anxious to support a movement that seemed to fulfill scriptural injunctions concerning the "redemption" of the remnants of the "House of Israel," interpreted by the Mormons to be America's indigenous peoples. Another practical benefit of the Lamanite mission, if implemented successfully throughout the Great Basin, was much hoped-for relief of white settlers from the temporal demands associated with Young's "feed rather than fight" policies.

George Washington Hill was one of those called to labor among the Indians, and Young assigned him to head the mission. Hill's first task was to find a suitable location for a continuation of the farming experiment begun at Franklin the summer before. The search took him north and west of Brigham City to an area about halfway between present-day Plymouth and Tremonton. In a report to President Young, Hill commented, "I went to look for a location[.] selected for permanent location a section of country lying betwen bear river and malad about twenty miles from corinne with good land and plenty of grass[.] water plenty but a heavy job to get it out."[2] The site had merit, including thousands of acres of fertile land needing only a plow and the diverted waters of the Malad River to make it productive. Young approved the location and asked the missionaries to gather there.

Sagwitch and his band of approximately seventy lodges returned from the Promontory region sometime in late winter. On February 22, 1875, Sagwitch and his wife, listed as Mogogah, but probably Beawoachee, along with fellow Shoshone Ohetocump and his wife, Minnie, entered the Mormon Endowment House located in the northwest corner of the temple block in Salt Lake City. They participated in sacred temple rituals and received the Mormon endowment. Afterward, Apostle Wilford Woodruff performed another ceremony that, according to Mormon belief, "sealed" each couple's marriage in an everlasting union.[3] Only a few Native Americans had received the Mormon endowment, and none had ever been sealed. Woodruff recorded the significant event in his journal: "This is not ownly the birth day of George Washington. But it was the day when the first Couple of Lamanites were together as man and wife for time & Eternity at the Alter in the Endowment House according to the Holy Priesthood in the last dispensation & fulness of times. Wilford Woodruff Sealed at the Altar two Couple of Lamanites. The first Couple was Indian Named Ohetocump But Baptized and Sealed by the name of James Laman. His wife Named Mine. 2d Couple Isiqwich [Sagwitch] & Mogogah."[4]

Sagwitch's band likely formed the core group of about two hundred Indians who joined Hill and the recently called missionaries at the new Indian farm in late April or early May. On May 5, 1875, Hill wrote to Brigham Young from the "Camp at Malad Dams," reporting that "the Indians are doing all they can[,] ploughing with their own horses[,] holding the plows themselves and seem to be very anxious to learn to work[,] are well pleased with their location here." Hill expressed anxiety over the fact that "the land is drying up very fast" and added that "we want to get to work on the Dam as soon as we can."[5] "Taking hold of their work well," the Shoshone converts and the missionaries filled the newly plowed ground with a hundred acres of wheat, twenty-five acres of corn, five and one-half acres of potatoes, and between six and eight acres of peas, beans, squashes, melons, and other vegetables.[6]

The Shoshone who worked alongside Hill exercised great faith in their Mormon hosts and in the farming experiment. By choosing not to pursue their traditional springtime food-gathering activities, they traded a tried and tested lifestyle for one that could promise no results until the autumn harvest. Without the spring harvest, the natives were left nearly destitute, having as usual exhausted most of their food stores during the cold winter. Hill worried about the condition of his charges, and wrote to Young: "The Indians feel well are very mutch encouraged with their prospects only one thing troubles them and that troubles me as mutch as it does them and that is something for them to eat untill it grows so that they can keep on at their work—they are willing to work every day but they are like other people, they cannot work mutch without eating."[7] It is not known whether Hill's request for food was granted, but the Shoshone continued to labor diligently at the farm.

After the Indians finished planting their crops, they began working in earnest on damming the Malad River. It soon became apparent, however, that the job could not be completed in time to divert water onto the dry ground and save the already-planted crops. Alvin Nichols, bishop of the Brigham City Ward, recommended the Indians plant their crops instead in the Bear River City field, a communally held Mormon property that he offered to them free of charge for the season.[8] Hill also had discovered that water from the Malad was alkali and generally unhealthy. He accepted Nichols's offer and

Endowment House, Salt Lake City. Sagwitch and his wife Beawoachee,
listed as Mogogah, entered this building, located in the northwest corner of
the Temple Block in Salt Lake City on February 22, 1875. They received
the Mormon "endowment" and afterwards their marriage was "sealed" in
an everlasting union. They were the second Native American couple ever
to participate in that Mormon ordinance. F. I. Monsen and Company,
photographers, ca. 1885. Photograph courtesy LDS Church Archives, Salt
Lake City, Utah.

reported that in "the latter part of may moved our camp on to bear
river on account of the water being bad in malad."[9]

His decision was based on other considerations as well. In a
letter to Young, Hill noted that "taking into consideration the heavy
job of getting out the water and fencing the land and the lateness of
the season I accepted the offer of what land we wanted in bear river
field and went to work."[10] As had been the case with the abandoned
Franklin farm the year before, Hill and the other missionaries again
told Sagwitch and his people to relocate, leaving behind the freshly
turned soil and wilting crops as evidence of their conversion to
Mormonism and an agrarian life.

The new farm, located just outside of Bear River City, five
miles from Corinne, looked very promising, offering as it did an
abundance of land and water for the Indians' use. The missionaries

and the Shoshone immediately went to work, preparing the land and planting "nearly one hundred acres of wheat[,] about twenty five of corn[,] five and a half acres of potatoes[,] three to four acres of other stuff."[11] Hill soon discovered that this land also was not all he had hoped it would be. After farming there all summer, he concluded that "I do not think they could have selected a poorer peace of land in utah of the same size than bear river field." Hill found the difficulty of irrigating the field especially frustrating: "There was quite an amount of the land that was recomended to me that when we come put the water on, it was higher than the water so that it would not water." Nevertheless, the crops grew well where they could be watered, and even the wheat that could not be irrigated "was short but [had] tolerably fair heads."[12] Under Hill's direction, Sagwitch, his people, and the missionaries began building a canal from the Bear River to their fields.

The dedication and civility of the Indians at the camp impressed visiting newspaper reporters. One *Deseret Evening News* writer viewed the Indians as "exceedingly industrious, working as faithfully and almost as expertly as white people." He noted that the young Shoshone men "do the laborious work, and attend to it without murmuring . . . They have their own horses, and plow, sow and do other farm work with readiness."[13] It must have been a truly unusual sight—proud Shoshone warriors using their prized Indian ponies at the plow, a people who cherished mobility trading all of their resources for a sedentary farming life. The nature of the new work necessitated the replacement of traditional gender roles with ones that eliminated hunting, raiding, and warring and placed husbands in the fields with their wives. The transition must have been difficult, though Anglo witnesses reported positive responses from the Indians.

Many of the natives were apparently very happy with the camp and wished to make it their permanent home. A reporter noted that the Indians "declare their intention to wander about no more, but to lead industrious and respectable lives, at peace with all their fellow creatures." He added that the Indians were presently camped out, but expressed "great anxiety to begin to build houses and live in them like white people, and as soon as the site of the settlement is decided upon, which will be when a canal now being constructed is fully located, the erection of dwellings will be commenced."[14] In the early part of June, large numbers of Shoshone, "Pab Utes," and Bannocks began to arrive at the camp from all directions, joining the core group of Indians under Sagwitch.[15] The influx amazed Hill. He recorded in his journal, "I did not send any word to those Indians who were situated at a great distance, as I expected to labor only with those who were near the settlements. Still those that were located at a distance of from four to eight hundred miles apparently knew as much about my actions as those did among whom I was then stationed, for they came in from every quarter to see and hear me."[16] Like a magnet, the camp began pulling Native Americans to it from every point on the compass.

Hill's experience was not unique. He had witnessed only one part of a larger religious movement involving Native Americans and Mormonism. While this movement enjoyed enthusiastic support in Utah's northern reaches, reports from Nevada, Arizona, Idaho, and all parts of Utah confirmed that the whole region was alive with a kind of Native American religious revivalism. In Salt Lake City, for instance, aging Indian interpreter Dimick B. Huntington became overwhelmed by hosts of Native Americans coming to the territorial capital seeking baptism. In a June 1875 letter to Apostle Joseph F. Smith, Huntington reported: "They are coming in by hundreds. There has been 2,000 baptisms already. I have more or less to baptize every week." Huntington added that he had become aware of nine tribes on their way to be baptized and then concluded, "O Joseph, how I do rejoice in it! They are coming in by hundreds to investigate, are satisfied and are baptized." The number of natives demanding baptism became so great that Huntington hired builders to erect a baptismal font in his front yard.[17]

In the St. George area, photographer Charles R. Savage witnessed the same phenomenon when he happened on a huge gathering of "Shebit" (Shivwit Paiute) Indians who had gathered for Mormon baptism at a pool north of the city. As the religious service began, Savage was impressed that "these swarthy and fierce denizens of the mountains knelt before our Eternal Father with more earnestness of manner than some of their white brethren. I shall not forget the sight—some three or four hundred persons kneeling, Indians and Caucasians, side by side; men who had faced one another with deadly rifles seeking each other's blood were mingled together to perform an act of eternal brotherhood."[18]

A California newspaper reporter noted that all of the Indians in Loanville, Nevada, had gone to Utah to join the Mormon faith,[19] and in June 1875 at Kanosh, Utah, Mormon bishop Culbert King baptized eighty-five Indians, including the settlement's namesake, Chief Kanosh, who reportedly spoke "with much earnestness, exhorting his followers to industry and good works."[20] Meanwhile, at Mount Pleasant, Utah, fifty-two members of Joe's band personally built a baptismal font by damming up a stream, thus facilitating their entry into Mormonism.[21]

Mormon leaders expressed their excitement over these events in the church's newspaper in Salt Lake City. Beginning in late 1874, articles reported that the conversion of hundreds of natives had been in response to appearances of heavenly personages who told the natives to request Mormon baptism, renounce their nomadic ways, and take up farming.[22] To the editors, who undoubtedly voiced popular Mormon thought, this turn of events was nothing less than the fulfillment of Book of Mormon prophecies and an additional witness to the truth of the Mormon gospel. A July 1875 editorial answered those of a more cynical bent by assuring the public that the recent baptisms of Indians had only been performed when the elders had "been convinced that they were sincere and had a reasonable understanding of the nature of the ordinance, and the responsibilities involved in accepting it." The editor also insisted that whether applicants for baptism be of Caucasian, African, or American extraction, they must be allowed membership in the Lord's kingdom, because "God is no respector of persons." The editor concluded by assuring his readers that with the Mormon gospel also came instruction in the habits of industry and honesty, which would bring "peacable fruits of righteousness."[23]

While the Mormons openly rejoiced in their new converts and made significant efforts to settle them as farmers, Fort Hall's Indian agents struggled to support their charges. The reservation that had been home to various Shoshone and Bannock bands since 1869 had never been alloted enough foodstuffs to care adequately for its residents or to meet treaty obligations. Fort Hall agent James Wright soberly wrote to the commissioner of Indian affairs on February 6,

1875. "We have flour enough on hand to issue to them until April 1st. We can also let them have potatoes occasionally. We have beef for one more issue. Now what will be done with these people . . . They cannot get out to hunt, there are no roots to be had, [and] fishing time will not have come." Wright pleaded, "Surely the Committee on Indian Affairs will allow us money to subsist these people on their reservation."[24]

By the following week, Wright reported that he had purchased some cattle without prior approval to feed the "suffering" Indians and hoped that the department would approve his "act of mercy" on their behalf. He added, "What the Indians are to do after this weeks issue I am unable to tell. I will issue flour, and coffee as long as I have it to issue."[25] Not long after Wright penned these dismal reports, he resigned and was replaced in July 1875 by William H. Danilson. The new agent assessed the reservation's food supplies and discovered that the resources on hand could only furnish each Indian with one meal a day for two days each week. Faced with the prospect of absolute starvation on the reserve, he broke with policy and sent the Native Americans out from Fort Hall to fend for themselves.[26]

Conditions were not much better for the Shoshone at the Wind River Reservation in Wyoming Territory. Agent James Irwin reported that after the spring planting "the Indians were permitted to go out and hunt until supplies could reach the agency."[27] Many of the hungry Indians thus evicted chose to join relatives and friends on the lower Bear River, where the Mormons welcomed them and offered both food and lessons in farming.[28]

George Washington Hill joyfully greeted these refugees and began to teach them the rudiments of agrarian living. He also held meetings almost daily wherein he explained Mormon doctrines and invited the converted to be baptized. Hill soon found that his activities as a proselytizer took most of his waking hours and left little time for farming. To speed up the process, he developed a visual aid to illustrate the tenets of the Mormon faith as well as the Indians' Israelite origins as expressed in the Book of Mormon. A daughter-in-law of Hill's described his teaching methods in the following terms:

> Sometimes they received [the Mormon gospel] very readily. It seemed as though they were anxious for it. Of

course, there were some who were not. He had to talk
more to some. But he was a good hand to talk to them. He
had a scroll with pictures of the authorities and the Book
of Mormon. It was a big scroll, about that square [18
inches], and he used to have that when he talked to the
Indians, and turned to different characters and told them
about their forefathers. I do not know what became of that
scroll, but I know grandpa had it. It had nice large pictures of the different Nephites and different leaders. The
Book of Mormon tells about them. He had pictures taken
on purpose for that, so that they would have something to
look at. They were like children and he could explain it
to them better. I have seen him have this scroll and talk
to the Indians, and show them the different pictures and
they were quite interested in it.[29]

Hill had ample opportunities to use his teaching scroll. On
June 7, 1875, he assembled a large number of recent arrivals and
"preached to quite a crowded congregation when they were calling
for Baptism so loudly we went to the water and I Baptised one hundred and sixty eight before coming out of the water, and 7 the next
morning."[30]

Thus went the mounting conversion of Indians to the Mormon
faith. So great were the numbers of natives asking for baptism that
Hill's account of his activities in the summer of 1875 eventually
omitted all description of farming and settlement activities and
instead focused on trying to list each Indian's name correctly so that
it could be forwarded to Salt Lake City for inclusion on the church's
permanent membership record. In a report Hill sent to Brigham
Young on August 25, 1875, he tallied the Indian baptisms: "I find by
looking over my work that I have baptised this season if I have not
made a miss count eight hundred and eight whitch with 102 that I
baptised two years ago and sixteen I baptised last summer and fifteen baptised by James H. Hill makes a total of nine hundred and
thirty nine that belong to this mission."[31]

The Indians' enthusiasm, devotion, and desire to emulate their
white brethren in many facets of life showed that Hill's tally represented more than mere statistics. Perhaps no event better epitomizes

the apparent Shoshone desire for acculturation than the Pioneer Day festivities held in Brigham City on July 24, 1875. Hill came to the celebration with eight hundred native converts, almost certainly including Sagwitch and his band. At about 11:00 A.M., Brigham City residents witnessed an imposing sight in front of the courthouse as three hundred Shoshone men and women drew their horses into a triangular line on the square while local bands played spirited tunes and artillerymen fired off several blasts. Then an Indian convert called James Brown gave a brief address. Afterward, the Indians corraled their steeds and joined their Scandinavian, English, and Welsh brothers and sisters in the Brigham City bowery. The speakers included the mayor, two city judges, resident Apostle Lorenzo Snow, and James Brown and John, two of the Shoshone converts. They addressed the audience with great zeal and spirit and "bore testimony of the Lord's visitation among them." They also said that they "had warm feelings towards the people, admired the fine appearance of the young people, desired to become civilized, build, plant and become like their white brethren." Before the day was out, all present joined in a mighty shout of Mormonism's sacred cry: "Hosanna! Hosanna! Hosanna! to God and the Lamb."[32]

The leaders in Brigham City must have been fully impressed, because on August 1, a delegation of dignitaries from the county seat, including Apostle Lorenzo Snow, visited the mission on the Malad. They could barely squeeze into a bowery filled with a thousand Indians, including about 450 Shoshone from Wind River, 150 Bannocks from the Idaho area, and a large group of local Indians, including Sagwitch's band. The silence and attentiveness of the Indians astounded the apostle and his poetess sister, Eliza R. Snow. As Hill concluded his sermon, three hundred Indians demanding immediate baptism swept him out the door and to the river.[33] Hill's success continued, adding scores of Indian converts to the church rolls, including Shoshone chieftain Pocatello.[34] Hill must have been a little overwhelmed in early August to hear that an additional five hundred Indians were en route to the camp to join with the Mormons.[35]

Successes in befriending, teaching, converting, and settling Native Americans made George Washington Hill and the Mormons ecstatic, while agents from the adjoining reservations grew increasingly concerned. Fort Hall agent James Wright visited the Mormon

Indian farm in May 1875 and found several hundred Indians there, mostly Shoshone from the Wind River Agency, though he discovered some Indians from Fort Hall who, he noted, must have "run off without my knowledge." He reported to the commissioner of Indian affairs that "These Indians are being operated upon by the Mormans, many of them Baptized, others taken through the 'Endowment House' (whatever that is or means) and then called 'The Lords Battle Axes.'" He cautioned that "All this means mischief" because it had a demoralizing effect on those Indians left behind at Fort Hall. He urged that all Indians not on their proper reservation be "removed from Utah" as soon as possible.[36]

Wright was even more certain of his position by the end of June 1875. He reported to the commissioner on June 31 that it was now "impossible" for him to keep the Indians at Fort Hall. "They go away in the night and when they return deny that they have been there and when pressed get mad," he noted, adding that "Unless the Indians are very soon taken out of Utah there will be trouble." In the same letter he plead for additional resources that would enable him to adequately supply, and thus keep, the Indians at Fort Hall.[37]

Wright's successor, W. H. Danilson, was even more direct. In a July 31 letter to the commissioner, he stated that he "exceedingly" regreted having to release the starving Indians from the reservation, noting that "Large numbers have gone and are still going to Utah to get washed and greased and enrolling themselves in the cause of the Mormons." He added that the Mormons had been teaching the Indians that they were the "chosen ones" to establish the kingdom of God on earth and that they should hate the government and distrust its agents. "The whole Mormon influence is bad and calculated to turn these people hostile to the government their only true friend," Danilson declared.[38]

The presence of so many Indians in the area also annoyed the residents of Corinne, just five miles from the Indian camp. The ever-increasing population of Indians on the fringes of the town caused the editor of the *Corinne Daily Reporter* on July 9, 1875, to write, "The valley is swarming with Indians who belong to the Fort Hall agency, and should be kept on the Snake River reservation. We are informed that the authorities at Fort Hall say that it is impossible for them to keep the Indians where they belong while the people are constantly making them presents and urging them to stay here."[39] The editor's tone in the following three weeks turned from annoyance to near panic as the number of Hill's charges swelled to nearly two thousand souls.

Corinne's residents were familiar with the Shoshone. The annual site for distribution of government annuities to the reservationless Northwestern bands had since 1863 been on the lower Bear River near Corinne. The city's "gentile" citizens had lost patience with the yearly gathering of Sagwitch's and other Shoshone bands, whom they denigrated as "bloody dogs," "filthy vagrants," and "varmints" who clogged the streets and put a "stench" in the air.[40] It was impossible to miss the Native Americans in Corinne. They could be regularly seen walking the streets, "foraging on garbage," holding weddings and other native celebrations, playing leap frog with each other and marbles with white children, selling and swapping horses, catching rides on passing trains, gleaning in the fields, and causing the resident dogs to offer them "open air serenades."[41] The Shoshone were occasionally guilty of more serious offenses including thefts of food.[42]

While Mormons viewed the Indians as fallen but noble children of God, the residents of Corinne saw them only as depraved and wretched, "fit subjects for a section of the hog ordinance."[43] The daily issues of the Corinne newspaper frequently included brief but mostly negative and racist references to the Shoshone. The tone of such writing exhibited the gross lack of regard that Corinne's citizens had for the Indians. One news item, for example, gloated over a recent railroad accident in which an Indian was run over and crushed. The editor concluded, "Poor lo, that his brains should lubricate the flange of a railway car is serious enough, but think of it, to send a red man headless to the happy hunting grounds on a narrow-gauge! Hurrah for the Utah Northern, the guillotine of the savage."[44] In another railroad accident where an Indian man had a leg severed after falling off the train, the editor concluded, "We pity the wounded savage, but would rejoice had the ponderous flange passed over his wind pipe."[45] With a less violent slur the Corinne editor villified a Shoshone woman in his city: "A squaw, an idiot by birth, and demented by cultivation, with features that would outcast a baboon from the society of its peers, daily straggles through our streets with a hideous looking brat strapped to her back."[46] Nat Stein summed up his fellow citizens' irritation with the Shoshone in the following excerpt from a poem published in the Corinne paper in 1871:

> But the Indians, shorn of glory which in former
> time was theirs,
> Only come our crumbs to gather or to borrow
> paltry wares.
> Then we feed them on our bounty, and to bid
> them to be good,
> Let them make their presence useful doing
> chores and chopping wood.
> Thus we solve the Indian problem, by a method
> mild and clear,
> Though for dealing with a savage you shall
> find no Quakers here![47]

Corinne's citizens found it confusing and unsettling that the local "savages" had become the object of concerted relief efforts by the Mormons. Strongly anti-Mormon and suspicious of any project directed by Brigham Young, the residents of Corinne immediately ascribed less than holy motives to Hill's conversion campaign taking place just five miles from their doorstep.

Founded as a shanty town along the transcontinental railroad line, Corinne had quickly become a permanently established "gentile island" in the midst of a sea of Mormons. Many of Corinne's permanent residents felt that their city had a larger mission to crush economically, and then religiously, Young's polygamous kingdom. One noted gentile visitor to Corinne summed up the feelings of his colleagues thusly, "And here we are at Corinne, the sworn enemy of the New Jerusalem. From Rome to Carthage in three hours! All the Utah Territory belongs to the Saints. Corinne alone, this thorn in the flesh of Mormonism, has dared to hold its own, in spite of Brigham Young, and to act as a city of refuge to those apostates from the faith of the Prophet who have been fortunate enough to escape the avenging sword of the Danites."[48]

The Corinne daily paper was certainly up to the task of promoting the campaign against the Mormons, publishing in most issues brief references, often full editorials, condemning some aspect of Mormonism, while advertisements for the paper proudly referred to it as "The great anti-Mormon newspaper."[49] The Mormons did little to foster a change of heart in their gentile neighbors and in fact often fanned the flames of bad feelings. Young, who viewed Corinne as a gross impurity on the hem of Zion's fabric, was both vocal and persistent in his condemnations of Corinne. In one especially colorful earlier attack on gentile intruders in general, Young had declared, "Our outside friends say they want to civilize us here . . . they mean by that, to establish gambling holes—they are called gambling hells—grog shops and houses of ill fame on every corner . . . also swearing, drinking, shooting and debauching each other . . . That is what priests and deacons want to introduce here; tradesmen want it, lawyers and doctors want it, and all hell wants it. But the Saints do not want it, and we will not have it."[50]

Young did more than make incendiary statements. Even before the railroads had joined at Promontory Summit in 1869, he initiated a cooperative program to ensure that Mormons produced and marketed most of the goods they needed among themselves, effectively closing Utah's doors to the products and "vices" of gentiles. It was not uncommon for a Mormon who traded with gentiles to be brought before a church court to be tried for his membership. Brigham City was the county seat for Box Elder County, where Corinne was located, and it happened to have one of the most succesful cooperative programs in the Mormon kingdom. The Brigham City Mercantile and Manufacturing Association had been founded in 1870 under resident apostle Lorenzo Snow's careful direction and by 1875 was economically vigorous and competitive. Freighters who loaded goods at Corinne and delivered them to the Idaho and Montana mines made up the largest share of Corinne's business, but the city's merchants also valued local trade, especially in the off season. Mormons who ventured to Corinne's business district usually traded home-grown goods for hard currency, a commodity in short supply in the Mormon and gentile settlements alike. This somewhat annoying barter arrangement bothered the merchants and was condemned by the Corinne paper, which complained that the "Church of 'pigs eye' can sell goods for cash but not buy merchandise or [the buyer] will be cut off [excommunicated]."[51]

A greater economic threat to Corinne than the Mormon system
of cooperatives was the Mormon-built Utah Northern Railroad. As
the narrow gauge crept ever closer to Franklin and beyond, the residents of Corinne properly worried about losing the whole of their
Montana trade to the Mormons, who could thus load teamsters' wagons at least a hundred miles closer to the Montana mines than could
Corinne. At least a few of Corinne's merchants relocated their ware-
houses to Franklin in anticipation of the coming dramatic swing in
freighting business. Mormon leaders even hinted at an extension of
the line directly into Montana. Though not a feasible goal, the threatened extension served to anger residents of the gentile city, who realized that without the trade with the mines to the north, Corinne
would soon go the way of other railroad shanty towns.[52]

In sum, Corinne was a city locked in battle with the Mormons,
whose religious doctrines, economic exclusiveness, and political
monopolies seemed to the people of Corinne to be the epitome of
evil. Yet another factor would prove to be the most potent agent in
souring Mormon-gentile relations and in harming Native Americans
in the process. It was the continuing fallout from an event that had
occurred eighteen years earlier.

In 1857, Indians had allied with paranoid Mormons in southern Utah to massacre a company of Arkansas immigrants headed for
California. The bloody affair at Mountain Meadows resulted in the
murder of dozens of men, women, and children and instantly became
a national news story and an evidence of the "evil" intentions of the
Mormons. Adding to this controversy were rumors about a secret
Mormon society known as Danites, who at Brigham Young's command would allegedly dispatch to the nether world all the enemies of
the kingdom. In their small and openly anti-Mormon town, Corinne's
citizens worried that they too would become victims of Mormon
hatred and over time adopted a seige mentality from which the
Mormon threat came to be seen as very real and imminent.

Corinne's newspaper editors heightened the sense of fear by
publishing articles hinting at the possible future union of Indians
and Mormons in an attack on Corinne. In the late fall of 1871, for
instance, the editor of the *Daily Corinne Reporter* noted, "There are
said to be five hundred Indians encamped across the river, near the
Mormon settlements. It is said they have allied themselves with the

Danite hordes for the coming struggle."[53] Beginning in September 1871, Corinne's paper for months carried advertisements for a new book titled *History of Mormonism*, which dramatically exposed the gruesome and bloody details of the Mormon attack at Mountain Meadows.[54] Several of the city's merchants offered the book, which no doubt found many buyers. Church and civic organizations in Corinne also ensured that the Mountain Meadows Massacre remained fresh in the minds of its citizens by paying guest lecturers to speak to sell-out crowds about it.[55]

Corinne's citizens very early came to doubt the noble intentions of the Northwestern Shoshone, seeing them as likely allies to the Mormons. After all, the Indians' reliance on the United States government was limited to a small distribution of goods every fall, after which the reservationless Shoshone roamed freely through the rest of the year, usually aided by the Mormons. When the Northwestern Shoshone held a "grand war dance" in 1873 to honor the Modoc Indian victory over government soldiers in northern California, the people of Corinne felt that their concerns about disloyal Indians had been confirmed, and editor Dennis Toohy wrote that "They ought to be skinned alive for their insolence."[56] As the Indians gathered near Corinne in late 1874, Toohy's editorial successor, Horace W. Myers, predicted that the natives would surely unite with the Mormons in any action they initiated against Corinne. The government needed to protect his city from the "Latter day pets" who frequented the area.[57]

While the Mormons and Indians never intended an attack on Corinne's citizens, the gentiles had been accurate in noting the close association of the two groups. Church policy had always allowed Indians to have full access to all aspects of Mormon religious practice, including its sacred temple ordinances. Through the spring and summer of 1875, George W. Hill sent several of the farm's Native American converts to the Endowment House in Salt Lake City to receive their endowment, the most sacred of Mormon ordinances, wherein they promised obedience to God's laws in return for assurances of great eternal rewards. Sagwitch had received this ordinance on February 22, 1875.[59] Two of Sagwitch's sons—Soquitch, with his wife "To-ancy," and Yeager, with his wife "Tam-py-yoke"—participated in the ordinance on April 4, 1875, and then had their marriages sealed in an additional ceremony. (On February 17, 1886, Yeager was also sealed to his second wife, Yampatch Wongan).[60]

As part of the temple ritual, the Indians received a sacred cloth undergarment to be worn thereafter as a reminder of covenants entered into and as a protection from harm. The garment stretched from head to foot, and must have been difficult to wear for a people familiar with simpler and less extensive clothing. The meanings attached to the garment, however, made its wearing desirable. One reporter humorously noted an incident in which Chief Pocatello nearly tore shirts and skirts from "white" passersby in order to ascertain that they also wore the endowment garment. Pocatello then proudly declared, as he pointed to his own garment, "Me good Mormon too."[61] Indians could feel pride in wearing a symbol of Mormonism's highest spiritual achievement, as well as take comfort in promises of protection against harm to garment wearers.

Participation in such Mormon ceremonies as the endowment bewildered and alarmed agents James Wright and W. H. Danilson at Fort Hall, who saw potential danger in a Mormon-Indian religious alliance. Wright visited the camp in May 1875 and confirmed that many Indians had been taken through the Endowment House. He expressed concern that they were afterwards reportedly referred to as "the Lords Battle Axes."[62] Reports circulating in non-Mormon newspapers said Mormons had taught the endowed Indians that once clothed in the sacred garments, "Gentile bullets would not penetrate them."[63] The *Salt Lake Daily Tribune* charged that Mormons baptized Indians "in their dirty, degraded ignorance, and acknowledge them as communicants of their Church in full fellowship, and pass all they can through the Endowment House, where, doubtless, the usual oaths are administered to them, to kill the murderers of the Prophet, Joseph Smith, and those accessory thereto, knowing them to be such wherever found, and to obey the Priesthood."[64]

Such charges failed to concern the Mormons, who continued to send Indians to the temple block for ordinances they believed to be essential for heavenly exaltation. The Indians also participated in other temple ordinances, including proxy baptisms for deceased ancestors.[65] The gentiles grew ever more concerned as the Indians were won over to the church and initiated into Mormonism's most important ordinances.

The Mountain Meadows Massacre, which already was a well-known event in Corinne, became even bigger news during the summer of 1875 when the federal court charged John D. Lee, a resident of southern Utah and a leader in the massacre, with murder and placed him on trial at Beaver. As the trial progressed, reports were telegraphed to papers far and near. By carrying complete coverage of the proceedings, the Corinne paper renewed details of the massacre in readers' minds and added greatly to already intense feelings. The trial ended on August 7 without a verdict, nine jurors having voted for acquittal and three for conviction. The anti-Mormon papers roared their denunciations of the miscarriage of justice and predicted future massacres by Indians and Mormons.[66] The *Idaho Statesman* declared that from the time the Lee trial began, Mormon authorities had "been looking around to see what revenge they could get on the Gentile population."[67]

Corinne's dry tinder only needed a spark. It came in the Corinne *Daily Mail* on August 9 and 10. Editors W. S. Cooke and S. S. Johnson staggered their readers with a seven-line headline:

MORMONS MEDDLING WITH THE INDIANS!
MOUNTAIN MEADOWS TO BE REPEATED!!
CORINNETHIANS TO BE THE VICTIMS!!!
INDIANS CONGREGATING IN THE VALLEYS—
SQUAWS AND PAPPOOSES BEING
SHIPPED AWAY!
OTHER PREPARATIONS OF WAR![68]

A vitriolic piece the next day recounted Mormondom's failed attempts to destroy Corinne, then suggested that Brigham Young had decided to make a new attempt by bringing his "battle-axes" into service, and claimed that "they might burn the town and butcher some of the inhabitants."[69]

Rumors circulated wildly. They included reports that an Indian woman had warned several residents of Corinne to flee an impending massacre, a Mormon girl employed by a local family had received a private dispatch warning her to "flee from the wrath to come," and four non-practicing or "Jack" Mormons had already made quick exits from their homes in Corinne.[70] With each telling, the rumors

Corinne posse ready to protect their city from anticipated Indian attack,
August 10, 1875. Photograph made from Compton Photographic Archives
glass negative courtesy Special Collections and University Archives,
Merrill Library, Utah State University, Logan, Utah.

characteristically became grander and more detailed. Though they
later failed to hold up, such rumors confirmed to the town that a massacre was imminent and heightened the residents' state of frenzy.

As a result, on August 10 Corinne's citizens prepared for a
siege. Women and children were placed in one of Corinne's only
masonry structures, the Central Hotel, or quickly sent out of town by
train, wagon, or foot.[71] One Corinne resident, Mrs. N. Jenson, might
have spoken for all the panicked residents when she tremblingly
declared to a friend that "she and all the rest would soon be num-
bered among the dead except they fled immediately, as the Indians
had been ordered by the leaders of the church at Brigham city to
burn the town."[72] Mrs. Jenson successfully begged her friend for a
ride out of town, while other women "screamed and fainted and men
rushed frantically from one place to another."[73] Corinne's "Night of
Terror" had begun.[74]

Meanwhile, the men swarmed to Corinne's depot, where they
broke open boxes of arms belonging to the federal government and
prepared themselves for war.[75] A contingent rode out to the Malad

bridge three miles from town to act as guards. As night fell, the frightened guards strained their eyes among the shadows and thought they saw a large party of Indians approaching the bridge on their way to destroy Corinne. The frightened men fired off frantic rounds that supposedly caused the Indians to whirl and run.[76] The distant gunfire prepared those at Corinne to believe the wild reports brought hastily back by the guards. Added to their statements was the new rumor that Indians had attempted to cut off Corinne's water supply by breaching the earthen dam on the Malad River.[77]

Mayor E. P. Johnson needed nothing more. He immediately wired Governer George W. Emery for troops to protect the supposedly threatened citizens, and Emery responded by ordering Captain James Kennington and fifty troops from Camp Douglas to guard the city.[78] George Washington Hill learned of the scare the next morning from Mormon Indian Jim Brown. Greatly surprised by the rumors, he declared the charges "as base of a falsehood as could have been invented," adding that "the Indians were attending to their own business and interfering with no body neither were they thinking of interfering with anybody."[79] The troops arrived by midday on August 11. After studying the evidence at Corinne, Kennington, along with Mayor Johnson, reporter W. H. Clipperton from the *Salt Lake Tribune*, and "Frenchman" interpreter Louis Demers headed toward the Indian encampment to finish their investigation. Harvest had just begun at the farm, and Indian Jack found Hill and most of the Indians cutting wheat in their fields.

He reported that the soldiers wanted an "interview" with Hill and "some of the chiefs" at Corinne. Hill sensed how dangerous and alarming the situation had become and "immediately repaired to camp," where he handpicked some of the chiefs to accompany him. Included was Chief Sagwitch, along with Sagwitch's interpreter Ejupitchee, or John, as well as Indian Jack and Jim Brown.[80] The party mounted and headed toward Corinne. On their way, they met Kennington and the others. Mayor Johnson introduced Hill to the captain, who then reported that he had come to investigate the attempted attack on Corinne. Hill answered that the charges were false but said "if that was his buisiness we had better go to my camp to do our talking."

Once settled in Hill's tent, the missionary faced the accusations directly. Asked about a possible attack on Corinne, he replied that the Indians had no disposition to attack Corinne, they were engaged in harvesting their wheat, and they wished to settle themselves, build houses, live in them, and cultivate the earth for their living. They knew that they could not do this and fight the government.[81] Hill further argued that the Shoshone could not have been at the bridge the previous night because "I was up until the Indians had all gone to sleep, and their ponies were scattered all over the prairies. It was utterly impossible for the Indians to have gathered up their ponies and started for Corinne without my knowing it." Besides, Hill added, "they never leave the camp without informing me." When the captain suggested that Hill might have been asleep during the Indians' departure, Hill replied, "I wake easily and there could not be a stir in camp without my knowing it." Mayor Johnson then asked in a tone of disgust, "Do you mean to say that your Indians have not threatened to attack Corinne?" Hill replied, "I mean to say that no Indian has threatened to attack Corinne, and I challenge any one to give the name of any Indian who has done so, and I will immediately send for him and have the matter settled. If you, Mr. Johnson, do not know the name of the Indian I will go with you through the camp, and you can point him out to me, and I will have him at once fetched in and the matter forthwith investigated."[82]

Kennington and the mayor grilled Hill and the chiefs with numerous questions about the whereabouts of the Indians the night previous, the number of Mormon converts among the Indians, their tribal affiliations, whether the Indians had cut the water off from Corinne or threatened to burn the city, why so many Indians had gathered at the camp, how long they intended to stay, what number of the Indians in camp were prone to drunkenness, and what claims the Indians had made on the lands in Malad Valley.[83] Hill became irked that he and the peaceful natives should have to endure such accusations and became sickened as he realized that the situation could very well mean the end of his proselytizing and farming efforts with the Indians.

He became so frustrated at the injustice of the situation that, as he confided to President Young, he "felt very mutch like turning loose, but finaly thought mild ness was the best policy." Kennington tested Hill's determination to remain calm when he asked "Do they [the Indians] make distinction between mormons and other whites?" Hill sharply replied, "They make distinction from treatment, they like their friends better than their enimies." Hill answered all of the questions curtly but honestly and to the apparent satisfaction of the captain. In his letter to Young, he went on to lay blame for the false scare on the people of Corinne themselves, suggesting that they had wanted "some goverment patronage and did not know how to get it only by circulating Lies of the Blackest dye." Hill further argued the innocence of the Indians by asking his visitors to find anything at all in the camp of a "warlike nature."

"If you will go out upon the farm, you will see the Indians hard at work harvesting, with many of the squaws and papooses gleaning, and others scattered all over the camp, while the Indians' horses are grazing in every direction over the prairie, as far as you can see," he challenged Kennington, adding "Did you ever, Captain, hear of Indians going to war under such circumstances?"[84] Confident that no attack had been attempted or seemed likely, Captain Kennington took Hill aside, told him that his orders were "to drive those that did not belong here away," but promised that he would be satisfied if the visiting Indians would leave by Friday the thirteenth at noon. He also assured Hill that he would not interfere with the local Indians.[85] Hill, along with Sagwitch and the others, had answered serious charges raised by the government and successfully negotiated a deal allowing the core group of Indians, including Sagwitch's band, to remain at the farm.

The *Deseret Evening News* and the *Corinne Daily Mail* ran lengthy comment on the Indian scare in their respective August 11 issues. The Mormon Church's organ, the *News*, predictably condemned Corinne's residents for making outlandish accusations, suggested that they likely had an economic motive in mind when they invited the soldiers to their city, and added, "it must occur to the most obtuse that no people on the earth are more interested in having the Indians in their neighborhood peaceable in every sense of the word than the 'Mormons.'" The Corinne paper asserted that the Mormons were "trying to get the control of a race of people who are ignorant and vicious enough" to destroy Corinne.[86]

What seemed to be so clear in the Mormon press, however, was not so obvious to Governor Emery. On the morning of August 12, the governor escorted two additional companies of soldiers to Corinne to personally investigate the situation and to back up Kennington's edict of the day before.[87] Brigham Young also sensed the potentially explosive nature of the situation and booked passage the same day on the Utah Northern to Brigham City, where he conducted his own investigation.[88] As the sun crept over the Indian camp on the morning of the twelfth, the place was unusually quiet. Most of the nonresident Indians had already begun their long journeys back to the Wind River range, Crow country, Blackfoot country, and numerous other homelands. The remaining Indians had not been included in Captain Kennington's edict and went out to their fields to continue harvesting their crops, which had matured nicely over the course of the summer. It seemed somewhat ironic that after a summer that witnessed the addition of many hundreds of new Indian converts to Hill's Lamanite mission, the eviction order left him with only his original converts of 1873 and 1874, including Sagwitch and his band.

Despite Kennington's assurances, Hill felt uneasy about the prospects of the negotiated peace and sent Indian Jim Brown to Corinne as a spy "pretending to sell a beef hide but in reality to see what he could find out." At about two o'clock, Hill's fears appeared to be realized when Indian Jim frantically rushed back to the fields "very bad excited" with word that a large military body wished to have another audience with him.[89] The Indians hurriedly harnessed a team, and Hill, Sagwitch, and a few other Indians headed for camp. On the way, they met Captains Kennington and Carpenter, along with interpreter Louis Demers.[90]

Carpenter had already conducted a quick investigation in Corinne. He could only document a few incidents that might have given rise to the scare. One was the alleged tampering with Corinne's water supply from the Malad ditch. Another was a recent incident wherein an Indian woman had been pushed off a CPRR train by a brakeman near Corinne. Carpenter felt that Corinne's citizens had acted wisely in responding to the situation, and he ultimately blamed the Mormons for creating the situation by befriending and converting so many Indians.[91] He did conclude that it seemed very unlikely that any Indians had fired on the guard at the Malad bridge on the evening of August 10.[92]

Captain Carpenter met up with George W. Hill as he was "coming from the corn field with a few Indians where they had evidently been at work." The captain was not ready to take additional testimony or consider the issue further. Nullifying Kennington's agreement of the day before, Carpenter informed Hill that "all the Indians must leave the farm and go to their reservations before noon the next day, or he would be compelled to drive them therefrom by force."[93] Hill responded by pointing out that Carpenter had erred in his command. He informed the officer that the nonresident Indians had already left for their distant homes, leaving only the resident natives, who could not go back to their reservation because they had never been given one.

Hill added that he had known these Indians for twenty-eight years and that they "were at home on their own land where they had always lived, had never sold their country nor never had agreed to go to any reservation." According to Carpenter, Hill grew increasingly agitated as he declared that the Indians still at the farm "had a better right to the country than any body else[,] that they would not know where to go to, that the d——d people in Corrine had told a pack of d——d lies about them and that it was just a plan for them to get possession of the land."[94]

When Captain Carpenter strongly reiterated his demand that all Indians vacate the camp, Hill replied, "Well, major, we had just as well under stand one another at once, and if I understand you aright, if these Indians have not broke camp by tomorrow at 12 oclock that it was an open declaration of war. Is that so?" Carpenter replied, "Well yes, I suppose so." Hill felt despondent, after seeing the agreement with Kennington so quickly invalidated, resulting in a situation that would force the Indians to flee for their lives. He warned the captain that he was "bargaining for a longer job than he thought," and added with disgust that "it was a hard matter for me to believe that my country had sank low enough to issue an order of that kind."[95]

Hill was certain that the government, once rightly informed of the Indians' circumstances, would allow them to remain at the farm. He proposed to the military detachment that they telegraph to Washington, D.C., a statement he would make, any response to which he would gladly honor. Until then, he proposed, the Indians should be allowed to continue in their harvest. The captain said he would send the statement, but "the orders must be obeyed" in the meantime.[96]

Sagwitch, who had been quiet through the meeting, now stepped forward. As he began to address the group and contemplated what the eviction order meant for his people, he was filled with anguish and sorrow and rage. Sagwitch had witnessed the near annihilation of the Northwestern Shoshone at the hands of United States troops at the Bear River Massacre in 1863 and, since then, had watched whites steal Shoshone lands, cheat his people, and condemn them as an inferior race. He had courageously led his band in a new direction, hoping that accepting a new religion and a settled agrarian life would finally ensure his beleaguered followers the peace and plenty they had long been denied. But now the soldiers had told him that he and his people must leave their fields and run or again be victims of a massacre, a prospect that must have sickened him.

Louis Demers recorded that as Sagwitch began to speak, "The old chief almost . . . cried as he begged us not to bring the soldiers upon them."[97] Sagwitch turned to the presiding officer and asked "what he had done, who he had killed, or what he had stolen that he must come with his soldiers to Drive him from the Bread he had been working for all Summer."[98] When Sagwitch had completed his statement, George Hill apparently turned to the old chief and tried to persuade him and the others to remain with him at the camp and make a stand against the soldiers.[99] Sagwitch snapped at his old friend, "don't talk to me, you have lied to me and my heart is sick."[100]

The despondent chief apparently alluded to an earlier pledge by Hill to permanently settle the Indians in Bear River Valley, a promise he could not keep in light of the soldiers' claim that the government, not the Mormons, owned the land. Interpreter Demers claimed that "The Chief Sang-witch" went so far as to say of Hill, "He heap lie."[101] Sagwitch's pleas for his people did touch the officer, who promised that "he would be as gentle as he could" in moving the Indians out. Hill cynically piped up, "What that term means, we well understand."[102]

After the military contingent had left, Hill called the Indians together and informed them of the situation. He promised them that "it would all come out right" and then advised them to return to their former haunts.[103] The captains' ultimatum had been taken seriously by the Indians. Even though the deadline was not until the next day at noon, the Indians all departed from camp by nightfall on August 12, leaving behind not only the crops they had worked so hard to plant and nurture but also most of their personal belongings. The edict ordering the group's departure had included George Washington Hill, and he likewise escaped with little more than his clothing.[104]

On Friday August 13, not a soul could be found in the previously bustling Indian village. The camp lay in deserted silence through most of the morning until four or five men from Corinne, allegedly including a "States Marshall," rode into camp with the stated purpose of hanging Hill. Whatever their intentions, the men did not find Hill, but they quickly went through the camp, stealing "everything to which they took a fancy." Among other things stolen were Sagwitch's chickens, eleven beaver traps and a muskrat trap, copper kettles, axes, and rabbit skin robes in which the Indians wrapped their children.[105] Hill soon learned of the robberies, which seemed to be the ultimate indignity. He wrote to the editor of the *Ogden Junction* documenting the thefts. About the loss of Sagwitch's prized poultry, Hill recorded:

> The first trophy of the war was two of poor old Tsyquitche's chickens. The old Indian had bought a few chickens this spring thinking to enjoy the luxury of an egg now and then, but the honest blacksmith found the chickens in camp with no Indian to protect them, and the temptation was greater than he could bear. Finding three small boys, they tried to hire them to run the chickens down for them, by offering a reward of twenty-five cents, but the first boy had a sore toe. They tried another; he had a sore leg. The other said he would not steal them unless the other boys would help him, so the honest Corinneite had to shoot them.[106]

Meanwhile, the federal troops at Corinne, who could have protected the Indians' possessions, instead packed their gear and returned to Camp Douglas on August 14, putting an official end to the so-called Indian scare.[107] After fleeing the Indian farm, Sagwitch led his family and a portion of his band to the home of Amos Warner in Willard, a small Mormon community just south of Brigham City. Warner, a trusted Mormon friend, was also the adoptive father of Frank Beshup Timbimboo Warner, Sagwitch's son who as a toddler was wounded in the Bear River Massacre.[108] Warner viewed Sagwitch and his group as family and did what he could to make the refugees comfortable.

After staying with the Warners just a few days, however, Sagwitch became restless. He resolved that his people should have the fruits of their labor and finally decided that he would risk a return to the camp to finish the harvest that had been so abruptly interrupted. On August 20, Amos Warner penned a hurried letter to George Hill informing him that Sagwitch and one of his sons, as well as Indian John, had already left for the camp. The remaining Indians also expressed a desire to return and harvest the wheat and potatoes themselves, rather than paying others to do it for them. Warner asked Hill if he thought it "safe for them to go and tend to their crop or not" and relayed a question from one of the remaining Indians about where to put the crop once harvested, "whether he shall take it to Hansen Glen or Brigham City or Willard City."[109] It seemed apparent that, despite the losses they had endured at the Indian farm the week before, Sagwitch had not cut all ties with his Mormon brethren and that his followers still trusted Hill and the Mormons enough to consider placing their yet-unharvested crop for safekeeping in one of the three nearest Mormon settlements.

When Sagwitch and his braves returned to the Indian farm, they found conditions to be still highly unsettled. The people at Corinne remained on full armed alert, having heard that Pocatello and at least fifteen hundred of his braves had not returned to their reservation as commanded but had encamped near Logan, where they were "being supported entirely by 'Mormons' and are under the control of the 'Mormon' Church."[110] The *Salt Lake Tribune* reported that 150 lodges of Indians "recently expelled" from the Bear River valley had encamped on the Logan River, where they were being fed twenty beeves and a supply of flour by the Mormons. The reporter condemned the "bloody priests" for their kindness to the Indians then, alluding to the Bear River Massacre, added "thus the good work done by Government, through Gen. Connor, is being all undone by Brigham Young."[111]

Feeling that the amassed Indians stood poised for "another" attack on Corinne, the burg's citizens posted a large number of guards at the portals of their city. Governor George W. Emery prevailed upon General Sheridan to authorize a company of men to be stationed at Corinne "until the Mayor of the city considers all danger of a Mormon-Indian invasion over."[112] Company C of the Fourteenth Infantry arrived from Omaha on August 25.[113] Clearly, conditions at Corinne made it unsafe for Hill or the Indians to be seen anywhere near their camp or the fortified city.

While Corinne's citizens exhibited an unfounded paranoia about the prospects of an Indian attack,[114] they accurately assumed that the natives, including Sagwitch, were angry enough to consider fighting. In a private letter to Brigham Young on August 25, Hill confided that the Indians "are anxious to fight the soldiers and want me to go with them."[115] According to one account, the gathered warriors even called Hill's attention to a Book of Mormon promise that "They should go through as a lion among the beasts of the forest or as a young lion among the flock of sheep," as a portent that the Indians would succeed in battle because of their allegiance to God. One of the chieftains followed the recitation of the scriptural passage by the request, "Now you lead us, and we will do that."[116] In fact, the Indians staying near Malad reportedly strutted around the town exhibiting their "Endowment garments" and claimed that the Great Spirit would soon come, after which they would "heap kill um dam Gentile."[117] Hill responded by telling the Indians not to fight because "they are not prepared and if they fight now they will [be] killed off and I do not want it done."[118]

Hill had contemplated battling the soldiers and reclaiming the farm by force but soon decided that such a course could not succeed. After weighing the options carefully, he concluded in his letter to Young that there were "but a few indians here now, namely old Tsy quitches band of maybe seventy Lodges and they are poorly armed with very Little Ammunition and not prepared for any kind of a fight."[119] Hill was torn between the realities of the ruined Indian camp and the scriptural challenge to "gather the Indians in from their long dispersion and make of them one nation again."

Realizing that it was impossible to harvest the remaining crops or to gather the Indians again in a group, Hill finally suggested to

Sagwitch and those with him that they "scatter one in a place all over the country" and that if they went to Fort Hall "he [God] would gather them back from there again." With that, the Indians once again turned from their crops and lands, unsure of their future course, but apparently still true to their Mormon faith and obedient to "Father" Hill.[120] From that time on through the end of the year, Hill attempted to keep his flock together but found that the people of Corinne kept such close watch that such an effort required much "manovering and shifting from place to place" to remain undetected.[121]

As Hill and the Indians departed a second time from their home on the Malad ditch, newspapers far and near began to devote lengthy reports and editorials to the Corinne affair. Not surprisingly, Mormon papers heartily condemned Corinne for the incident, charging that the residents of the commerce-strapped city had created the scare to disgrace the church and to benefit from the business that the soldiers could provide. The editor of the *Deseret News* poked fun at the gentile city, declaring, "All the world is laughing till its sides ache over poor scared Corinne's last convulsive kick," and suggested that in the future, the proper mocking salutation to a resident of Corinne should be "How's your hair?"[122] The editor more seriously assessed the horrible injustices the Indians had endured, losing the products of an entire summer's labor "at the point of the bayonet, in deference to the demogogish and partisan misrepresentations of a few unprincipled white men,"[123] and argued that the citizens of Corinne should pay the Indians "every cent of a just indemnification" for their losses.[124] Editors from the *Ogden Junction* and *Salt Lake Herald* expressed similar sentiments.[125] Meanwhile, the *Corinne Daily Mail* and *Salt Lake Tribune* filled their papers for weeks with editorial justifications of the incident and condemnations of Brigham Young and the church for setting the situation in motion.

The Corinne scare also became big news outside Utah Territory, with national newspapers anxious to cover an incident that initially appeared to be as interesting as the well-known Mountain Meadows Massacre. Papers in California and New York condemned Mormon involvement with the Indians. The editor of the *Sacramento Union* warned the Mormons that they were "playing with matches at the open door of a powder magazine" and threatened that twenty thousand armed men could be raised within twenty-four hours "to settle polygamy and the Church of Latter-day Saints." "If Corinne is attacked by the Indians," he added, "let Brigham Young see to it that Salt Lake does not smoke for the outrage."[126]

A few papers saw the affair differently, with the editor of Montana's *New North West* calling it "almost incredible" to believe that an Indian attack had even been contemplated, while the *Helena Independent* labeled the Corinne affair a "hoax."[127] The *Omaha Herald* was by far the most generous to Mormon interests as it reported the scare, declaring, "The charge that Mormons have sought to influence Indians, or that Indians have intended to slay and slaughter 'Gentile' citizens of Corinne, is a preposterous slander upon both Mormons and Indians." The *Herald* editor agreed with the Mormon position that Corinne initiated the scare for economic reasons: "Corinne has been slowly sinking in wealth and urban importance for so long that she has reached that deplorable layer from which her municipal officers and wealthy citizens determined to raise her. They thought that by the injection of a little currency into her veins, life might be resuscitated."[128]

Brigham Young also had a good deal to say about the Corinne scare. He held that the Mormon Indians at Malad had been innocent of all of Corinne's indictments. In a private letter to associate W. C. Staines on August 27, Young reasoned that the charges against the Indians defied logic and noted that the Indians had not sent their women and children to a safe site before the scare, no war dances or war paint had been observed, the ponies needed for the attack were all on the prairie grazing, and the supposed attack on the Malad bridge was unlikely because Shoshone always attacked at dawn rather than in the middle of night. Young pointed the finger of blame at Corinne, suggesting that the economically suffering city had invented the scare, hoping the results would include a "road to wealth" for the town.[129] To a reporter for the *Omaha Republican*, Young complained about the constant misrepresentation the Mormons suffered in the press and used the Corinne scare as an example, saying, "[the] Corinne Indian scare was the most ridiculous lie that was ever hatched . . . the object of which is to make public sentiment against us so strong that an army can be sent to drive us from our homes, which we have spent our lives in beautifying, so that they can revel in our deserted houses."[130] Young concluded, "Well, let them work away; they will get their reward in the next world, if not in this."[131]

Native Americans had been the most affected victims of the Corinne scare, and their responses varied. Agent William H. Danilson at Fort Hall noted that some of the Indians he spoke with at the reservation felt that "the Mormons have deceived them very much and just at present [they] do not seem disposed to put confidence in them." Danilson mentioned that the evicted Indians had been "thoroughly frightened" by the experience.[132] Ironically, the successful eviction of the peaceful Indians from their ripening crops at Bear River created a significant problem for the government. Danilson reported to the commissioner of Indian affairs that many of the displaced Indians had found refuge at Fort Hall, greatly swelling the population there. He wrote, "The question naturally arises how are they all to be fed this Winter. The present allowance will not do it."[133]

Agent James Irwin at the Wind River Reservation in Wyoming Territory noted in his annual report in September 1875 that a number of his Indians had been "induced" to Utah where they "were baptized in the Mormon Church, and advised to leave their reservation and drive the Gentiles out of Utah, and take posession of their ranches and property." He noted that timely intervention sent the "deluded Indians" back to their homes and that those returning to his reserve "are generally ashamed of the whole proceedings."[134]

In the initial confusion after the scare, even those Indians most loyal to Mormonism, including Sagwitch, blamed the Mormons, along with the soldiers, for what had happened, though most of them retained their close affiliation with the Saints. Sagwitch and Little Soldier, Shoshone chieftains ejected from the Indian farm, each dictated for publication their own statements about the Corinne scare. Little Soldier declared, "[We] were making a good farm above Bear River City; and all they wanted was to be good Mormon and live in peace. But Corinne white man send talk all over the country, got soldiers come and drive Indian away; reason: Corinne man no like Mormon, heap like sell soldier whiskey make money. Indian no money. Corinne man no like shake hands. Now may be heap soldiers come kill Indian man, woman, and pappoose. Indian no sleep now, no potato, no wheat, no beef; no like Fort Hall Reservation; not good."[135]

Sagwitch made a statement to his translator and assistant Ejupitchee, or Indian John, who then dictated it to George Washington Hill "in behalf of Tsyguitch's band of Sho-sho-nees." Hill included a note with the transcription to the effect that Indian John desired that their statement "might go as far as corinne's talk had gone, that the white man might know for himself whether he was guilty as accused or not." Hill also assured the reader that the chief's statement was "just as he gave it, without any varnish."[136]

The white man of Corinne has had his say; I now want mine. I have been intimately acquainted with the white man from my childhood, and I appeal to any white man, when have I played false with him? When have I lied to him? When have I stolen anything from him? Whom have I killed or even threatened to kill? I have ever been an advocate for peace. I abhor war to-day. I want peace. I sue for peace to-day. I want to be at peace with all men, and I challenge Corinne today to produce one instance where I have transgressed the law or done aught to break peace with the white man. The white man roams the mountains all over, hunting for the gold and silver that belong to the Indian until he sells the land. When have I interfered with him? The railroads pass through my country and have scared the game all away. Still I have made no objection to this, nor do I want to. I want all men to have the privilege of doing as they like, undisturbed, and make all the money they can, and all I want is peace and to be allowed to make a farm in a small, very small, portion of the country I have always lived in and still want to live in. My father's bones lie on this soil and my mother's as well, and I claim the privilege of laying mine with theirs. I have always lived in peace, and I still want to, and lay down my bones in peace, and leave peace for my children.

Corinne has got up this excitement without any cause. There is no foundation in truth for it, and I do not want there to be any cause for it. I hold no hard ness at Corinne for what they have done, only I want it stoped, that we may return to our farm and go to work and build houses to live in, and be ready to do something next year, if our crops are all destroyed this year. We do not want to give it up and stop at this, but want to continue and make a success of our farming experiment yet for the benefit of my people. I ask the white man to say when have I killed any thing, except the wild game of my own country? Or when have I made any objection to the white man comeing into my country and killing my game? The white man is roaming all over my country and killing my game. Still I make no objection to his doing so, and all I want is to be let alone, with the privilege of making a small farm for the benefit of my people, and to be allowed to live on it in peace. I have not gone into the white man's country and intruded on him, and I do not think it is fair for him to come into mine and drive me from my own lands without any cause, and I ask the government to take the matter in hand and reinstate me and mine on our own lands, that we may live there in peace and friendship with all men.[137]

Brigham Young remained committed to "reclaiming" the Indian, even though the Corinne scare had effectively doomed the Mormon Church's summer-long efforts. At the October 1875 general conference of the church, Young again signaled his strong support of the Lamanite mission by calling a host of new missionaries to assist those called the previous spring, including Israel J. Clark, Cyrus E. Clark, Isaac E. D. Zundel, Garret Wolverton, Alvin Nichols, John Jones, Alexander Hunsaker, Charles Knudson, Willis Booth, Homer Call, Matthew Dalton, John Hubbard, Clinton Bronson, George Marsh, Orville Child, William T. Baker, Robert Holroy, Asa Garner, William McGregor, James M. Brown, Albern Allen, and William Davis.[138]

On October 25, 1875, George Washington Hill joined four of the newly called elders and headed for the upper Bear River Valley to the site where the missionaries and Indians had begun building a dam the previous spring, but had then abandoned it due to the lateness of the season. The logical course was to reclaim the site and

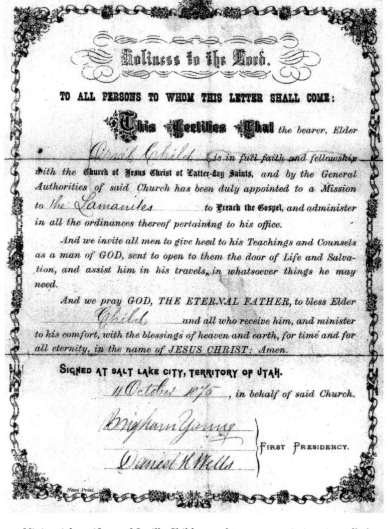

Ministerial certificate of Orville Child, one of twenty-two missionaries called to the "Lamanite" mission in October 1875, in the aftermath of the Corinne scare, with the charge to help establish a farm for the Shoshone in Box Elder County, Utah. Copy of original document courtesy LDS Church Archives, Salt Lake City, Utah.

pursue construction of the dam with vigor so that by springtime water would be available for an Indian farm that, unlike the previous location, was safely distanced from Corinne. The work went slowly, even after an additional five missionaries joined the group in late November. On November 22, work on the dam was concluded for the season due to foul weather and the limited number of missionaries available to help.

From that time until spring, an aging George Washington Hill traveled "from camp to camp" to visit his scattered converts and to inform them of the anticipated operations at the new site in the spring.[139] Meanwhile, Corinne continued its economic decline. Ironically, the Montana trade that was so important to the city began to drop off sharply after the scare. The exaggerated but effective news reports about bloodthirsty Indians on the Bear had made their mark in Montana, much to Corinne's chagrin.[140]

In November 1875, Corinne's paper, a source of much of the anti-Mormon sentiment that had played so important a role in the scare, ceased publication. The city had gambled and lost, much to the pleasure of one Mormon newspaper correspondent who wrote from Brigham City, "Poor Corinne! I did not visit its dying bed, but I could see its shadowy form away across the river, and it looked like the ghost of a miserable sinner silently passing away to Hades."[141]

Wintertime looked bleak for the Indians. Mormons from Bear River City harvested all that they could salvage of the Indians' crops, but the total amounted to only about two hundred bushels of wheat and another two hundred bushels of potatoes, certainly not enough to sustain hundreds of Indians through the cold months ahead.[142] The Mormons provided food to the Indians as a supplement to what they could hunt on their own. As Sagwitch and the other Mormon Indians settled in for a long winter, they hoped that their continued faith in Mormonism and agrarianism would bear better fruit the next season than it had in the previous two summers.

As the all-too-eventful year passed away, the citizens of Grantsville, south of the Great Salt Lake, did their part to help the Indians who had settled in their vicinity, distributing to "the poor and the Indians" rabbit carcasses gathered during a hunting contest.[143] It would be a cold, hard winter indeed.

5

Lemuel's Garden

*Our Indians feel first rate[,] take hold well[,] have no fault
to find of them[.] they attend well to meeting and some of
them understand themselves very well in fact are very good
preachers. They some of them fully sense the situation[.]
They say they understand mormonism now and like it
well[.]*

George Washington Hill, August 15, 1876

*My fathers bones lie on this soil and my mother's as well,
and I claim the privelage of laying mine with theirs. I
have always lived in peace, and I still want to, and lay
down my bones in peace, and leave peace for my children.*

Sagwitch, August 31, 1875

As a warmer sun began to break the icy hold of winter in early
1876, no one could have been happier than George Washington
Hill. The aging missionary to the Indians had spent much of the cold
wintertime traveling from one Indian camp to another to keep in contact with the Shoshone converts, who were his responsibility by
assignment and his friends through long and intimate association.
He was more than a little anxious to settle the dust of the Corinne
scare of 1875 by regrouping the natives for another season of farming and worship.

Hill exhibited tremendous zeal and dedication to this cause. It
seemed as if nothing was more important to him than seeing his converts comfortably settled as "civilized" farmers. Unfortunately, many
of the twenty-two men Brigham Young called as missionaries to the

139

Shoshone had little sense of commitment, or they hesitated abandoning their own life-sustaining farming and business interests long enough to teach the Indians how to plow, plant, and build houses. The early start Hill hoped for at the farm had not been possible simply because none of the other missionaries showed up to work. Hill became extremely frustrated and must have lodged a complaint with the church president. In mid-March, Brigham Young sent pointed letters to at least six of the missionaries, noting, "We are given to understand that you have not yet commenced your labors on the mission to which you were called at our last October conference. We hope that you will not longer delay attending to this call, but will report yourself 'on hand' to Bro. Geo. Hill of Ogden, now helping to make a farm on the Malad, at as early a date as practicable. We desire to see this mission prosper, and that all the brethren called thereto will labor with all diligence, faith and wisdom in accomplishing its objects."[1]

While Young's clerks posted such letters, Hill kept busy with other arrangements, including the acquisition of a plow and other tools for the farm.[2] On April 4, he headed for the farm. With him was missionary Orville Child and two substitute workers—James Brown, who was sent in the place of his father, James M. Brown, and William Eggleston, who had been enlisted by Robert Holdroyd to take his place. Willis H. Booth sent no replacement but declared that his health was too poor for him to be of service to the mission. As the party passed through Willard and Brigham City, they found that the missionaries residing in those cities were not yet ready to join them at the farm. By April 5 Hill and his few assistants reached camp and began setting up for the season, and by April 10 the Indians had joined them.[3] Given Sagwitch's role as a leader and spokesman at the farm in the previous two years and the fact that many of the still-loyal Shoshone converts were part of his band, it is likely that he arrived early and brought a large contingent of followers with him.

Hill chose to return in 1876 to the lands between the Bear and Malad rivers where he and the Indians had begun working in the early spring of 1875, before their temporary removal to the site near Corinne. A. Milton Musser, who served the Mormon First Presidency from 1858 to 1876 as a traveling bishop, visited the site Hill had chosen and described it as a "high, dry, semi-sandy plain, some 200 feet above the waters of the rivers." Musser noted that a mile of fence on the north and a mile and a quarter of fence on the south, both stretching from river to river, would serve to enclose some nine thousand acres of land.[4]

Under Hill's direction, the Indians and missionaries plowed an enthusiastically large plot and prepared it for crops. They planted eighty acres of spring wheat and another eighty acres of fall wheat, seventy-eight acres of lucerne (alfalfa), six acres of potatoes, seven acres of corn, and four acres of other vegetables.[5] Hill and the Shoshone had planted crops in this soil the previous spring but had been forced to abandon it due to a late start and the difficulty in getting water onto the fields. Not wanting another failure for lack of water, Hill obtained the services of Mormon surveyor Charles Hardy to map the best route for an irrigation canal to the fields. He completed the survey, which also included a study of the lands to be used for farming purposes, by May 4. The survey report dictated the backbreaking construction of a canal sixteen-and-one-half miles long, most of the way carved into hillsides. Not overwhelmed by such difficult construction requirements, Hill optimistically reported to President Young that there would be "7 thousand five hundred acres of land below where our canal would come out."[6]

By April 12 some of the delinquent missionaries had arrived at the camp. After they were settled and had begun laboring with the Indians in planting crops and digging the canal, Hill used his time to begin the legal procedures necessary to solidify the claims of the Shoshone to their lands. He reported that on May 8 he returned home to Ogden in order "to try and raise some money to homestead land for the Indians to secure them from being driven as they were last year."[7] In applying for homesteads on behalf of the Shoshone, Hill utilized an 1875 amendment to the 1862 Homestead Act that for the first time allowed Native Americans to be considered as American citizens with the right to file on public lands. The amendment did require that those Indians who successfully homesteaded relinquish forever their tribal affiliations and rights to government annuities.[8]

Having determined that it would cost about $16.50 to homestead one Indian, Hill visited the cooperative store in his hometown of Ogden and asked the various clerks, undoubtedly his friends, for help. Between the fourteen men present, $15.50 was raised. He then appealed to the "moneyed men" of the city for donations to the noble cause. All of them turned him down. One fellow Ogdenite, Michael Beus, did pay the full cost of a single homestead application. In Salt Lake City, President Young's office offered $33 to the project. All told, Hill had acquired just enough money to homestead four Native Americans. On May 19, 1876, he filed claims on eighty-acre plots on behalf of Indians John Moemberg and Charles Ahbuck and two unnamed Indians who filed under missionary James Brown's name.[9]

By the next day Hill returned to the farm, where he directed the temporary removal of the entire camp of missionaries and Indians to a site on the Malad River several miles north and slightly west of their fields. Construction had begun at that site the previous fall on a large rock dam. Once finished, Hill anticipated that the dam could divert a large body of water through a canal to the farm land. The success of the Indian farm ultimately hinged upon the completion of the water system. It cannot be overemphasized that in seeking to establish themselves as farmers, the Shoshone were engaging in work that was absolutely foreign to them—plowing and planting crops, using their ponies to drag loads of rock, and digging deep trenches several miles long. Sagwitch and the other leaders must have played a role in sustaining in their people the kind of faith needed to stick to the difficult and strange work. Perhaps the abuses suffered at Corinne the year before had solidified the loyalties of those Indians who chose to return to the farm in 1876. One thing is certain, that the Indians who returned were committed to their farm and to Father Hill's gospel. A. Milton Musser noted in 1876 the dedication of the Indians at the farm and wrote that "a more orderly, prayerful, and persevering colony of men and women would be hard to find."[10] Hill echoed those sentiments in an August 1876 letter to Young: "Our Indians . . . attend well to meetings and some of them understand themselves very well in fact are very good preachers. They some of them fully sense the situation[.] They say they understand mormonism now and like it well[.]"[11]

Mormon Church policy encouraged Native Americans to participate in every aspect of the faith. In keeping with that policy, Sagwitch's people conducted most of the Sunday worship services, offering prayers and sermons in their native tongue. Surviving evidence suggests that one of the Indians might have been selected to serve as the bishop of the farm. Brigham Young noted in a September 1876 letter that "their bishop and teachers are of their own people and they hold their meetings and pray and preach as intelligently as their white brethren according to their capacity."[12] A letter Hill wrote to Young in August 1876 also establishes that someone in camp functioned as a bishop and hints that it might have been a Native American.[13] Missionary Matthew Dalton, in a personal reminiscence, mentioned the presence of an Indian he called "Bishop John" at the camp.[14] If indeed church leaders ordained a Native American as a bishop in 1876, it was certainly the first such occurrence in Mormonism.[15]

The Indians continued work on the dam and canal, allowing George Hill to return to Salt Lake City to file more homestead applications. In a missionary report, Hill noted that on June 3, 1876, he "made citizens of and homesteaded land for seven Indians." The tract book recording homesteads only shows filings for Dina Pitsy, Shosho Nits, and Noyl Watt. It is likely that clerks did not file the remaining four homestead applications because the Indians ultimately failed to comply with requirements dictating permanent residency on the property and the construction of dwellings there.[16] On June 24, Hill returned again to the land office and filed homestead applications on behalf of three more Indians: Signe Ticker, Poor Owa, and Pahnea Tonik. Hill was jubilant that by the end of June, fourteen natives had begun the homesteading process. The Indians themselves fully supported the homesteading effort, so much so that many, as visiting church leader Musser noted, "sell their ponies to obtain means to meet the expense."[17]

Work continued on the canal and dam until July 14, when Hill called everyone back to the fields to begin the harvest. The Indians had made great progress on the dam, having placed five hundred loads of rock in the channel of the river. Construction of the canal had moved more slowly, with just three miles completed. This, however, represented an immense effort, especially considering the fact that the canal's route had required a thirty-foot deep cut in a steep mountainside. The Indians had been zealous workers on both projects.[18]

When Hill and the Indians returned and began their harvest, they happily discovered that even without irrigation, their harvest yielded "some 400 bushels of wheat, some oats, and a good show of corn, 'spuds,' melons, squashes, &c." The lucerne had also done surprisingly well, sending its roots eighteen inches into the dry soil and producing a fair crop of hay in the process.[19] Despite this apparent success, it seemed clear that all of the crops had suffered from the lack of water and from an infestation of hungry grasshoppers. Most upsetting to Hill was the discovery of grazing damage by the farm's own cattle to the spring wheat due to the careless watch kept by two of the missionaries.

Hill vented his anger in a letter to Brigham Young wherein he complained of the burdens associated with running the farm nearly alone. He wrote, "I suppose you think there is about twenty or twenty five of us here[.] Well there is about five as a general thing and we have two wagons here that belong to the missionaries and when it comes wood hauling time I expect they will run away as others have done when the spring got far enough along that the grain needed watering[.] Oh they must go and water their grain they would be back in a few days say four or five at the farthest[.] Well when they get away they forget to come back and that is the last we see of them."[20] Isaac E. D. Zundel, one of the twenty-two missionaries called to the work in October 1875, would have agreed with Hill. He later reminisced, "I began to labor among the Indians under the direction of Geo. W. Hill; and being a young man I felt keenly the responsibility of my sacred calling . . . Twenty-five brethren were called . . . to study the Indian language; they all began to do so, but one by one they tired of it, till finally I found myself a lone white student among the red men."[21] Even after the season of work had ended and Hill's anger had subsided, he could only say of the missionaries that "some have never exerted themselves at all, some come and done a few days work and to all appearances have quit for good, [and] some have enjoyed the spirit of their mission and done well."[22]

With or without the help of others, Hill greatly desired that the farm prosper, having devoted himself to its success. He also realized that the Indians had given up most of their other options when they settled at the farm and that their very survival now depended upon a good irrigation system, plentiful crops, and patented homesteads.

Isaac Eberhart David Zundel (1840–1920). Called on a mission to the Indian
farm in October 1875, he was appointed director of the project in 1878, and
in September 1880 was set apart as first bishop of the newly formed
Washakie Ward. Fox and Symons, photographers, Salt Lake City, Utah, ca.
1880. Photograph courtesy LDS Church Archives, Salt Lake City, Utah.

After venting his frustration to Young regarding the lack of missionary support, Hill sorrowfully noted that the Indians "feel themselves entirely at the bottom of the hill[,] poor and destitute without wagons or other tools [and] without friends except their white brethren." Hill added that while the Indians "have no fault to find of them," they were aware that ". . . their white Brethren have taken up all the best land all that is situated close to water and timber and they have to take up with that that is not so good and where it takes a vast amount of labor to get the water out and where the timber is inconvenient." Through Hill, the Indians wished to appeal to "father Brigham" for their white brethren "to turn out and help them to get a start help them to get out their lumber and help them to finish their canal so that they can have the water on the ground that they can have full crops." Hill assured Young that the Indians had worked hard and would continue to do so but the scope of work was so vast that outside help was absolutely necessary.[23]

Within three days, President Young sent a conciliatory response to Hill, expressing his gratitude for the Indians who continued in "laboring energetically to accomplish the work designed for their benefit." However, he added, "We wish you to explain to the Indians that we are not by right bound to help them, only thro' the duty laid upon us by the Gospel to seek the Salvation of all the world. It is the government of the U.S. that has taken their land from them, not us. Nevertheless we will help them all we can."[24] Young offered to supply the farm with more shovels, spades, and hoes for digging the canal, encouraged Hill to "get your Cabins up as fast as you can," and promised the services of men from Cache and Box Elder valleys in hauling lumber to the farm as soon as their work would permit.[25]

Though Young might have sounded less than overwhelmingly sympathetic in his letter to Hill, he was nevertheless very impressed by the farm and its Mormon Indian occupants. So pleased was he, in fact, that he mentioned the farm to leaders in other Mormon communities having Indian populations. Writing to Lot Smith and other presidents of Mormon settlement companies on the Little Colorado in Arizona, Young discussed the Malad Valley Indians under Hill's tutelage and bragged that they were "assimiliating themselves as rapidly as we can expect to their new mode of life."[26] In a letter to

Dan Jones in Fairview, Utah, Young also mentioned the Indians on the Malad and noted that "notwithstanding some few drawbacks," they had enjoyed an excellent crop and were "in first rate spirits."[27]

While Young waxed enthusiastic, George Washington Hill and the Indians worked on. Meanwhile, the gentiles who still remained at the "dying burg" of Corinne kept a wary and concerned watch. Some citizens wrote to the *Salt Lake Daily Tribune* of their concerns over the new buildup of Mormon Indians in the valley. One correspondent warned that "Old Hill is 'nest hiding' among them, and says he will see the United States Government d——d before his pets shall leave the valley again."[28] Another writer calling himself "Jabez" wrote about the large numbers of Indians returning to the valley and threatened, "We can assure the Lamanite brethren and their Mormon friends that we are prepared to give them a warm reception . . . we mean business from the start, in proof of which we have only to refer to the prompt manner in which we checkmated the Indian move of last summer."[29]

At least for the time being, Corinne's threats fell on deaf ears, and the farm continued its bustling activity uninterrupted. The Indians finished their harvest in September by cutting the spring wheat with a reaper that they borrowed and learned to run themselves. Through late fall, the Indians hauled logs for their homestead cabins and made good progress toward getting many such structures erected.[30] In this task, missionary Matthew Dalton was most helpful. Dalton, who owned a sawmill, offered to supply a good amount of lumber to the Indians and to personally build one of the needed homestead cabins. He later recorded, "I sawed free of charge all the lumber needed for six houses, and then set to work and erected a very neat one room house with proper floor, bedstead and table, and turned it over for the use of Bishop John . . . The other brethren then each put up a house and thus we introduced to the Lamanites, the art of erecting houses, and living in them like white men."[31]

Most of the work on homestead cabins had been postponed until cold weather set in as the missionaries and Indians had been preoccupied through the summer and fall with farming and canal digging. It became cold enough during house construction in late fall that master mason Shadrach Jones warned against trying to build rock chimneys for the houses and urged Hill to look instead for second-hand stoves. The missionaries raised sixty-nine dollars and purchased four or five stoves for the Shoshone houses.[32] The missionaries also solicited nearby Saints for donations of stoves and furniture. Several cabins were soon nicely, if spartanly, furnished.[33]

Unlike its predecessors of the preceding two years, the farm, apparently intentionally, did not become a center for proselytizing new Indian converts. In summarizing his labors for 1876, Hill wrote: "We have not Baptised any Indians in our camp yet this year[.] we addopted the plan this year of making citizens of them as fast as we could get the [resources] to do it, homestead the land and make things shure and safe[.] in doing this we have not advanced in numbers but have established in firmness those that have already joined the church[.]"[34]

In late December 1876, after the approaching winter finally made further homebuilding impossible, most of the Indians headed to the Promontory Mountains, where they could find more abundant fuel supplies and forage for their stock. A few remained at the farm, camping in or near the homestead cabins they had built to prove to the government what they themselves had never questioned, that the land upon which they were building their lives and futures was theirs.[35]

During the winter, Brigham Young had time to reflect on the successes and failures at the Indian farm in the previous few years. He likely thought long and hard about the problems George Washington Hill had detailed in his many letters to church headquarters. Important factors were the ever-present shortages of tools, food, money, and, most significantly, dedicated missionaries to help in preparing the fields, hauling wood, building homestead cabins, and helping to build an irrigation system to water the fertile but parched soil. The efficient Young took steps to make sure that these issues would not be problems at the farm in 1877.

In the first week of January 1877, the aging Mormon leader asked his counselors in the First Presidency to post letters to several of the missionaries to ensure their involvement at the Indian farm. Bishops in Cache and Box Elder valleys also received letters asking them to urge their citizenry who had "the good of Israel at heart" to give what aid they could in goods and labor. Six of the missionaries received nearly identical very firm letters that suggested nothing less than the uncertainty of their salvation in the next life should they not fulfill their responsibilities to labor with the Indians. Such letters included the following statement: "We are full well assured that the path of duty for a Latter-day Saint is not only the path of safety, but the path of salvation also, we therefore feel impressed not only for the sake of our brethren of the Lamanites but also for your own, to suggest that you show yourself alive to this duty and calling and perform the work to which you were assigned."[36] A kinder letter posted to George B. Marsh thanked him for his valuable assistance in the previous year, and said "We shall be happy when receiving his [Hill's] future reports to again see your name with that of your team on the list of zealous laborers in the work of saving the outcasts of Israel."[37]

The First Presidency felt very strongly that those called to work with the Lamanites should do their assigned duty. For 1877, they initiated a formal reporting system that would show just how much each man was doing at the farm. The presidency wrote to Hill and asked him to begin keeping quarterly reports to document the number of hours worked by each missionary and his team and the goods and labor donated by others. Hill responded to the request with characteristic frankness: "I commenced to keep their time but they was with me so Little of the time it made a bad Looking sheet so that I quit keeping their time correctly[,] but I will make out as concise report as possible and as nearly correct as possible."[38]

The First Presidency asked Bishop William B. Preston of Cache Valley to send men to help with the plowing. Church leaders suggested that since the snow usually melted in Box Elder Valley three or four weeks before it did in Cache, the brethren in Cache Valley might "render them most valuable help" by plowing the Indians' fields during the period of time that would otherwise simply be spent "in watching and waiting for the snow to disappear." When the First Presidency wrote to Bishop Alvin Nichols in Box Elder County, they apologized for the heavy burden that his congregants endured due to their close proximity to the Indian farm. Even so, the presidency felt that those residents could do more good for the Indians in less time and with less trouble and expense to themselves than could brethren living at a greater distance, "and they could put an occasional day or two on the farm without material loss to themselves or the County."[39]

The number of letters sent and the ecclesiastical leverage exerted made it clear that the Mormon Church's top ruling body wanted success at the Indian farm and was now willing to direct more resources to achieve that success than ever before. Such a strong posture soon had its desired effect. By January 28, Hill could write that he and the missionaries had already planted eighty acres of wheat and had another twenty acres broken and ready for planting as soon as frost conditions would permit.[40] Furthermore, Hill's report covering the first quarter of 1877 documented an impressive number of donations in cash, goods, and labor received by the mission, including hundreds of labor hours by the Latter-day Saints in several small towns in Box Elder and Cache counties. Hill also reported that the mission had already built another homestead cabin for the Indians and plowed ten acres for sugar cane and ten for potatoes and was presently plowing land for corn.[41]

The Indians who had wintered at the Promontory returned to the farm as soon as the weather allowed them to travel. Records do not say whether Sagwitch was among them or if he had stayed at the farm through the winter. Hill reported that the Indians were "generaly healthy" but sadly noted that sickness had claimed the lives of two of the small children. The Indians were in good spirits and were reportedly anxious to begin building a schoolhouse in which their children could be taught properly.[42]

By early 1877 George Washington Hill began to refer to the Indian farm as Lemuel's Garden, a term which probably suggested the Mormons' belief that the Indians had literally descended from Lemuel, a Book of Mormon figure, as well as Hill's determination that the dry sandy plain that they were settling would one day become a lush and productive Eden.[43]

Unfortunately, as the land became less forbidding, it also became more attractive to outsiders and more difficult to retain in Indian hands. Hill convened a council to consider the problem, and those present decided to try to secure all of the land in the vicinity to the Indians, "so as not to allow ourselves to be cut into," and then let the mission brethren file on surrounding properties, feeling that "we had rather choose our neighbors than to let some body else choose them for us."[44] With that decided, the missionaries helped the Indians file on additional homesteads, and work at the farm continued with increased fervor. In addition to farming chores, Hill had to make certain that fifteen additional houses had been constructed by the end of summer to satisfy requirements on previously filed homesteads.[45]

In the midst of this activity, Hill received an invitation that he could not easily ignore. Three hundred lodges of "Northern Indians" had sent word to him that they wished to have a meeting "as far from the white man as they can get easily" in order to receive instruction and baptism under his hands. The prospective converts included "Pabby Utes," "Boise Indians," "Northern Sho sho nees," "Bannocks," "Walla Wallas," "Cy use," "Nez per ces," and "Flat heads." Hill was thrilled that "the work is still spreading" and made plans to meet them in mid-May.[46]

In his next quarterly report on July 1, Hill announced that the appointed gathering had been very fruitful. Two hundred forty-nine Indians had been baptized. Hill temporarily denied baptism to an additional hundred Indians, "as we were wright under the Agents nose I thought we had stayed long enough." The converts begged to join Hill at the farm. He denied their requests simply because another grasshopper infestation had destroyed most of the season's crops and the farm's insufficient resources could not feed an enlarged Indian presence. It seemed apparent that in this marginal farming season, additional Indians would have starved at the Mormon farm almost as readily as they did on their government reservations, despite Brigham Young's gift of an additional twenty-six cows and the donation of a number of goods by nearby settlers.[47]

Hill did not plan to abandon his converts from the north, however. On June 23, he penned a letter to William H. Danilson, agent at Fort Hall, asking permission to come to the reservation and preach Mormonism to some of the Indians "that believe in the Principles of the Gospel as taught by the Latter Day Saints." Hill also asked permission to establish a mission near the fort where Mormons could help in "civilizing" the Indians and to teach them farming skills, thus relieving the government of the burden of supporting them.

Danilson sent a polite but firm reply just three days later. He informed Hill that Fort Hall had been assigned to the Methodist Episcopal Church and that permission would not be granted to "come upon the reservation to preach to those Indians or to carry on any missionary work whatever." Hill must have been upset by the agent's reply because in reporting the incident to Young, he mentioned his disgust for Danilson, who would not let an Indian get closer than a rod away from him because he was "afraid to touch their hands for fear they will Black his." Hill gloated, "He does not know that his Indians are all mormons and that he has not one methodist Indian on his reservation."[48]

As the summer progressed, unrest among several Indian tribes increased. The state of near starvation that had become the hallmark of life on the government reservations was becoming intolerable. Segregated reservation life also effectively left each tribe powerless and at the mercy of its federal hosts. Towards the end of summer, leaders of various tribes began a movement aimed at uniting all of the northern, western, and southern Indian groups "for self protection and for one other purpose." Under the leadership of Sagwitch, Pocatello, and several others, the group hoped to hold a grand council at the Mormon camp where the diverse tribes would exchange gifts and strike a "treaty of alliance." Sagwitch and the others soon made Hill aware of the plan and informed him that the other purpose involved him. The Indians told him that they wished to "gather in and bundle around as they say they do not sleep well now where they are." He also reported that a Bannock chief at Fort Hall had already told his followers that "they could not stay at the Agencies mutch longer that it was only a question of time they had got to come to me."

According to Hill, the Mormon farm had attracted the attention of a very large spectrum of Indians, and Sagwitch and several other chiefs wanted to make them feel at home. While the reservation Indians continued to suffer at their appointed reserves, the Mormon-sponsored Indians were moving swiftly forward with farming and homesteading opportunities and with a religion that seemed to recognize and honor them. Hill reported to Young that the Indians "in the Distance say that ink a pompey [Hill] has brought his children through the narrows safely [and] they want to do the same."[49] Though no records document the occurrence of such a gathering, they do show that Hill began making plans for it, taking special care that the chiefs not stay any longer than necessary, owing to the shortage of foodstuffs at the camp.[50]

As the Indian farm grew and became better established, Corinne's residents became increasingly concerned. The Mormon Indians and their hosts reminded the Corinne citizens of the problems they had experienced two years earlier. In April 1877, Corinne's city council appointed a committee to quietly investigate matters at the Indian farm. The committee returned to report, among other things, that the homestead laws had not been honored, since only five unoccupied shanties could be found.[51]

The citizens of Corinne soon worked themselves into a second "Indian scare," as the city's correspondents to the Salt Lake newspapers began writing impassioned columns detailing every element of the supposed Indian threat. One writer, while admitting that "no alarmingly hostile demonstrations have been indulged in to warrant another request for soldiers," still argued that the citizenry was at the mercy of "a pack of savages" and strongly argued that as a deterrent to potential attack and "for the sake of our wives and children, we must have troops."[52] Corinne's mayor met with Utah governor George Emery, asking for a deployment of soldiers to protect the city.

Emery finally held a public meeting in Corinne and soon thereafter decided to appoint a grand jury from the third judicial district to conduct a proper investigation. The investigative body filed its report on September 26, 1877. It concluded that Mormons provided all of the labor at the farm while the Indians, who "live and dress like all wild Indians," merely "loafed" and "roamed about." The grand jury more accurately reported that the Indians at the camp were more loyal to the Mormons than to the federal government, whose agents they apparently called "Amerikats." The committee charged that the Mormons had used the Indians as tools for the purpose of obtaining more land for themselves and argued that the presence of the Indians in the vicinity, also carefully calculated, served to scare off legitimate non-Mormon homesteaders.[53]

Six weeks before the release of the grand jury report, Ogden resident and self-proclaimed "Late Secret Service Detective" Ephraim Young had made similar accusations in an August 9 letter to the secretary of the interior. Young charged that George W. Hill, who he did not know and mistakenly assumed to be an Indian, had amassed a band of from four to five hundred well-armed Native Americans. He suggested that the Mormons might use the Indians to "redeem Utah from the 'Gentiles' & drive them out," and reported that Hill had attempted the previous year in Ogden to get Indians to vote and actually "offered them ballots at the polls." Young called for all the Indians to be confined on reservations and declared that "it behooves the Government to give us proper protection that we may not be caught and slaughtered like sheep."⁵⁴

Although Ephraim Young apparently did not have personal knowledge of the Indian farm he condemned, his letter was very effective in raising concerns at the highest levels of government. The United States attorney general became aware of Young's allegations and asked Utah's district attorney Sumner Howard to investigate. On September 11, Howard reported that the Indians were indeed "under the protection, and are the objects of the care and attention of the Mormon Church." He wrote that the Mormons had passed the Indians "through the Endowment House, where, by the peculiar ceremonies performed, their superstitious natures are purposely wrought upon; and it is not strange that every Indian looks upon the Mormons as their friend; and the 'Americans' as their enemies, and are led to believe that a conflict is pending between them." He thus concluded "every Indian that joins the Mormon church becomes at once disloyal."⁵⁵ Howard described the farm on the Bear River and noted that the Mormons had established "a sort of protectorate over the Indians contiguous to them," and were "pretending to teach these Indians to farm." Howard felt that the Indians had become filled with prejudice against "anti-Mormons," and suggested that George W. Hill be prosecuted for tampering with them.⁵⁶

Ephraim Young's letter also caused the commissioner of Indian affairs to ask Utah Territory's Indian agent, John J. Critchlow, to investigate. Critchlow visited Corinne on September 18. He listened to the complaints of Corinne freighters who accused the Shoshone of "obstructing the public highway" by making irrigation ditches across the northern road. He listened to and agreed with those who charged that the Mormons were using the Indians to secure lands for their own use and to discourage gentile settlement, though he acknowledged that the Indians and Mormons denied all such allegations.⁵⁷

Critchlow also visited the Indian farm and found Isaac Zundel and three other white men at work. He discovered that the mission had constructed six board houses and one made of logs on seven of the twenty-four eighty-acre Indian homesteads. Five hundred bushels of wheat had been harvested that season and stored by the Shoshone for their later use. Zundel told Critchlow that it was the goal of the mission to "have the Indians settle down and become good citizens of the Govt. and obey its laws." To that end, Zundel reported, the Mormons had furnished all supplies and labor gratis.[58]

Critchlow next traveled to Ogden and met with complainant Ephraim Young, who, he concluded, "seemed to know nothing definitely," and with other witnesses recommended by Young who "had no facts but gave me various rumors." Critchlow reported that the Mormons exercised a controlling influence over several small Indian bands but that he thought there was "no immediate danger, if any in the future." He felt that many of the complaints and charges were nothing more than the product of "the excited state of the Gentile mind" and found no evidence that the Indians had hostile intentions. Critchlow closed his report by casting doubt on some of the findings of the grand jury.[59]

Governor George Emery, feeling compelled to personally investigate the charges brought by his Corinne constituents, visited the Indian farm in late September. A few days later, he wrote the secretary of the interior to report he was certain that most of the Indians there belonged to the Fort Hall Agency. He had learned from the land registrar that twenty-seven Indians had filed homestead papers and that there seemed to be no way of stopping that legal process short of suspending federal law. He accused the Shoshone of stealing fruit from the orchards of white settlers and turning their stock into farmers' gardens and fields. The governor called for action on the part of Congress to keep the Indians on their reservations.[60]

Mormon leaders became increasingly concerned about the potential fate of their converts as various federal officials called loudly for the forced removal of the Shoshone to reservations. George Washington Hill and John Hess turned for help to the only friend they had in national government, Utah's territorial delegate to Congress George Q. Cannon. Cannon, a Mormon apostle who had been Brigham Young's counselor in the church's ruling First Presidency since 1873, was well acquainted with the Indian farm and with Mormonism's theological and temporal goals for Native Americans.

Hill and Hess wrote to Cannon on October 29, 1877, explaining that the Shoshone homesteaders could prove, through receipts in their possession, that they had made proper legal claims to lands in Box Elder County. They reported that eight homestead houses had already been built on eight parcels and that the Indians had pitched their lodges on the other properties. They also noted other improvements at the farm that served to validate their homestead claims. Hill and Hess included a listing of all of the Shoshone homesteaders, including the section, township, and range coordinates for each of the quarter-section claims. As for removal of the Indians to Fort Hall on the premise that the reservation was their rightful home, they declared "These Indians have never belonged to any reservations, they have abandoned their tribal relations, are living upon their homesteads, and are minding their own business."[61]

By October 1877, Utah Indian agent John J. Critchlow had come to agree with the assertion made by Hill and Hess that the Mormon Indians along the Bear River did not belong to a reservation. In a letter to the commissioner of Indian affairs, he reported "I have been advised by the Agent at Fort Hall that the Indians in the neighborhood of Corinne do not belong at that Agency, and that coincided with what the Mormons told me when there."[62] The Fort Hall agent with whom Critchlow had spoken was William H. Danilson, who had served as agent there for over two years and had become acquainted with Sagwitch and others during the Corinne scare in August 1875. Although Danilson already had a general familiarity with the Indian settlement in northern Utah, the commissioner of Indian affairs asked him to visit it personally to investigate allegations raised by the grand jury and others.

Danilson arrived at the farm on November 15, 1877. He found that forty Indian families were living there, they had about three hundred acres under cultivation, and they had constructed eight houses, each measuring about twelve feet square. Danilson called the Shoshone together for a talk. After interviewing them at length, he confirmed what he had already assumed, that all those present had been "born and raised" in Utah and were "renegade Indians who have never been assigned to any reservation." In fact he emphatically stated in his report "that the Indians whom I saw on Bear River do not belong to this Agency."[63]

Some of the Indians Danilson spoke with expressed a willingness to abandon their homestead claims and move to Fort Hall if the government would promise to adequately provide for them there. The majority, however, wanted to remain in Utah. Danilson felt that the "Bear River Indians," as he called them, should be assigned to a reservation and suggested Fort Hall as the most likely agency since many of the Indians had relatives and friends there. He cautioned the commissioner that such a move could not be contemplated unless additional supplies were provided to subsist the 240 people involved.[64] Danilson's assessments helped to calm the concerns of government leaders about the intentions of the Shoshone near Corinne, though his recommendations calling for their relocation to Fort Hall were ignored.

Through the summer and fall of 1877, critics of the Indian farm had been successful in filling the public mind with allegations of Mormon-Indian collusion against gentiles and with fears concerning a potential attack on Corinne. Their efforts did not go unchallenged, however. The Mormon Church press was predictably disgusted with what it viewed as a contrived issue and vocal in denouncing the efforts of those like Ephraim Young and the people of Corinne. The *Deseret News* characterized attempts to remove the "peaceful harmless Indians" from their lands as "brutal, merciless, and wholly unnecessary" and, as in 1875, charged that Corinne had invented a crisis in hopes of stirring up another lucrative "contractor's war."[65]

A correspondent to the *Deseret News* writing from Hampton Bridge, just a few miles from the farm, labeled the conclusions of the grand jury dishonorable and noted that he often saw Indians driving teams, plowing, harrowing, and engaged in lumbering and other labors that seemed to be solid proof of their desire to give up the nomadic life. Moreover, he continued, the Indians never bothered stock on the open range, as the grand jury had charged, and were so trusted in the area that many had credit accounts at the Deweyville store that they never failed to pay.[66]

Eventually, most of the fears and allegations about the Indians on the Bear River were found to be without merit. Even Governor George Emery, one of Corinne's great allies, chose not to station troops at Corinne after the release of the inflammatory grand jury report. Perhaps to placate his Corinne constituents however, he did authorize delivery of one hundred guns to the citizenry for the purpose of self-protection.[67]

Despite Corinne's posturing, the farm continued to progress. By summer's end, more than a dozen additional homestead claims had been filed, and the farm enjoyed a good enough reputation among businessmen to allow the purchase, on credit, of a reaper, a mower, a hay rake, and a cultivator. After the Indians and missionaries harvested the grasshopper-damaged crops, they continued to build homestead cabins using wood hauled from nearby mountains. Hampered by a shortage of lumber on the dry, sandy plain, the missionaries made numerous attempts to turn clay into adobe building blocks, apparently without success. As autumn approached, Hill tried several times to have a local judge inspect and confirm the new property boundaries. Once such boundaries had been approved, Hill intended to have fences built running from river to river, a move that would demarcate, perhaps politically as well as physically, the Shoshone's claims to the land.[68]

George W. Hill was anxious to foster a better understanding between Mormons and Indians and always needed additional missionary helpers who had a familiarity with Indian customs and language. Perhaps in a move to achieve both aims, he prepared an English-Shoshone vocabulary. The church press published and began selling it as homesteading and farming activities continued in 1877.[69]

The Indian farm lost two of its most constant allies during 1877. The death of Brigham Young on August 29, 1877 must have been keenly felt by many of the Northwestern Shoshone.[70] Though his successor, John Taylor, continued to strongly support the church's Indian programs, he could not, in some ways, replace Young, who had come to be seen as a "father" to many of the Indians who had known him personally during the thirty years he spent in their homeland.

Probably more significant to the Indians, however, was the release of Inkapompy (George Washington Hill) from his missionary duties among them at the end of 1877. In 1878, Mormon Church leaders assigned Hill to secretly minister and preach to Washakie's band on the Wind River Reservation. The following year, after church Indian interpreter Dimick Huntington died in February 1879, Hill

was asked to move his family to Salt Lake City and fill Huntington's
position. Church leaders chose Isaac Zundel as the new director of
the farm. Zundel, who the Shoshone called Biataibo (Piataipo), "Big
White Man," had served as a missionary at the farm since 1875.[71]

For all the uncertainty at the farm in 1877, including crop failures, grasshopper infestations, and gentile "intrusions," at least one
aspect of Hill's fatiguing efforts to settle the Indians on their own
lands had been noted and formalized. Lieutenant George M.
Wheeler, leading a survey for the U.S. Army Corps of Engineers,
included on his 1877 map of the Box Elder and Cache area the site
of "Indiantown" precisely where Hill, Sagwitch, and many others
had worked to establish Lemuel's Garden.[72]

As Mormon leaders in the Box Elder area gathered on March 2,
1878, for their monthly priesthood meeting, stake president O. G.
Snow read a letter he had just received from the church's acting
president, John Taylor. The content of the letter left no room for confusion about Taylor's support of the Indian farm on the Malad. He
requested teams, wagons, grain, tools, and other items for the
Shoshone village and asked that the Saints in Box Elder and Cache
valleys supply them. Box Elder Stake leaders assigned Isaac Zundel,
the new head of the mission, to visit leaders in Cache Valley to
gather their donations to the cause. By the time of the June 2 priesthood meeting, leaders reported that all of the requested assistance
had been provided.[73] The farm had begun a new era under the
administration of Taylor and Zundel.

One of the first changes initiated by the new leaders concerned
the missionaries to the farm. As early as October 1877, Isaac Zundel
had suggested to Taylor that six or eight of the brethren be called to
the mission with their families. He felt that their presence, and "the
instruction of their wives to the Indian women," could accomplish
more than could be taught any other way.[74] In February 1878 Zundel
again recommended his plan to Taylor and included a list of likely
candidates. Interestingly, Frank Warner, Sagwitch's youngest son,
who the Amos Warner family had raised, was on the list.[75] Taylor
must have approved the plan because a few families moved to
Lemuel's Garden in 1878, including those of Isaac Zundel and
Alexander Hunsaker. This change gave the farm stability it had
never before known. Year-round residential administrators now

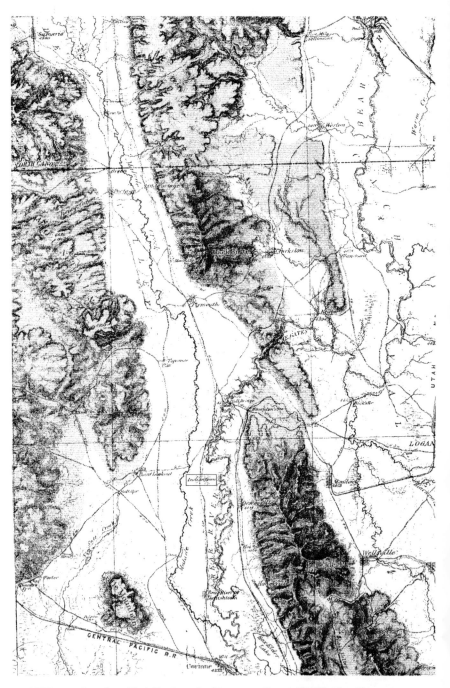

1877 map of northern Utah Territory, by Lieutenant George M. Wheeler. The map
shows Lemuel's Garden, the Mormon Shoshone settlement near the Bear River, as
"Indiantown" (outlined by a box not on the original map). Copy of map courtesy

replaced seasonal missionaries, who had traditionally returned to their homes from late fall until the following spring.

As a new season of work at the farm got underway, a final chapter of the "Indian Scare" of 1877 was played out. On about April 22, 1878, Utah Territory's Indian agent, John J. Critchlow, again inspected the Indian farm, as he had done the previous September. He did so under orders of the commissioner of Indian affairs responding to a December 1877 request by Utah's delegate to congress George Q. Cannon for an investigation. Critchlow was directed to ascertain if the Shoshone along the Bear River were "sufficiently advanced in civilization to manage their own affairs, support themselves, and entitle them to homesteads."[76]

After visiting the farm, Critchlow estimated that one-fourth of the Indian homesteaders had failed to make any improvements to their properties, but that the others had made signficiant progress, planting two hundred acres of wheat and another two hundred acres of corn, mostly using their own ponies. The Indians told him that they could have done much more if they had been able to obtain additional plows and harnesses. Critchlow inspected the homestead houses and witnessed that some of them were equipped with cooking stoves and "other rude furniture" that he thought showed some degree of progress towards civilization. He noticed several "quite intelligent Indian men" in the group wearing "citizen dress," who exhibited "evidences of improvement warranting the conclusion that they can and will support themselves."[77]

Critchlow reaffirmed his position of the previous year that the Shoshone at the settlement had never belonged to a reservation and that they posed no danger to nearby communities. Breaking with the assessments of other government representatives, he noted that their condition under Mormon tutelage was "vastly better" than would have otherwise been the case and judged the church's efforts to have been "in good faith for the benefit of the Indians."[78]

Rather than recommending forced removal to a reservation, Critchlow suggested that if the Mormons would continue to instruct and care for the Shoshone, he could see "no reasonable objection to their doing so, and thus relieve the Gov't of their care and support." Writing that he was neither a "Jack-Mormon" nor "one of those 'gentiles' who believes that everything Mormons do must necessarily be evil," he recommended that the federal government leave the Indians where they were and provide them with agricultural implements, harnesses, and other supplies, and he concluded that some of the Indians were "worthy of it and even of homesteads and citizenship."[79]

The federal government must have placed considerable faith in Critchlow's assessments. From that point on, no significant efforts were ever again made by the government to remove Sagwitch and Sanpitch's people to Fort Hall or to any other reservation. The Mormons would finally be allowed, without interruption or supervision, to operate their ministry among the Northwestern Shoshone and to teach them farming and ranching skills. Most important, the Shoshone would be allowed to remain in their home territory and seek an alternative to a future of meager federal handouts on one of the reservations.

Although the United States was finally willing to look the other way and allow what remained of the Northwestern bands to live in northern Utah, many Shoshone chose to straddle both worlds by retaining a relationship with the Mormon Indian farm in Box Elder County while also establishing a residence at Fort Hall. Sagwitch was one of those who utilized what was offered both by the United States government and by the Mormons. While maintaining close ties with Lemuel's Garden, Sagwitch also set up a home for his immediate family in Idaho, apparently in the Bannock Creek area several miles southwest of Fort Hall proper but within reservation boundaries. It is not known when he first became known to agency officials, but he was included in a census taken on November 3, 1878. The document listed "Seg-witch" as head of "lodge 119," which consisted of one man, two women, and one boy. The census also listed other Shoshone families from northern Utah including Sagwitch's son Yeager, fellow chieftain Sanpitch, and Mormon Jim.[80]

No records have been found that document how long or how consistently Sagwitch lived at Bannock Creek as opposed to Lemuel's Garden. It is likely that he lived sporadically at both sites between 1878 and the early 1880s. Had he been living exclusively in Utah during that period, he likely would have applied for homestead land at Lemuel's Garden when so many other fellow Shoshone were doing so.[81]

Sagwitch probably remained through the summer of 1878 at
the farm on Bear River. Several conditions hampered the success of
the farm that year, including irrigation problems. In fact, in an otherwise optimistic autumn 1878 report to President Taylor, Isaac
Zundel could only report that the crops had been "tolerably good
this year."[82] The next year proved to be just as challenging for the
two hundred Indians attempting to make a living from the land.[83]
The growing season in 1879 was especially hot and dry, and the
wheat grew on very short stalks. Harvesting the crop manually with
scythes would have been very difficult. One person's misfortune,
however, became a boon to the farm. Moroni Ward recorded that a
man named Quincy Nolton, representing his father-in-law Captain
William Henry Hooper, had brought a large herd of cattle from the
west and turned them on the Malad River range near the Indian
farm. Two hours after their arrival, 145 of them died from foraging on
poisonous larkspur. Native Americans at the farm helped herd the
remaining animals to safety. Nolton gave the Indians the dead animals, which they immediately skinned, selling the hides to the
Brigham City Cooperative tannery. The Shoshone raised enough
money in this way to purchase a header for cutting grain.[84] It was
reportedly just the second header ever used in the Malad Valley.[85]

Isaac Zundel asked Moroni Ward to oversee the operation of
the header, which was drawn by the Indians' ponies and run by the
Shoshone themselves. He noted some difficulties encountered by the
Indians attempting to run the large machine. "The drivers were
Indians wearing blankets which required the left hand to hold them
in place, leaving one hand to drive with and keep their two long
braids of hair out of the machinery." Difficulties aside, the harvesting crew still managed to cut over six hundred acres that fall.[86]

The Indians began to realize that even with new equipment,
their lands, although fertile, would continue to be relatively unpro-
ductive due to the perennial shortage of usable water. Through their
missionary hosts, Sagwitch's band petitioned Mormon leaders for
lands in well-watered Cache Valley where they could begin farming
anew. President Taylor apparently refused their request but began to
consider other sites for the Lamanite farm.[87] By the spring of 1880,
church leaders invited the Indians to relocate on the Brigham City
Cooperative's farm four miles south of Portage in Box Elder County.

When they negotiated the purchase of this land, church leaders also acquired the cooperative's improvements, especially its interest in a partially constructed canal that, when completed, would take water from a source near the town of Samaria in Idaho Territory south to the area where the Indians hoped to settle.[88]

The choice of the new land delighted Isaac Zundel, who assessed it to be "a place where the Indians will become self sustaining in time." In a report to Taylor, Zundel stated that the Indians were "well satisfide with this place . . . and they feel to thank you Bro. Taylor and the Council, for your kindness extended towards them . . . They feel a new determination to go ahead."[89] Isaac Zundel's daughter Phoebe later reminisced about her family's experiences at the new Indian settlement: "The year they built the houses in Washakie, we baked 18 loaves of bread every day. The Indian women had to be taught, and they were slow. Sundays we did not know whether we were to get dinner for our family of six or eight, or for 18 or 20. We had lots of visitors."[90]

Sagwitch's people set to work on the uncompleted canal in May 1880 and by mid-July had finished it. Disappointingly, the porous soil in one section of the ditch would not hold water, making the entire project worthless. Zundel decided to line that portion of the eleven-mile ditch with wood fluming to the tune of thirty-five to forty thousand board feet of lumber.[91] With such problems solved, the new home for Sagwitch and his people eventually proved fruitful.

A milestone in the development of the Indian settlement came in 1880. In September of that year, Mormon leaders officially recognized both the numeric size and devotion of the Indian congregation by authorizing the formation of an ecclesiastical congregation called a ward at the farm, with Isaac Zundel as bishop and Alexander Hunsaker as his counselor. The new unit was named Washakie Ward in honor of the great Eastern Shoshone chief who still lived on the Wind River reservation in Wyoming.[92] Within the year, the Washakie Ward gave its name to the new settlement and Washakie, Utah, was born.

It was also in 1880 that Frank Timbimboo Warner, Sagwitch's son, was assigned at the church's April conference to preach Mormonism as a full-time elder to his own people at the Washakie farm. Sagwitch must have been pleased to see that the religion he embraced in 1873 was now to be promoted by one of his descendants.[93]

Although missionaries had officially moved the Indian settlement to the site near Portage, many Native Americans, especially
those who were proving up on homestead lands near the old site, continued to farm at Lemuel's Garden. A good number of Indians also
applied for lands in the vicinity of the new farm at Washakie.
Sagwitch and his sons Yeager and Soquitch all applied for homestead
land near Washakie between 1881 and 1883.[94] Sagwitch filed his
claim on 160 acres near Washakie on October 6, 1883. In compliance
with the requirements of the Indian homestead amendment, Sagwitch
signed a declaration that stated: "I Tsyguitch, an Indian of Box Elder
County, Territory of Utah . . . do solemnly swear that I am an Indian,
formerly of the Shoshonee tribe; that I was born in the United States;
that I have abandoned my relations with that tribe and adopted the
habits and pursuits of civilized life; and that I am the head of a family,
that I desire said land for the purpose of actual settlement and cultivation."[95] With George Washington Hill and Alexander Hunsaker as
witnesses, Sagwitch affixed his mark, a dark black X, to the affidavit
and paid sixteen dollars in cash.[96]

The Washakie farm began to prosper. Soon the settlement
boasted several houses, outbuildings, and corrals, as well as a blacksmith shop and a cooperative store and, after April 1884, a post
office.[97] The Shoshone had long petitioned their Mormon hosts for
better educational opportunities for their children. In the past, such
requests had been filled in a sporadic and piecemeal fashion, probably owing to the fact that the seasonal missionaries, when they came
at all, spent most of their time helping with farming and irrigation
work rather than teaching school. Once the settlement became
established at Washakie, however, that situation changed. President
Taylor authorized the services of carpenters from the Logan Temple,
who moved the farm's meetinghouse from its site near Lemuel's
Garden to Washakie.[98] The relocated structure became home to a
formal school.

At the April 1882 conference, general authorities of the
Mormon Church called James J. Chandler, a well-qualified instructor,
to teach at Washakie.[99] By June of that year, the school was running
and was reported to be very successful. A reporter for the *Ogden
Daily Herald* noted, "He [Chandler] reports an average attendance of
35 native youths of both sexes at the school. The pupils take great

Indian Homestead under Act March
3. 1875.
Affidavit.

I Tsygwitch, an Indian of Box Elder
County, Territory of Utah, having filed
my application No 6206 for an entry
under the provisions of the Act of Congress
of March 3, 1875, do solemnly swear
that I am an Indian, formerly of the
Shoshones tribe; that I was born in
the United States; that I have abandoned my relations with that tribe and
adopted the habits and pursuits of
civilized life, & that I am the head of
a family, that I desire said land for the
purpose of actual settlement and cultivation, and not, directly or indirectly,
for the use or benefit of any other
person or persons whomsoever; and that
I have not heretofore had the benefit
of said act.   Tsygwitch X his mark
Alexander Hunsaker
Sworn and Subscribed before me this
6th day of October 1883
                          H McMaster
                               Register

Sagwitch's homestead application affidavit, October 6, 1883.
All Native Americans filing for homestead property under the
March 3, 1875 Indian homestead amendment were required to
sign similar statements. Note Sagwitch's signature mark at the
bottom of the document. Copy of document courtesy National
Archives and Records Administration, Washington, D.C.

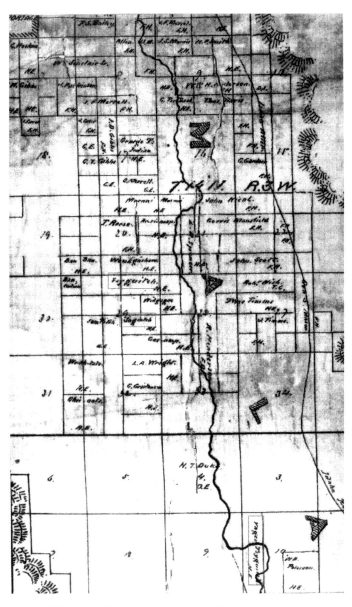

Detail from Box Elder County land map, 1884, showing lands homesteaded by several Native Americans, including "Tsyguitch" (Sagwitch), "Yager Tsyguitch" (Yeager), and Soquitch (these names are outlined by boxes not on the original map). Copy of map courtesy Gale Welling.

The United States of America

To all to whom these presents shall come, Greeting;

Homestead Certificate Nº. 4422.
Application 6206.

Whereas, There has been deposited in the General Land Office of the United States a Certificate of the Register of the Land Office at Salt Lake City, Utah Territory whereby it appears that pursuant to the Act of Congress approved 20th May, 1862, "To secure Homesteads to Actual Settlers on the Public Domain," and the acts supplemental thereto, the claim of Anna Tsyguitch widow of Tsyguitch deceased, has been established and duly consummated, in conformity to law, for the North West quarter of the North West quarter of Section twenty eight, and the North East quarter of the North West quarter and the North half of the North East quarter of Section twenty nine, in Township fourteen North of Range three West of Salt Lake Meridian in Utah Territory, containing one hundred and sixty acres according to the Official Plat of the Survey of the said Land returned to the General Land Office by the Surveyor General.

Now Know Ye, That there is, therefore, Granted by the United States unto the said Anna Tsyguitch the tract of Land above described: To Have and To Hold the said tract of Land, with the appurtenances thereof, unto the said Anna Tsyguitch, and to her heirs and assigns forever; subject to any vested and accrued rights for mining, agricultural manufacturing, or other purposes, and rights to ditches and reservoirs used in connection with such water rights

Homestead patent for Sagwitch's farm at Washakie, January 25, 1892. Because Sagwitch had died by the time the homestead application matured, the property was awarded to his widow Beawoachee, listed on the certificate as Anna Tsyguitch. Copy of document courtesy United States Bureau of Land Management, Salt Lake City, Utah.

as may be recognized and acknowledged by the local customs, laws and decisions of Courts, and also subject to the right of the proprietor of a vein or lode to extract and remove his ore therefrom, should the same be found to penetrate or intersect the premises hereby granted, as provided by law.

This Patent is issued upon the express condition that the title hereby conveyed shall not be subject to alienation or incumbrance either by voluntary conveyance or by judgment, decree or order of any Court, or subject to taxation of any character, but shall remain inalienable and not subject to taxation for the period of twenty years from the date hereof as provided by Act of Congress approved January 18.th 1881.

In testimony whereof, I, Benjamin Harrison, President of the United States of America have caused these letters to be made Patent and the Seal of the General Land Office to be hereunto affixed.

Given under my hand at the City of Washington the twenty fifth day of January in the year of our Lord one thousand eight hundred and ninety two, and of the Independence of the United States the one hundred and sixteenth.

L. S.

By the President. Benjamin Harrison.

By M. M.c Kean Secretary.

D. P. Roberts. Recorder of the General Land Office

Washakie Ward meetinghouse and schoolhouse, ca. 1920. Built at the Lemuel's Garden settlement in the late 1870s, this structure was moved in 1881 to Washakie. Photograph courtesy Mae T. Parry.

interest in their studies and are anxious to learn the English language. They are very assiduous in studying their lessons, and by the use of charts, blackboards, and objects, they are making satisfactory progress in their education. Their deportment is excellent."[100]

As educational opportunities improved at Washakie, other features of life at the farm became equally enviable. That the Indians owned much of the land they were farming meant that they enjoyed many more freedoms than did Native Americans at the Fort Hall and Wind River reservations. Although the Shoshone were settled in a permanent community at Washakie, Isaac Zundel and other farm leaders allowed them to participate in their traditional hunting and gathering circuit, as long as it did not interfere with essential functions at the farm, including the grain harvest. Because of this freedom, the Indians continued to travel to Bear Lake in early summer to fish and hunted rabbits and deer as needed. They also traveled west in late autumn to participate in the communal pine-nut harvest.[101]

Zundel also allowed the Shoshone to hold traditional socials and dances. Zundel's son David remembered such dances at

Lemuel's Garden lasting three or four days and two or three nights. After the Indians moved to Washakie, such dances eventually became uncommon. Zundel also allowed the Shoshone to use native medicines, including potions made of herbs and roots, and even grudgingly tolerated shaman-directed healing ceremonies, wherein the shaman would sing, and then "would vomit and stir up the vomit in the ashes."[102] Zundel encouraged the Indians to turn instead to the Mormon priesthood for blessings when sick and to utilize commercial medicines supplied periodically by Mormon general authority and medical doctor Seymour B. Young. Zundel also allowed the Indians to contract marriages in the traditional Shoshone way without formal ceremony.[103]

Meanwhile, fellow Indians living on neighboring government reservations faced conditions of near starvation, limited freedom, and intolerance of native customs. Many of those living under such conditions desired to join the Washakie farm. In late 1883, Isaac Zundel nervously wrote to John Taylor to report that "Washakie says he is determined to break the bands that the soldiers have around him and he has runners going to all the different tribes to get them to go to war with the goverment." He added, "Some have said that they are determined to join us and live as this people live. I have never as yet given them any encouragement to come and live with us."[104] Washakie did not go to war with the government, nor did the farm experience a large influx of newcomers, but Indians from the reservations continued to envy the better life enjoyed by their friends at the Washakie farm.

Not everything at the farm, however, was desirable. Housing for the Native Americans continued to be substandard. Though some Indians had small frame or log dwellings, many continued to live in grass and willow wickiups. Clothing, too, was in perpetually short supply. Modest crop yields, due to grasshopper infestations and water scarcity, kept new clothing and supplies out of reach. To make things worse, a devastating fire at the Washakie settlement on September 3, 1883, destroyed over three thousand bushels of wheat as well as haystacks, a corn crib, stables, and a corral.[105] Zundel reported the loss due to the fire and added, "If this had not happened we would of been able to of got the Indians some clothing for winter, but this will prevent us from doing so."[106]

Sicknesses took an enormously heavy toll on Native Americans at Washakie. The infant mortality rate due to illnesses was high, particularly in 1882. In that year, thirty-three children died—fifteen from measles, thirteen from whooping cough, and five from other illnesses. For a small settlement with a population of about 250 people, this was a wrenching loss representing more than 10 percent of the entire population and perhaps 30 percent of all the children. A correspondent for the *Utah Journal* commented on the heavy loss of life that year at Washakie and concluded that it had been due to the "lack of cleanliness during cold and changeable weather, insufficient clothing at summer time, irregular supplies of improper food, the wick-e-up mode of life and Indian habits generally."[107] It seems reasonable to assume that fatalities would have been far fewer if the Indians had enjoyed greater access to good housing, adequate food, and warm clothing.

The Mormon religion continued to be a major influence doctrinally and culturally among Sagwitch's people. Outsiders visiting a typical Shoshone Sunday worship service usually came away with the conclusion that the Indians were truly devoted to their adopted religion. One visitor remembered experiencing "their noisy meetings in which they 'sang' in the oldtime Indian way their chants without words."[108] Another visitor a few years later noted that "to hear the Lamanites sing in a strange tongue, to listen to the remarks of the speakers, and to gaze reflectively upon the swarthy visages of the descendants of Father Lehi formed an intellectual entertainment of no ordinary interest."[109]

It is significant that with the exception of the recitation of sacramental prayers, every aspect of the Indians' Mormon worship was conducted in their own language.[110] Sometimes their devotion and diligent obedience seemed to exceed that of the white missionaries called to lead them. In a report to Box Elder Stake leaders, Isaac Zundel related that the Indians had upbraided him after noting that his behavior was not consistent with the church's code of health, which forbade smoking. He confessed, "I went to preach to the Indians with the pipe in my mouth. They soon told me I was a pretty father to puff away at a pipe, so I have thrown it away."[111]

Native Americans living at the farm interpreted several occurrences of the next few years as additional evidence that their faith in their adopted religion had been well placed, resulting in even greater commitment to Mormonism. Isaac Zundel reported one such experience to President Taylor in 1880:

> We have had a great manifestation of the power of the Lord. About five months ago, three of our young thrifty women commenced laughing and making fun of those that prayed and said it was all foolishness to pray. Shortly after they were taken sick, or rather a noumbness came over them. They commenced to wither away; untill there was nothing left but skin and bone. Two of them we have just layen in the grave, and the other one is expected to die every day. They are all three sisters. At the graves I cautioned them not to make light of the things of God. After we returned to our homes, There wase two aged women, they began to talk and said the Lord had no hand in the matter. They ware also taken immediatly And yesterday morning They came with tears in their eyes wanted us to administer to them, which we did. one of them is on the improve, the other one is worse, and there is a quite a feeling among the Lamanites. And some of them is all most afraid to speak for fear they say something that will not be right.[112]

Another case involved the death and resuscitation of Mrs. Ammon Pubigee when she was a girl. Her husband told the story thus:

> She was miserable and one night she went to bed and she had a dream. Somebody talk and tell her 'You shall hear coyotes howling first thing in morning.' Got up early and heard coyotes howl before daylight and she worse that morning. Pretty weak. Coyotes howl mean she would pass away. She tell her parents. Next night she passed away— died. Never wake up in morning. Her mother ask her 'How you feel?' She doesn't any words so she come to her and feel her. No breath. Hands stiff. Cold. Her heart not beating so her know she is dead. Her mother feel very

sorry. She thought she lost her boy and her daughter, too.
All die. About 3 or 4 o'clock she began to breathe. Her
body became warm and she get up out of her bed and she
told her mother: 'My spirit go back to presence of my
Father.' When her spirit in Spirit World where God is, He
had a beautiful home. Everything is quiet and happy. She
saw God and His Son Jesus Christ, and they sent her
back. 'You are not sick, you better go down in your body.'
So she goes down in her body and wake up again. Then
she was instructed how to live on earth. After while she
be all right. After that she have dream and vision.[113]

The telling of this story had a profound influence on the other
Indians at the farm. They would gather in a circle with the woman in
the center and ask her to retell the story over and over. They also
made her a beaded dress and a saddle and would lead her around
the camp on a horse. The practice continued until Isaac Zundel
finally put an end to it because, according to his daughter, he felt
that they had gone too far and "were worshipping her instead of the
one they should."[114]

A more telling example of the Shoshone commitment to the
new religion was their donation, under the direction of Sagwitch, of
thousands of hours of labor toward construction of a Mormon holy
building, the Logan Temple. Records from the Box Elder Stake show
that the Shoshone on the Malad donated more to the project than the
residents of the nearby communities of Honeyville, Deweyville,
Plymouth, Malad, or Snowville and almost as much as the people of
Calls Fort, Portage, and Bear River City.[115] By late 1883, the Indians
had donated a total of $8,000 in labor to the project, based on a
working wage ranging from $1.25 to $2 per day.[116] This was a significant contribution by any standard, but was especially so for the
Indians who had little time to spare because their homestead lands
demanded nearly all of their time just to coax a modest crop from the
dry soil.

Native Americans from the Malad farm began helping at the
Logan Temple site in 1878, when two men from the camp went to
work on the building.[117] In 1879, sixteen Indians from the farm
worked at least part of the summer on the temple.[118] It was not long

Logan Temple under construction, 1879. Sagwitch and his people donated
substantial service hours in quarrying, hauling stone, and mixing mortar for
the temple's construction. Charles R. Savage, photographer. Photograph courtesy of Oneita Hyde Waite. Copy courtesy Nelson Wadsworth.

before work routines became well established. The Indians usually
left their farm in parties of six workers, took an ox team to
Collinston, and there caught a train to Logan, worked for two weeks,
and then returned home.[119]

The Indians did a variety of jobs at the temple construction
site, including mixing mortar and plaster, helping at the Franklin
quarry, and hauling stone to the masons.[120] Sagwitch made his support very visible by personally taking his turn, despite his advanced
age, in the construction labor. His sons Soquitch and Yeager also
made great contributions to the work. Yeager remembered "with
pleasure" his work on the temple and also recalled friendly wrestling
bouts with the "white" boys after the work day was completed. It was
noted that "the Indians could usually beat the white boys at this
sport."[121]

As a work party returned home after its two-week stint, a
majority of the Native Americans at the farm anxiously gathered at

Logan Temple nearing completion, early spring 1884. Even after exterior masonry work had been completed, some Native Americans from Washakie continued to help with construction by mixing plaster for the structure's interior. Photograph from the author's collection.

the meetinghouse "to shake hands with the 'missionaries' and hear the latest news from Logan."[122] Temple building quickly became a primary expression of their religious devotion, and the construction laborers worked with enthusiasm. Shoshone work parties labored on the temple through 1882, when exterior work on the building was completed, and then continued with the more limited task of mixing plaster for the structure's interior. The temple was subsequently dedicated in May 1884.[123]

On March 10, 1885, Sagwitch entered the Logan Temple, and over the next four days, he participated as a representative or proxy in sacred Mormon ordinances on behalf of deceased relatives. On March 10, he was baptized on behalf of his father, Pin-in-netse, his brothers Sewahhoochew (Síhípihuiccuu) and Anga-poon-moot-say, and an uncle, Quash-i-wat-titsi-say. In the following few days, he also participated in the Mormon temple ordinance called the endowment on their behalf. It seemed fitting that Sagwitch had the opportunity to honor his deceased father and other family members in a structure he had personally helped to build.[124]

After Sagwitch finished with the ordinances, he returned to his homestead at Washakie in time for spring planting. Prospects looked good for the farm in 1885. Isaac Zundel reported to John Taylor in March that the farm was in a "prosperous condition," and John Hess reported the following month that the Shoshone were "verry buisey puting in grain and repareing watter ditches" and that a "general good feeling" prevailed among the Indians.[125] In the June report to President Taylor, Zundel and Moroni Ward optimistically noted "The interests of the Mission were never in a more prosperous condition than at present. There is a good prospect for a bountiful harvest. The Indians are well united and a good feeling is existing among them in general."[126] The situation for Sagwitch, however, was about to turn sour.

On Friday, July 24, Isaac Zundel traveled from Washakie to Lemuel's Garden to do some maintenance work on the header the Indians were using to cut their wheat. After working with Sagwitch and other Shoshone men Friday and Saturday, Zundel announced that he would hold a church meeting with them the next morning. When time came for the religious service, he noticed that Sagwitch had saddled his horse. Zundel walked over to where Sagwitch and

his son Yeager were standing to see what was happening and
engaged Sagwitch in conversation. As Zundel reported:

> I asked him where he was a going[.] he told me he was a
> going to Bear River City[.] I asked him why he did not
> stop and attend to our meeting to which he flew in a pas-
> sion and called me all sorts of names[,] said I was the
> Devil and that I talked like the devil[.] while I was listen-
> ing to his remarks his son stepped up and slapped me in
> the face and then drew his knife on me[.] I first thought to
> knock him down . . . I then pushed him to one side and
> walked two or three steps from him[.] he then sprang and
> grabed his bow and arrowes[.] I had made up my mind if
> he went any further I would be forced to kill him[.] This is
> something I have always dreaded to do but in the case of
> self defence I supposed I would be justifyed.[127]

The standoff somehow ended without injury to Sagwitch,
Yeager, or Zundel, but it left Zundel shaken. He immediately
hitched his team and drove back to Washakie where he called the
"leading Indians" together to report the episode. They were also disturbed, and Zundel reported that news of the altercation "caste a
deep gloom over the Indian Village." Zundel explained to Taylor that
he was especially surprised because he had "never had any words
with either of these men and I supposed we were on the best of
terms."[128] The situation was so unusual that Zundel asked President
Taylor for advice in handling the "emergency."[129]

Even Sagwitch's descendants do not know what prompted
Sagwitch and Yeager to react so forcefully that day, though family
stories suggest that they were venting anger over perceived impro-
prieties in the way the farm was being run by Zundel.[130] Family
accounts also say that Bishop Zundel had grown resentful of what he
viewed as Sagwitch's undue and improper influence over the
Shoshone and that the situation came to a head when Zundel
accused Sagwitch of breaking the Sabbath. According to family lore,
Sagwitch had replied that white people worshipped God one day a
week, while the Indian worshipped Him seven days a week. The
heated argument then followed.[131]

In an August 1885 letter to President Taylor, Zundel reported that the Indians involved in the altercation had left the settlement and that no other Indian "sanctions the actions of those Indian[s]." John Hess, writing to Taylor in late September, noted "The sircomstance that we wrot you about of the Indian drawing a knife and thretening Br Zundel the feeling manifest at that time only Existed with the purpitreter and one other[.] they boath left soon after and have not Returned."[132]

Family accounts say that after the altercation with Zundel, Sagwitch left Washakie and took his family and a few other families to Bannock Creek in Idaho. This seems reasonable considering Sagwitch's earlier residency there between 1879 and the early 1880s. By 1885, Bannock Creek was home to around two hundred Shoshone. Using farming skills learned at Lemuel's Garden, Sagwitch planted several crops at Bannock Creek. Among his plantings were reportedly the first potatoes grown in that area. It was said that other Indians in the region would come to investigate the "strange crop" that he was growing.[133]

The family traditions record that representatives from the Washakie farm including a Shoshone named Brown came to Bannock Creek to sue for peace. Sagwitch was reportedly told that "Bishop Zundel and the rest of the LDS officials from Salt Lake City wanted him back in Washakie, that it didn't look good that their chief had moved away and there was a lot of talk about the fight, and they told him to come back to Washakie."[134] It was probably in late November 1885 that Sagwitch finally returned to the farm at Washakie, where he again began to cultivate and improve the 160-acre parcel he had filed a homestead claim on two years earlier. John W. Hess noted Sagwitch's return in a December 7 letter to John Taylor: "The Indian that had the row last Sumer with Brother Zundel has Returned to the mishion and we hear that he is verry sorry for what he has dun and intends to make every thing Right."[135] With Sagwitch again settled at the Indian farm, the work of the mission could continue unhampered by the unsettled conditions his absence had caused.

Toward the end of 1885, President Taylor wrote to John Hess suggesting that Indians from the Washakie farm be sent on unofficial missions to live among and preach the gospel to their "Lamonite

Bretherin" on nearby government reservations. Hess responded with enthusiasm to the plan and suggested that several of the men living at Washakie would be good candidates for such a program since many "are learnin verry fast in temperal things as well as the princepals of the gospel and cood soon be yaused in that way if needed."[136] Such a plan was the only way to preach Mormonism on the restricted government reserves. It is not known if Taylor's idea was put into effect, but his plan served to show that the LDS Church president placed a high level of confidence in the Mormon Indians at Washakie. It was also clear that church leaders felt good about the progress the mission had made in its spiritual goals for Native Americans.

By the mid-1880s, the Indian farm was also beginning to enjoy economic success. That success was at least partially attributable to diversification into livestock production on the farm. A visitor to the farm in 1885 noticed that the Indians "do not care to raise much more of the cereals than they require for their own consumption." At the same time, he noted that the farm owned a good number of sheep and was paid to take care of another two thousand sheep. Horses, which had traditionally been an important part of the Shoshone culture and economy, continued to be valued at Washakie. The Indians purchased French and Morgan stallions and pursued an agressive breeding program to upgrade the quality of their Indian ponies.[137]

Missionary John W. Hess had noticed as he worked with the Shoshone over the years that they seemed better adapted to animal husbandry than to farming. He proposed to President Taylor in January 1886 that their church lend the Washakie farm twenty-five to thirty cows and one thousand sheep to join the three hundred sheep already owned by the mission. With proper care and breeding, Hess reasoned, the herds would grow rapidly. After a few years time, the loaned stock could be returned to the church, while the increase would remain the property of the mission. President Taylor approved the plan, and the farm almost overnight became one of the larger ranches in northern Utah.[138]

Farming did not cease to be important though. Isaac Zundel reported to John Taylor in April 1886 that two hundred acres of grain had already been planted that spring and that the farm was running ten plows, three harrows, and two drills. Other Shoshone work parties were operating five horse-drawn scrapers to prepare the irrigation ditches for another season of use. Zundel noted that the Indians were taking hold of their work that spring "better than ever, and a good feeling prevails among them."[139]

Considering the reports being brought back to the farm by Shoshone visiting the government reservations in early 1886, Zundel must have been relieved to note a general feeling of solidarity and peace at the farm. The agent at Fort Hall purportedly had tried to turn the Shoshone against the LDS Church by telling the leading men of the tribe "that the Mormons will soon all be used up," and that "Mormonism will soon fall." The rumors had been the cause of several large meetings at Fort Hall wherein some spoke against Mormonism and others ardently defended it.[140]

The situation at Fort Hall ultimately had no real effect on the Washakie settlement, but other, internal disputes were less easily dismissed. In May 1886, Zundel wrote John Taylor for guidance in handling a problem the farm had never before experienced. A few of the Indians had requested that the church assign them tracts of land that they could own and run independently of the mission.[141] These were presumably Indians who had not applied for homestead lands and thus had always worked communally on the Mormon Church's property. Zundel gathered the community together and spoke with them "upon the subject of unity, & the great benefits derived there-from." Many of the gathered Shoshone were surprised that President Taylor had not given permission to divide the farm. After much discussion, Zundel was able to disperse the "dark cloud" and regain support for the farm as a cooperative.[142]

With that threat to the economic solidarity of the community answered, farming, ranching, and house building work could continue. John Hess wrote to Taylor in early September 1886 that the farm had gathered enough materials to build ten houses for the Indians that fall "if the Devel or some one else Dont inter fear."[143] It was important for the community to get several houses built before winter, not only to satisfy the immediate housing needs of several Indian families but also to solidify Shoshone claims to homestead lands. A January 1886 deadline for making final proof on five homestead properties had already been missed. Isaac Zundel wrote to George Washington Hill for help in trying to save those claims.[144]

Houses at Washakie, Box Elder, Utah, ca. 1920. The log structure at far left,
reportedly the first built at the new settlement, was the home of Soquitch
and Towange Timbimboo. The other homes in the picture were owned by
Grouse Creek Jack, Mammie Wongan, and the Parry family. Photograph
courtesy Mae T. Parry.

As Hill investigated the status of the homestead properties at
Lemuel's Garden, he became greatly concerned. He learned that a
government agent had just completed an investigation of land claims
in the area in late September and had found four Indian entries that
he concluded were fraudulent because required improvements were
not visible as promised. As Hill investigated, he found that while
acreages had been plowed and crops planted several years earlier,
those plots by and large had been allowed to go back to weeds, and
the small houses erected on the properties had not been maintained.
One had fallen over in a bad storm; the others had been "hauled
away makeing pig pens[,] corralls and so on." Hill held back from
blaming Zundel and attributed the failure to follow through on the
property improvements to the move to Washakie, which had "taken
the Indians away from those Entries." Still, the failure to maintain
those properties had placed them in jeopardy, and action needed to
be taken if any of them were to be saved.[145]
  Hill felt that the homestead entries for Pah nea Tunips and Per
Dash were not defendable, but that properties on which Jim Brown,

Sho Sho Nitz, and Wig E Gitch had filed could be saved "by the Brethren going to work and building houses on their original entries."[146] Consequently, on October 14, 1886, John Hess asked President Taylor to call seven carpenters from Brigham City and Bear River City on a mission to build houses for the Indians.[147] The men were called and immediately reported to the farm. By November 8, Isaac Zundel could report that all seven men were busy at work, three Shoshone houses had been completed, and another ten were anticipated.[148]

By the beginning of December, when weather conditions made further construction impossible, the carpenters had built six houses and were ready to build more as weather permitted. The completed houses were sixteen feet square, with plastered ceilings, shingle roofs, two doors, and two windows, "making a very warm, snug, and healthy little house." The leaders at Washakie regretted that they could not build "expensive" houses for the Indians but felt that smaller homes would do for at least awhile because most of the Indian families were small and the Indian women inexperienced at taking care of a house.[149]

The missionaries at Washakie soon discovered that moving the Shoshone out of native housing and into Anglo-inspired structures necessitated the acquisition of a good number of additional household items. They reported to Taylor: "We find that one convenience calls for another. while the indians live in their lodges with their fire in the centre, they can readily do their cooking, with very few cooking utensils. But on leaving the lodge and getting into a house, we find many things are wanted, such as, beadsteads, chairs, tables, etc, besides a stove, which seemes almost indispensible."[150]

The shortage of housing and household goods would take some time to resolve. Zundel and the other missionaries were also anxious to equalize the work load at the settlement by increasing the productivity of allegedly lazy Indians. Zundel and the others documented their frustrations in a letter to John Taylor: "Some of the Indians are as industrious as could be expected, while others are lazy and indifferent, and dont care whether they work or not, for they all eat out of the same crib. We have not been able to manage this differently, as they are so hospitable to one another, that were we to withold supplies from certain ones, they would become offended."[151] The missionaries proposed a system that would reward individuals according to merit. With Taylor's approval, they drafted articles of association for the Washakie Cooperative Association. It dictated a system of joint corporate ownership and payment of dividends according to individual contribution. Zundel was sure that it would mean "onward progress" for the mission and that the Indians "would take hold with a zeal."[152]

As plans for a Mormon economic cooperative at Washakie took shape at the beginning of 1887, so also did an impressive number of new Shoshone houses. By the end of February, twenty-two structures had been built, including nine on Shoshone homestead properties and thirteen more at the Washakie townsite.[153] Washakie, Utah, was becoming a small city. Numerous improvements were also made at Sagwitch's homestead property. Whether he and his family accomplished most of the work on their own or received assistance from mission carpenters is not documented. It is known, however, that by October 1890, when his widow received title to the property, Sagwitch's homestead included a log house measuring sixteen by eighteen feet, which had a floor and shingle roof, and a stable, stack and stock yards, cellar for storage of foodstuffs, chicken coop, pig pen, and 160 rods of fencing. The property and improvements were valued in 1890 at $1,000.[154] After many years of setbacks, disappointments, and backbreaking labor, Sagwitch was well on his way to proving to the government that the cozy and productive farm he had homesteaded could legally be awarded to him, but he did not live long enough to receive a proper patent to his property.

A headstone marking Sagwitch's grave in the Washakie cemetery informs those who visit the peaceful site that he died March 20, 1884. In view of recently discovered documents, it now seems likely that he lived until 1887, making this marker, placed at Sagwitch's grave in 1963 by the Sons of Utah Pioneers Ogden Pioneer Luncheon Club Chapter, innacurate. We may never know with certainty when Sagwitch died. Washakie Ward records that probably contained such information reportedly burned in a September 1887 fire that consumed the Washakie Cooperative store and all of the mission's records. A second fire on July 5, 1891, almost certainly destroyed what records might have survived the first conflagration.[155] References to Sagwitch's passing are absent from surviving Logan, Ogden, and Salt Lake City newspapers. It is truly sad, but not so surprising, that the death of a

Descendants of Sagwitch gathered for dedication of the monument marking his gravesite west of Washakie, Utah, May 25, 1963. The marker was donated by the Sons of Utah Pioneers, Ogden Pioneer Luncheon Club Chapter. Photograph courtesy Mae T. Parry.

man of such obvious note and historical importance could be missed entirely by the larger Anglo culture that had displaced Sagwitch and his people and occupied their lands.

It is clear that Sagwitch was alive in March 1885 because Logan Temple records document his presence in Logan at that time.[156] It also appears that Sagwitch was living in November 1886 because Isaac Zundel noted, in a November 30, 1886, letter to John Taylor concerning Sagwitch's son Frank Warner, that Frank's *"father,* brother, & relations *are here"* at Washakie (italics added).[157] On February 22, 1887, Sagwitch's son Frank wrote to the Commissioner of Indian Affairs to request a land allotment at Bannock Creek under the 1887 Dawes Act, where, as he wrote, "His father had a home." This could imply that Sagwitch was still alive in February 1887.[158] Sagwitch's grandson Moroni Timbimboo, born August 1, 1888, was told by his father Yeager that his grandfather Sagwitch died roughly two years before he was born. That would suggest a death date possibly sometime in the fall of 1886 or early in 1887.[159]

Moroni Timbimboo was consulted before the 1963 headstone was placed at Washakie and probably provided much of the information for the marker, including Sagwitch's date of death. It is possible that he provided the specific day, March 20, correctly but innacurately provided 1884 rather than 1887 as the year of death. Although we may never know that, we do know something of the circumstances surrounding Sagwitch's passing.

The Washakie settlement's white administrators in the 1880s—Isaac Zundel, his brother Abraham Zundel, and missionary Moroni Ward—were all polygamists during the time that they lived at the Indian farm. All three men had become increasingly concerned about their safety as the federal government stepped up both the passage of new anti-polygamy legislation and the enforcement of existing laws. Arrest, prosecution, and imprisonment were very real threats to all Mormon polygamists by the mid-1880s. In April 1885, Zundel had addressed the issue in a letter to President Taylor: "In consideration of circumstances connected with my family affairs I have deemed it wisdom to consult you for advice as to the best policy for me to pursue in order to secure myself and family as much as possible from becoming subject to persecution. In my present position I am very much exposed, and while I do not feel in the least degree to flinch or leave my post I desire to be cautious in all my movements."[160]

By 1886 federal marshals were even more determined in their efforts to track down and arrest polygamists. Zundel wrote to John Taylor on November 8, 1886, that he and the other brethren at the mission "expect to take for the mountains in the morning as we have received word that an attack is designed against this place." Zundel hoped that they could "remain in the hills near by with safety."[161] To help protect Zundel and the others from arrest, Sagwitch, with his wife and about nine other Shoshone, moved with him to Rough Canyon in the mountains west of Washakie. Moroni Timbimboo told how his grandfather Sagwitch and the others helped Zundel:

> This bishop was a polygamist at that time. He stayed with
> them Indian camp up there, tried to hide himself from the

officers. My father always tell a story about that. He said
the bishop, Issac Zundel, had a blanket. They give him a
blanket, I guess, so them officers looking for polygamy
wouldn't know him. He would come out with a blanket all
wrapped up and—I guess he paint up too—and just act
like he was an Indian and hid around there in that camp
with them. Then after this was going on, they finally catch
up with Bishop Zundel.[162]

With help from Sagwitch and later others, Bishop Zundel avoided
arrest and prosecution for polygamy until 1889.[163]

Living at Rough Canyon was difficult at best. The camp did not
offer even the modest amenities the Native Americans enjoyed at the
Washakie settlement. Sagwitch's wife Beawoachee reportedly "said
she had had enough" and moved back to the Indian farm.[164]
Following her departure, Sagwitch contracted a cold that quickly
turned into pneumonia. As the old chief suffered with the illness and
became increasingly weaker, a relative, Hitope Joshua, who was also
living in Rough Canyon, took her two-week-old baby and rushed to
Washakie to tell Sagwitch's sons about their father's condition.
Yeager and Soquitch soon arrived at their father's bed and could tell
that he needed more care than could be given there. A stretcher was
hurriedly constructed, and four men began carrying their beloved
father and leader towards the settlement. His condition worsened as
they traveled, and the men finally stopped and gently laid him on the
ground. Sagwitch died a short time later. He was buried at the exact
place where he died. Significantly, in the years that followed, over
two hundred of his people chose to be buried near him.[165]

The Shoshone Nation lost a great leader and spokesman that
day. His courage and hunting prowess early in life had been an
important factor in saving his people from starvation and enemy
threats. His leadership was critical in fighting federal troops at the
bloody Bear River Massacre and in regrouping what remained of the
Northwestern Shoshone afterward. Sagwitch's ability to correctly
assess and then respond to a changing world helped him and his people during the tremendously difficult period that followed the arrival
of the Mormons in 1847. His oratorical talents allowed him to effectively lead his people and to successfully negotiate with outsiders. By

embracing Mormonism in 1873 and leading his people into that faith, Sagwitch was instrumental in giving them a new set of beliefs concerning God and life. By exhibiting stalwart dedication to his new religion, Sagwitch inspired many of his followers to do the same. As a result, his people came to live a very different life than that of Native Americans confined to the government reservations.

Some of the most sweeping events in the history of the American West occurred during Sagwitch's lifetime. Taken together, they effectively changed the beliefs, customs, and lifeways of the Shoshone. As a leader among his people for nearly forty years, Sagwitch saw those forces at work. He proved to be an exceptional guide through those times.

Epilogue

Sagwitch's Legacy

Here is a town laid out with school houses and church, homes, farms and every convenience found in settlements no older than Washakie. Many neat homes are found here. Grains of all kinds and lucern is abundant. The farms, lots, and corrals are fenced; every kind of modern farm machinery is in use, and from a wandering, useless being, the noble Red Man has become an independent farmer, and some of them are getting rich.
　　　Correspondent, Deseret Evening News, May 26, 1898

I don't believe in chiefs too much myself. I didn't claim to be a chief on account that we believe in Mormonism and I believe it is more than a chief to believe in Mormonism.
　　　Bishop Moroni Timbimboo, December 9, 1970

W hen Sagwitch died, he left a legacy of leadership that spanned four decades. There were many among his people who had never known a time when Sagwitch had not been one of their leaders, and it must have been very difficult for many to adjust to the fact that a virtual institution among them was dead.

Although Sagwitch remained a central figure among his people until his death, Washakie farm administrators by the mid-1880s had begun to coordinate farm business through other men. Isaac Zundel told a newspaper reporter in late 1884 that "Shosnoitz" and "John Momemberry" were the "leading men" at the farm.[1] Due to several factors, these new leaders probably played a more limited governing role than Sagwitch had. The process of acculturation into mainstream

Encampment of Northwestern Shoshone from Washakie, Utah, on the Logan Tabernacle grounds for the city of Logan's semicentennial celebration, May 6, 1909. Photograph courtesy Utah State University Special Collections and University Archives, Merrill Library, Utah State University, Logan, Utah.

American society and away from a tribal society was one factor. The Indians' devotion to Mormonism, which left little room for a separate authority structure among its adherents, must have also been a significant issue. When Sagwitch's grandson, Moroni Timbimboo, was asked in a 1970 interview if he had served his tribe as a chieftain, he replied "No, I don't believe in chiefs too much myself. I didn't claim to be a chief on account that we believe in Mormonism and I believe it is more than a chief to believe in Mormonism."[2] In some ways, it could be argued that Sagwitch was the last chieftain of his people, at least as the Shoshone had traditionally utilized and responded to that role.[3]

The devotion to Mormonism that Sagwitch fostered among his people continued after his death. Arguably, it would have been difficult for those living at a church-sponsored farm to be contrary to the faith. Still, the devotion of the Indians at Washakie seems to have been exceptional, judging from the writings of churchmen and reporters who over the years visited their spirited but reverent worship services.[4] Shoshone parents manifested that kind of zeal in naming their newborn children after Book of Mormon figures or church leaders. Names such as Moroni Timbimboo, Ammon Pubigee, Nephi Perdash, and Joseph Smith Tosahpanguitch became common.[5] Adults, too, sometimes forsook their own Indian names in favor of scriptural replacements.

Mormon leaders created a Shoshone-friendly ecclesiastical organization that remained distinctly Indian by allowing most elements of the worship services to be held in the Shoshone language. Leaders also staffed auxiliary organizations—including the Relief Society, Sunday School, and Young Men's Mutual Improvement Association—with Shoshone members. In the twentieth century, Native Americans provided all of the staff for these organizations. Even the bishopric soon included Indian counselors and finally, in 1939, a Shoshone bishop.[6]

The Shoshone at Washakie culturally incorporated Mormonism, and it affected nearly every aspect of their lives. Through the years, Saints from Washakie manifested their devotion through a high level of church attendance, temple worship, and the generous payment of tithes and offerings. In fact, the Washakie Ward was one of very few units to register 100 percent compliance in a 1922 churchwide drive titled "Every member a tithepayer."[7] LDS Church leaders rewarded the devoted congregation in 1939 with the construction of a new brick meetinghouse paid for jointly by the congregation and church headquarters. Apostle George Albert Smith dedicated the structure.[8] The Washakie community also participated as actors in the production of a 1950 church film about the Book of Mormon titled *The Stick of Joseph*.[9]

Sagwitch's descendants manifested strong commitments to their Mormon faith. Frank Timbimboo Warner, Sagwitch's youngest son, became one of the first full-blooded Native Americans to be sent out as a proselytizing missionary for the faith. He served a total of

Elder Frank Warner, formerly Beshup Timbimboo, at far right, with Sioux and Assiniboin converts to Mormonism during Christmas celebration, December 25, 1914, at Fort Peck Reservation, Wolf Point, Montana. This was during the second of three missions that Warner served for the Mormon Church. Photograph published in *Liahona: The Elders Journal* 12 (30 March 1915): 641.

Washakie Ward bishopric and others at Washakie meetinghouse, ca. 1925. Left to right, Hyrum Wongosoff (Sagwitch's stepson), John Pabowena, Moroni Timbimboo, Yeager Timbimboo, Bishop George M. Ward, unidentified woman, and Katch Toyadook. Yeager Timbimboo served as first counselor to Ward for many years; Katch Toyadook was second counselor. Photograph courtesy Mae T. Parry.

Washakie Ward Relief Society, 1918. Standing, left to right: Cohn Zundel, Lewis Jones Neaman, Positze Norigan, Sadie Peyope, Towenge Timbimboo, Yampitch Timbimboo, Mary Ann Ward, Helen Young (school teacher at left center), Amy Timbimboo, unknown, Ivy Hootchew Bird, Annie Hootchew, unknown, Minnie Woonsook, Hitope Joshua, Hazel Timbimboo (child), Joan Timbimboo (child), Minnie Zundel, Evans Peyope (child). Seated, left to right: Poe ne Nitz, Boe be nup, Jane Pabowena, Mary Woonsook, Anzie Wagon with Eddie Wagon on her back in a cradleboard. Photograph courtesy Mae T. Parry.

three missions, one of them to his own people at Washakie, the other two to the Sioux and Assiniboin Indians in the Wolf Point and Fort Peck, Montana, areas, before he died in 1919 of influenza.[10] Soquitch, Sagwitch's oldest son, served the Washakie Saints for many years as an ordained elder in Mormonism's Melchizedek priesthood who had a calling to visit the homes of the Shoshone and give priesthood healing blessings to the sick. His wife, Towange Timbimboo, served as a counselor in the Washakie Ward Relief Society, the Mormon women's organization, for many years.[11]

Yeager Timbimboo, another son of Sagwitch, proved to be an exemplary churchman. In 1891 he began working as president of the Washakie Ward Young Men's Mutual Improvement Association. In 1907 LDS Church leaders ordained him a high priest, and he

Shoshone from Washakie and others gathered for filming of a Book of
Mormon motion picture, *The Stick of Joseph*. Harold S. Rumel, photographer,
ca. 1950. Photograph courtesy LDS Church Archives, Salt Lake City, Utah.

began serving as a counselor to Bishop Alexander Hunsaker.[12] In
1926, church president Heber J. Grant invited Yeager to speak at
the faith's general conference held in the tabernacle on Temple
Square in Salt Lake City. With Bishop George M. Ward standing at
his side as translator, Yeager delivered what reporters at the time
called a "profound" address. Even the non-Mormon *Salt Lake
Tribune* ran a lengthy article about Yeager's talk, commenting that
the thoughts expressed by the Indian "were listened to in most profound silence" and noting that "it is probable that if a zephr had
come into the great building during the speech it would not have
been heard."[13] Yeager told the congregation that since his baptism,
he had felt: "to live a righteous life and I advise this people now to
do likewise. I feel that the earth is the Lord's and that the fullness
thereof is His and that we are His children. I feel that everything we

have—brains and all—comes as a blessing from the Lord, for which we should be thankful."[14] Noted Mormon photographer George Edward Anderson gathered Yeager and his family together afterwards for a photograph, which the *Deseret News* then published.[15]

Yeager's son Moroni Timbimboo followed his father's example of church leadership and served in many capacities in the Washakie Ward, including several years as a bishop's counselor. In 1939, Apostle George Albert Smith ordained him a Mormon bishop of the Washakie Ward; he was officially the first Native American to hold that ecclesiastical position. He chose fellow Shoshone Nephi Perdash and Jim John Neaman as his counselors, thus organizing the first all-Indian bishopric in the church.[16]

Besides holding specific ecclesiastical appointments, many of Sagwitch's descendants have served their church as proselytizing missionaries. In 1935, Mormon leaders called Moroni Timbimboo, then serving as first counselor in the bishopric, to serve a short-term mission to the Indians at the Fort Peck Reservation at Wolf Point, Montana.[17] Other descendants, including Brian Parry, Darren B. Parry, and Jeffery B. Parry, have proselytized in various parts of the United States and in England, while one grandson, Jon Warner, served in the Northern Indian Mission among the Sioux Indians on the Standing Rock Reservation at Fort Yeates, North Dakota, and Rosebud, South Dakota, and also among the Cheyenne and Crow Indians in Montana.[18] In 1990, Jon Trent Warner, a direct descendant of Sagwitch, became one of the first Mormon missionaries to proselytize in Bulgaria, at that time still governed by a Communist regime.[19] The religion Sagwitch embraced in 1873 thus continues to be embraced and sponsored by many of his descendants.

The Washakie settlement, which was still new and raw at the time Sagwitch died, soon became well established and, for the most part, prosperous. Many of the Indians owned homestead parcels, while others benefited from the use of lands that had been purchased by the LDS Church. In the early years of settlement, specific ownership of the land was not an important issue to the Indians. They felt comfortable holding their resources in common. Mormons, who had tried and failed to establish a United Order, a communal economic society, in the 1860s and 1870s, could only laud the virtues of their Indian brethren. In describing the Washakie cooperative, Bishop Zundel

Moroni and Amy Timbimboo family with grandfather Yeager, 1934.
Photograph courtesy Mae T. Parry.

Elder Jon Trent Warner, Sofia, Bulgaria, 1991. Warner, a direct descendant
of Sagwitch, served from November 1990 to February 1992 as one of the
Mormon Church's first missionaries in Bulgaria. Copy of photographic slide
courtesy Christian Mark Elggren.

Bishop Moroni Timbimboo (1888–1975) and Hitope Joshua (ca. 1844–
ca. 1940) at newly built Washakie Ward LDS meetinghouse, ca. 1940.
Timbimboo was the first Native American bishop in the Mormon church.
In 1887, Hitope Joshua ran with her newborn baby in arms from Rough
Canyon to Washakie, Utah to get help for Sagwitch, who lay dying of
pneumonia. Photograph courtesy Mae T. Parry.

said, "There have been some good dividends, and what is more important, the settlers are not robbed and swindled by traders. All profits
beyond the legitimate expenses of the concern, is applied to the benefit of the colony at large—repairing, where such is necessary, etc., with
which none seem dissatisfied, where all work in unison."[20]

Unfortunately, a series of disasters kept the cooperative from
becoming as successful as it otherwise could have been. Cricket
invasions continued to curtail the Indians' crops, greatly limiting the
availability of saleable surpluses. Fires also took a heavy toll,
including blazes in 1887 and 1891 that destroyed the cooperative's
store and an 1889 fire that reduced to complete ruin the profitable
sawmill the Indians had built and operated in southern Idaho.[21]

While Western societies considered the accumulation of
wealth to be an important value, it was not a driving force to Indians
whose culture dictated that people use, eat, and stockpile only that
which they need. The communal spirit that the Mormons so envied
in the Indians also served to foil church leaders' attempts to encourage industry by rewarding the hardest workers and limiting the distribution of goods to those who did not perform. The Native
Americans simply shared their goods with all members of the settlement, regardless of their individual contributions.[22] In at least two
periods of the farm's history, church leaders went so far as to introduce a wage system at Washakie, which marginally increased productivity but spawned a number of problems, including serious
charges that farm administrators withheld wages or shortchanged
payments.[23] Philosophically, the two cultures who shared Washakie's
soil defined wealth and success differently.

Both cultures could agree upon the importance of agriculture
and animal husbandry. The Indians made good use of the Samaria
Canal that they had completed in 1880. It delivered useable water to
the settlement, allowing for the irrigation of garden spaces as well as
some two hundred acres of cropland. The Indians raised potatoes
and other vegetables as well as the lucerne and grains needed by the
community. They raised the latter crops by dry farming because of
the limited water supply and the difficulties in delivering it to the
fields.[24] When the beet sugar industry became established after the
turn of the century, Washakie's settlers tested the viability of the crop
on the grounds of the Utah Sugar Company experimental farm near

Fielding, Utah. Some thereafter planted the new crop in their own fields. The Indians at Washakie also supplemented their agricultural and stock-raising income by making and selling gloves, moccasins, and beadwork.[25]

The Shoshone considered the farm and range lands at Washakie and at the old Lemuel's Garden settlement near Tremonton to be important assets in their farming and ranching operations. By the early 1880s, the "proving up" periods on the earliest homestead applications near the Malad began to expire, and the U.S. government began to award property patents to many of the Indians. In 1883, government officials approved patents for at least a dozen Indian applicants or their widows living in Box Elder County.[26] By the early 1890s, homestead applications, including Sagwitch's claim, filed on lands near the new settlement at Washakie began to mature. Sagwitch's widow, listed on the patent as Anna Tsyguitch, substantiated her claim to the homestead on October 28, 1890, and was awarded the deed to Sagwitch's 160-acre parcel on January 25, 1892.[27] Sagwitch's son Soquitch received a similar patent deed in 1891.[28] The land holdings of the Indians finally seemed secure.

As Washakie moved into the twentieth century, its residents faced new problems and opportunities. The most significant challenges were legal in nature. Many involved land disputes, with the United States government, neighboring settlers, and the LDS Church.

In 1931, Indians from Washakie, in league with other remnants of the Northwestern Shoshone tribe living in Utah, Idaho, Nevada, and Wyoming, initiated legal action against the government of the United States. The band requested nearly seventeen million dollars as compensation for the loss of fourteen million acres of land in Box Elder, Rich, and Cache counties in Utah and other lands in southern Idaho. The lawsuit also requested an accounting of annuities promised as part of the 1863 Treaty of Box Elder but never received by the tribe.[29] Several residents of Washakie testified in the case. Although the lawsuit did not succeed, it represented an important first step on the part of the Shoshone, who sought redress for the wrongs they had suffered, and it paved the way for additional and more successful litigation later on.

In the late 1930s, LDS officials initiated a new economic program at Washakie. Earlier Mormon involvement in the life of the community had been primarily tutorial: a few white families helped the Indians learn farming skills during the week and guided them in their Mormon worship on the Sabbath. A new policy, prompted by concerns over the low standard of living of many of Washakie's settlers, brought greater church involvement in the settlement's economy. In the early 1940s, the LDS Presiding Bishopric hired A. Fullmer Allred as farm manager to oversee Indian labor in communal fields and to pay wages to those employed. The church also began to replace the Indians' "shacks" with new standardized structures. A writer for the weekly church section of the *Deseret News* declared, "As each shack is wiped out and replaced by a better home and each Indian family accepts more and more of the responsibility for a better home life, this Indian village will become one of the bright spots of northern Utah."[30] Of course, many Indians continued to work their own lands or to seek employment away from the settlement. The Mormon Church's increased administration and financial involvement seemed to signal a philosophical change in how its leaders viewed the Indians. Church leaders, not recognizing the complexities of cultural diversity, increasingly came to see the Indians at Washakie as "wards of the church," rather than as capable equals.

Early in the twentieth century, non-Indians began raising funds for a marker at the site of the Bear River Massacre near Preston, Idaho. Such efforts sought to honor the soldiers who died on the battlefield or the role of Mormon women in nursing wounded troops back to health. No consideration was given to the very different story told by Sagwitch's sons and other survivors who still lived at Washakie. Nor was any effort made to interpret what the horrendous loss of Indian lives had meant to those most deeply affected.

The first effort to mark the battle site was mounted in 1917 by the Franklin County Historical Society. The organization raised money for a marker through the sale of a pamphlet titled "The Passing of the Redman." As one citizen remarked, "If ever any soldiers deserve to have their memories perpetuated for deeds of service and sacrifice—then the battle ground at Battle Creek deserves to be so marked."[31]

Construction of the proposed monument did not go unchallenged. Sagwitch's youngest son, Frank Timbimboo Warner, responded in a letter to the *Franklin County Citizen*. As a wounded survivor of the massacre, he could speak powerfully on the issue. After suggesting that the proposed marker would be nothing more than a "monument to cruelty," he noted that former soldiers had boasted of taking "little infants by the heels and beating their brains out on any hard substance they could find." Warner clearly understood how a political agenda could taint the interpretation of the past. Commenting on the fact that the massacre of his people had officially been labeled a battle, he noted, "I can't help but reflect how some men can make distinction between a battle royal and a massacre. I've heard a Mr. Dyer who took part in this battle, make the statement that that was a royal battle, but the battle of General Custer was a horrible massacre."[32] Warner's enlightened remarks were little heeded. It was the distractions of World War I and not his letter that initially blocked efforts to mark the battle site.

It was not until 1932 that a committee of citizens finally erected a marker at Battle Creek. Survivors of the massacre, including Sagwitch's sons Yeager and Soquitch and a good number of Shoshone from the area attended the dedication. One Native American later charged that Mormon leaders at Washakie forced the Indians to attend the "degrading" service in full costumed regalia.[33] The wording on the marker, which still stands today, documents a flawed interpretation of the massacre. Besides mentioning the death of Indian men it notes that "combatant women and children" were also killed. This inaccurate and incomplete marker stood alone as an interpretation of the site until 1990. On October 18, 1990, National Park Service officials, under authorization from chief historian Edwin C. Bearss, conducted the formal dedication of the massacre site as a national historic landmark. As part of the dedication proceedings, the name was officially changed from the Battle of Bear River to the Bear River Massacre, and officials placed new signage reflecting a more balanced history near the original marker.[34]

In 1963, family members, in cooperation with the Ogden Pioneer Luncheon Club chapter of the Sons of Utah Pioneers, placed a monument at Sagwitch's grave near Washakie, Utah. Seventy-nine years after his death, a carved granite stone finally marked the location of his final resting spot.[35]

Even as whites and Indians marked sites significant to the history of the Shoshone living at Washakie, that community's population

Dedication of Battle of Bear River marker, September 5, 1932. Moroni and Yeager Timbimboo attended the ceremony. Photograph courtesy Mae T. Parry.

Hazel Timbimboo Zundel, her husband Wallace Zundel, and Mae
Timbimboo Parry with Utah Governor Michael Leavitt. In the 1980s and
1990s, Sagwitch's descendants played active roles in the successful fight to
rename the Battle of Bear River as the Bear River Massacre and in efforts to
repatriate the remains of unidentified Native Americans and were
recognized by the Utah Arts Council and Governor Leavitt for outstanding
artistic contributions with beadwork. Photograph courtesy Mae T. Parry.

On June 1, 1971, Bruce
Parry, a direct
descendant of Sagwitch,
began serving as
director of Indian affairs
for the state of Utah. He
held the post for thirteen
years. Photograph
courtesy Mae T. Parry.

continued a slow decline. In fact, during the entire twentieth century, Washakie experienced only a few brief periods of population growth. In 1884 Washakie had boasted 259 residents and in 1892, 260.[36] By 1900 the settlement was reduced to 187 members and by 1920 to 114.[37] Several factors contributed to the declining population. Illnesses continued to take a horrible toll on Indian lives, especially on the young. Indian agent Lorenzo D. Creel visited Washakie in January 1915. He concluded that the colony was "gradually decreasing" and blamed much of the decline on a high infant mortality rate. Creel noted that of seven children born in the colony in 1914, only two had survived into the first month of 1915.[38]

Out-migration also contributed to the population decline. Some residents, unsatisfied with the limited economic opportunities at Washakie, began moving out early in the twentieth century. Many who left Washakie joined relatives and acquaintances at the Fort Hall reservation. Once there, the government enrolled them, and they became eligible to participate in relief programs and to receive annuities. When the LDS Church's assistant historian, Andrew Jenson, visited Washakie in 1920, he noted that many of the former residents of the settlement "had become discouraged" and moved to Fort Hall.[39]

Population losses early in the century, though significant, were not as great as those brought by World War II. The government drafted several of Washakie's young men into active service. It also employed a good number of Washakie's residents as civilian defense workers at Hill Field, the Ogden Air Depot, and other nearby military installations.[40] Others obtained employment in private industry. Many who were thus employed moved to communities closer to their work. At the end of the war, some chose not to return to their old homes. With new skills learned while employed at government facilities during the war, they were in great demand for their services in the booming postwar economy. Returning Washakie soldiers also brought new perspectives and a broader experience with them. Some, like Lee A. Neaman, who became the first Native American to graduate from Utah State University, took advantage of the G.I. Bill to further their educations. [41]

During the 1950s, out-migration and the death of the settlement's oldest members further depleted Washakie's population. By

1960, numbers had dropped so low that the community could no longer staff a full-fledged Mormon ward. As a result, church leaders dissolved the Washakie Ward eighty years after its founding.[42] The Washakie Branch that replaced it offered Sunday worship services but fewer meetings of auxiliary organizations. Still the population continued to decline. An entry in the Washakie Branch's manuscript history for September 30, 1965, is telling: "The moving away of the Neamans, Barelas and the Snows has left our Branch Membership sadly depleted. It is growing increasingly difficult to carry on even as a Branch because of our decrease in membership."[43] An entry in the same history for December 31, 1965, proved to be the final historical note for the branch. The writer reported, "The moving of the Pubigee family to Idaho brings our total Branch Membership to ten . . . The end of this year finds us with a very sad and vacant feeling concerning our Branch . . . We hope that every member of this Branch will be able to accept this as the will of the Lord and conduct themselves accordingly."[44] Stake leaders dissolved the Washakie Branch in January 1966, and invited the few residents still remaining at Washakie to worship with the Portage Ward Latter-day Saints, who met a few miles to the north.[45]

By 1970 only a few houses remained at Washakie. The Mormon Church had adopted the policy several years earlier of burning residential structures located on church-owned lands as soon as the Indians vacated them. This policy was effective in clearing the property for new uses, but it also ensured the quiet death of the settlement by giving the Indians little to return to. Many of Washakie's settlers viewed the policy as a violation of their rights and as an insult on the part of the church they loved and so long had served. Formal complaints voiced by those affected were aired in meetings with high-level LDS Church officials.[46] Though leaders promised to be more considerate in the future, it was clear that the church was not interested in continuing to oversee the nearly abandoned settlement. By the mid-1970s, most of the lands had been sold to a private party for a ranching operation, and the Washakie colony ceased to exist.

In 1988, the Northwestern Shoshone adopted a new constitution reaffirming their rights and powers as a federally recognized tribe. Appropriately, they also purchased 185 acres of land at the old

Washakie farm, with plans to someday construct a tribal headquarters building there.[47] In June 1996 the band was awarded a $1.8 million housing grant from the federal government. They hope to use the money to develop 15 low-income homes at Washakie for the band and to set up a staffed office to administer the grant.[48]

Notes

Preface

1. Brigham D. Madsen, *The Shoshoni Frontier and the Bear River Massacre* (Salt Lake City: University of Utah Press, 1985).
2. Ibid., 20–21.

Introduction

1. Warren L. D'Azevedo, ed., *Great Basin,* Handbook of North American Indians, vol. 11 (Washington: Smithsonian Institution, 1986), 98–99, 102–5.
2. Ibid., 171–72.
3. Ibid., 161–72; A. J. Simmonds, "The Fremonts and the Shoshonis," *Herald Journal/Cache (Logan),* 3 December 1993.
4. "Our Indians," *Corinne Reporter,* 8 November 1873.
5. D'Azevedo, *Great Basin,* 262–335.
6. Ibid; Brigham Madsen, *The Northern Shoshoni* (Caldwell: Caxton Printers, 1980).
7. Mae Timbimboo Parry, interview by Scott R. Christensen and A. J. Simmonds, 9 March 1988, Special Collections and University Archives, Utah State University, Logan, 2; George Washington Hill, "George Washington Hill papers, 1842–1883," LDS Church Archives, Salt Lake City; Logan Temple, "Indian ordinances record, 1885–1886," LDS Church Archives, Salt Lake City.
8. Julian H. Steward, *Basin-Plateau Aboriginal Sociopolitical Groups,* Smithsonian Institution, Bureau of American Ethnology Bulletin 120 (Washington, D.C.: GPO, 1938; reprint, Salt Lake City: University of Utah Press, 1970), 19, 41–42, 179. Parry, interview, 2–3; D'Azevedo, *Great Basin,* 266, 268.
9. Merlin R. Hovey, *An Early History of Cache Valley* (Logan: Cache Chamber of Commerce, ca. 1923) 4; Joshua T. Evans, "The Northwestern Shoshone Indians, (a) Under Tribal Organization and Government, (b) Under the Ecclesiastical Administration of the Church of Jesus Christ of Latter-day Saints as Exemplified at the Washakie Colony, Utah" (M.S. thesis, Utah State Agricultural College, 1938), 23; Steward, *Sociopolitical Groups,* 178–79, 200.

10. Parry, interview, 2.
11. Ibid., 3; Steward, *Sociopolitical Groups*, 179.
12. Phoebe Zundel Ward, interview by Charles E. Dibble, 31 July 1945, Special Collections, Marriott Library, University of Utah, Salt Lake City; Parry, interview, 3; Steward, *Sociopolitical Groups*, 19; D'Azevedo, *Great Basin*, 266; A. J. Simmonds, "Fires Now, Fires Back Then in Cache," *Herald Journal/Cache* (Logan), 19 August 1994.
13. Parry, interview, 2–3; D'Azevedo, *Great Basin*, 268.
14. Parry, interview, 3; D'Azevedo, *Great Basin*, 267–68; Steward, *Sociopolitical Groups*, 179.
15. Parry, interview, 2–3.
16. Ibid., 2; Steward, *Sociopolitical Groups*, 178; D'Azevedo, *Great Basin*, 266–67.
17. Parry, interview, 2; Steward, *Sociopolitical Groups*, 179; D'Azevedo, *Great Basin*, 268; "The Shoshones," *Deseret News*, 18 November 1874.
18. Steward, *Sociopolitical Groups*, 179; D'Azevedo, *Great Basin*, 267.
19. D'Azevedo, *Great Basin*, 268.
20. Parry, interview, 6.
21. Ibid., 2–3; D'Azevedo, *Great Basin*, 272–73; David Zundel, interview by Charles E. Dibble, 31 July 1945, Special Collections, Marriott Library, University of Utah, Salt Lake City.
22. D'Azevedo, *Great Basin*, 271, 630–40; *Deseret Evening News*, 27 August 1868.
23. D'Azevedo, *Great Basin*, 271–72; Steward, *Sociopolitical Groups*, 179.
24. David Zundel, interview.
25. Charles E. Dibble, "The Mormon Mission to the Shoshoni Indians, Part Three," *Utah Humanities Review* 1 (July 1947): 290.
26. D'Azevedo, *Great Basin*, 276; Steward, *Sociopolitical Groups*, 180; Jack S. Harris, "The White Knife Shoshoni of Nevada," in *Acculturation in Seven American Indian Tribes*, ed. Ralph Linton (New York: Appleton–Century, ca. 1940), 53.
27. Steward, *Sociopolitical Groups*, 178; D'Azevedo, *Great Basin*, 276.
28. Parry, interview, 1, 8; Steward, *Sociopolitical Groups*, 179–80.

Chapter 1

1. Mae Timbimboo Parry lists the names of Sagwitch's parents as "Pininnetze" and "Woowahrotoquap." She supplied the 1822 Sagwitch birthyear date; Parry, interview, 6. Amy Timbimboo lists the names of Sagwitch's parents as "Pin-in-netse" and "Woo-roats-rats-in-gwipe" and records Sagwitch's year of birth as 1823; Amy Hootchew Timbimboo, "Genealogical Records," n.d., in possession of Amy Hootchew Timbimboo, Clearfield, Utah. Sagwitch's headstone, erected in 1963, lists the names of his parents as "Beneanear" and "Woometadsegih" and his birth year as 1822. Hovey recounts an interview with Sagwitch, who said that he was four years of age when the horrible

winter came, causing his family to leave Cache Valley and the buffalo in northern Utah to die; Hovey, *Early History of Cache Valley*, 4. Evans discusses a conversation between Logan resident Thomas Galloway Lowe and Sagwitch. Sagwitch mentioned that he had been about four years old during the great winter (believed to be 1825–26) when all of the Utah buffalo died. Assuming that Sagwitch was referring to that year, he would have been born in 1821 or 1822. Evans, "The Northwestern Shoshone Indians," 23. Harris, "White Knife Shoshoni," 62–63. Sagwitch's descendants say that he had one brother, Sewahhoochew, and three sisters, Bowjanapumpychee, Duabowjanapumpychee, and Payhawoomenup. However, Sagwitch performed Mormon temple ordinances in March 1885 for Anga-poon-moot-say, who, he told temple workers, was also his brother; Logan Temple, "Indian Ordinances Record, 1885–1886," LDS Church Archives, Salt Lake City.

2. Parry, interview, 1. In the Western Shoshone dialect, mud or muddy is said as *pasakwinappeh*. "Sagwip" could easily be a derivative of that term. Wick R. Miller, *Newe Natekwinappeh: Shoshoni Stories and Dictionary*, Anthropological Papers 94 (Salt Lake City: University of Utah Press, 1972), 124.

3. Warren Angus Ferris, *Life in the Rocky Mountains: A Diary of Wanderings on the Sources of the Rivers Missouri, Columbia, and Colorado, 1830–1835* (Denver: Old West Publishing Company, 1983), 125.

4. Parry, interview, 7.

5. Ferris, *Life in the Rocky Mountains*, 372. Parry describes the application of this initiation procedure upon her father Moroni Timbimboo (1888–1975) when he was a young boy; Parry, interview, 7.

6. Parry, interview, 1, 7–8.

7. Ibid., 8.

8. Ibid., 2.

9. "Shoshone Indians," *Salt Lake Daily Herald*, 9 August 1874; Parry, interview, 18.

10. Parry, interview, 1, 8. Miller translates to talk or speak as *taikwaG* and *taikkwa*; Miller, *Newe Natekwinappeh*, 136.

11. "Shoshone Indians," *Salt Lake Daily Herald*, 9 August 1874; "The Indians on the Corinne-Indian Ejectment," George Washington Hill to editor, 31 August 1875, *Deseret Evening News*, 15 September 1875.

12. Parry states that Hewechee was Sagwitch's second wife; Parry, interview, 11. Entries by Amy Timbimboo state that Sagwitch married Hewechee in 1840, meaning that he had to have married Egypticheeadaday sometime before 1840; Timbimboo, "Genealogy." Egypticheeadady, "Coyote's Niece," is a phonetic spelling for Ica-ppíh-tí-cciattattai, a name formed from phonetic spelling for *ica-ppíh* or *isapai-ppeh* meaning "coyote," *tí* or *cci* meaning "little," and *cciattattai* or *ata* meaning "niece"; Miller, *Newe Natekwinappen*, 158, 165. The recorded entry for Yeager on the day he received his Mormon endowments (5 April 1875) lists his mother's name as "Ew-Wach." Yeager

would probably have supplied the name to the recorder personally, though cross-language misunderstandings could mean that it was recorded innacurately. Church of Jesus Christ of Latter-day Saints, "Endowment House Endowments Register, Book J, Lamanites, 14 June 1869–9 August 1875," Special Collections, Family History Library, Salt Lake City. Crum and Dayley give the Shoshone term for dove as *haiwi* or *haaiwi*; Hewechee, "Mourning Dove," is a common phonetic spelling for Haai-wicci. Beverly Crum and Jon Dayley, *Western Shoshoni Grammar*, Occasional Papers and Monographs in Cultural Anthropology and Linguistics, vol. 1 (Boise: Boise State University Press, 1993), 266.

13. Parry, interview, 14; Steward, *Sociopolitical Groups*, 215; Harris, "White Knife Shoshoni," 49–50.

14. Parry, interview, 11. Miller translates "young man" as *tuittsi*. The *cci* would be a diminutive ending meaning "small, little, or young"; The proper linguistic spelling for the name is Tua-na-ppucci. Soquitch is a common phonetic spelling for Soo-Kuiccih, composed of *soo*, "many," and *kuiccih*, "buffaloes." Miller, *Newe Natekwinappeh*, 114, 134, 142.

15. Mae Timbimboo Parry, unrecorded interview by Scott R. Christensen, 7 January 1995.

16. Parry, interview, 8, 10.

17. "The Pioneers of 1847," *The Historical Record* 9 (May 1890): 82–83; Church of Jesus Christ of Latter-day Saints, "Journal History of the Church, 1830–present," LDS Church Archives, Salt Lake City, 31 July 1847, 1.

18. Andrew Jenson, "Washakie Ward Manuscript History, 1847–1930"; Parry, interview, 5.

19. "Journal History," 1 August 1847, 2.

20. The statement was made by Nelson Higgins during a conference held in Salt Lake City August 22, 1847; "The Pioneers of 1847," *The Historical Record* 9 (June 1890): 98.

21. Parry, interview, 6, 11. Crum and Dayley translate "cottontail rabbit" as *tapun*. The diminutive ending *cci* means "small, little, or young"; Crum and Dayley, *Shoshoni Grammar*, 285.

22. Steward, *Sociopolitical Groups*, 177–78.

23. Ibid., 179–80. The name of Sagwitch's fellow-chief Kwudawuatsi is composed of three elements, *kwŧ ttih*, "to ejaculate," *wŧa*, "penis," and the diminutive ending *cci*.

24. Ibid., 180.

25. Parry, interview, 8.

26. Parry, interview, 17; Glen Fostner Harding, *A Record of the Ancestry, Family and Descendants of Abraham Harding: A Glover and Planter, Who Lived in Boston, Braintree, and Medfield, Massachusetts* (Ogden: Empire Press, 1979), 377; Laurine R. Liljenquist, "Experiences Related," n.d., Special Collections and University Archives, Merrill Library, Utah State University, Logan.

27. "Journal History," 24 May 1852, 1.

28. Thomas Witton Ellerbeck, "Diary, December 1852 to December 1853," LDS Church Archives, Salt Lake City, 5 September 1853. Ellerbeck was Brigham Young's chief clerk in this era.

29. "Talk with the Shoshones or Snakes," *Deseret News*, 7 September 1854; "Journal History," 4 September 1854, 1.

30. "Journal History," 12 October 1849, 1–3; *Deseret News*, 21 September 1850; "To the Saints: Latest News—Washington—Congress, &c," *Deseret News*, 12 June 1852.

31. "Journal History," 12 October 1849, 1–3.

32. Lorin Farr to Brigham Young, 16 September 1850, "Journal History," 16 September 1850, 1.

33. "Journal History," 9 May 1850, 1.

34. Ibid., 10 July 1851, 1.

35. *Deseret News*, 14 May 1853.

36. "Eleventh General Epistle of the Presidency of the Church of Jesus Christ of Latter Day Saints, to the Saints in the Valleys of the Mountains, and Those Scattered Abroad throughout the Earth," *Deseret News*, 13 April 1854.

37. *Deseret News*, 24 November 1853; "Journal History," 28 February 1854, 1; *Deseret News*, 1 December 1853; "Eleventh General Epistle," *Deseret News*, 13 April 1854.

38. John V. Bluth, "The Salmon River Mission: An Account of its Origin, Purpose, Growth and Abandonment," *Improvement Era* 3 (September 1900): 801–15, (October 1900): 900–913.

39. Dibble, "Mormon Mission to the Shoshoni," 280. Dibble quoted a document by George R. Hill titled "Life and Labors of George Washington Hill."

40. Dibble, "Mormon Mission to the Shoshoni," 281–83; Lawrence George Coates, "A History of Indian Education by the Mormons, 1830–1900" (Ph.D. diss., Ball State University, 1969), 207–21.

41. "Twenty Fourth of July Celebrations," *Deseret News*, 13 August 1856; Douglas Campbell, "'White' or 'Pure'; Five Vignettes," *Dialogue* 29 (Winter 1996): 35.

42. A. J. Simmonds, "The First Settlements, 1855–1860," Special Collections and University Archives, Merrill Library, Utah State University, Logan, 18–19.

43. Joel E. Ricks, ed., *The History of a Valley: Cache Valley, Utah-Idaho* (Salt Lake City: Deseret News Publishing Company, 1956), 29.

44. Isaac Clark to Brigham Young, 14 July 1851, Brigham Young, "Incoming Correspondence, Brigham Young Papers, 1832–1878," LDS Church Archives, Salt Lake City.

45. Ricks, *History of a Valley*, 28–31.

46. Ibid., 28.

47. Ibid., 33–34; Mary Ann Weston Maughan, "Journal," in *Our Pioneer Heritage*, ed. Kate B. Carter, vol. 2 (Salt Lake City: Daughters of Utah

Pioneers, 1959), 382–84; Mildred Allred Mercer, ed., *History of Tooele County* (Salt Lake City: Publishers Press, 1961), 19–20.

48. Parry, interview, 2–3.

49. Jacob Forney to Commissioner of Indian Affairs (hereafter cited as C.I.A.), 15 February 1859, U.S. Department of the Interior, Records of the Bureau of Indian Affairs, Record Group 75, "Letters Received, 1824–1881," Microcopy 234: "Utah Superintendency, 1849–1880," U.S. National Archives (hereafter cited as Interior, "Letters, Utah"), Roll 899.

50. Ricks, *History of a Valley*, 42–44; Victor Sorensen, "The Wasters and Destroyers: Community-Sponsored Predator Control in Early Utah Territory," *Utah Historical Quarterly* 62 (Winter 1994): 26–41.

51. Joel Edward Ricks, ed., "Memories of Early Days in Logan and Cache County," Special Collections and University Archives, Merrill Library, Utah State University Logan, 15 March, 12 April, 17 May 1924; Peter Maughan to Brigham Young, 4 June 1857, Young, "Incoming Correspondence."

52. Brigham Young to C.I.A., 12 September 1857, Interior, "Letters, Utah," Roll 898.

53. Jacob Forney to C.I.A., 5 November 1858, Interior, "Letters, Utah," Roll 898.

54. Madsen, *Shoshoni Frontier*, 102–3; "Indian Murders," *Deseret News*, 3 August 1859; "The Indian Massacre," *Deseret News*, 17 August 1859. Major Isaac Lynde was commander of the 7th Infantry investigating the Ferguson-Shepherd Company massacre. He concluded that initial reports that the emigrants had provoked the massacre by first killing two Indians were "utterly false." Major Isaac Lynde, Headquarters, Bear River Expedition, to Major F. J. Porter, 20 August 1859, U.S. Congress, Senate, *Message from the President of the United States to the Two Houses of Congress*, 36th Congress, 1st session, 1860, Executive Document 2, serial 1024, vol. 2, "Report of Secretary of War, 1st Part," 236.

55. Samuel Smith to Jacob Forney, 1 August 1859, Jacob Forney to Alfred Cumming, 2 August 1859, Interior, "Letters, Utah," Roll 899; "Emigrant Cruelty and Indian Revenge," J. C. Wright to editor, 1 August 1859, *Deseret News*, 3 August 1859; "Indian Troubles on the California Road," *Valley Tan*, 3 August 1859; "Indian Difficulties," Jacob Forney to editor, 9 August 1859, and J. H. Tippetts to Jacob Forney, 6 August 1859, *Deseret News*, 17 August 1859; Madsen, *Shoshoni Frontier*, 103.

56. Governor Alfred Cumming to General Albert S. Johnston, 3 August 1859; Major F. J. Porter to Major Isaac Lynde, Humbolt Expedition, 6 August 1859; and Major F. J. Porter to Lt. Ebenezer Gay, 6 August 1859, "Report of Secretary of War, 1st Part," 1860, 210, 213–14.

57. Jacob Forney to C.I.A., 10 August 1859, and Jacob Forney, Notice, n.d., Interior, "Letters, Utah," Roll 899; Jacob Forney to Major F. J. Porter, 22 September 1859, "Report of Secretary of War, 1st Part," 1860, 239–40.

58. "The Massacre of Emigrants on the California Road," *Valley Tan*, 17 August 1859; "The Late Indian Difficulties," *Deseret News*, 24 August 1859; Lydia

Walker Forsgren, *History of Box Elder County, Utah, 1851–1937* (Brigham City: Daughters of Utah Pioneers, Box Elder County Camp, 1937), 150–51. Forsgren incorrectly dates the 1859 Devil's Gate attack as occuring in 1860. Although this history states that Sagwitch's "squaw" was killed in a separate encounter, it is clear from a careful reading that the author is making reference to the Devil's Gate attack. Lt. Ebenezer Gay to Major F. J. Porter, 15 August 1859, "Report of Secretary of War, 1st Part," 1860, 219–20. The same letter is reprinted in *Valley Tan*, 24 August 1859 under "Correspondence." Madsen, *Shoshoni Frontier*, 104.

59.   Lt. Ebenezer Gay to Major F. J. Porter, 17 August 1859; Major Isaac Lynde to Major F. J. Porter, 20 August 1859; and Major Isaac Lynde to Major F. J. Porter, 2 September 1859, "Report of Secretary of War, 1st Part," 1860, 235–36, 238.

60.   Peter Maughan to Jacob Forney, 22 August 1859, and Peter Maughan to Brigham Young, 25 August 1859, Young, "Incoming Correspondence"; "The Late Indian Difficulties," *Deseret News*, 24 August 1859; "The Indian War at the North," *Deseret News*, 31 August 1859; "Journal History," 27, 29 August 1859; "The Walters Family Record, January 1914," Special Collections and University Archives, Merrill Library, Utah State University, Logan.

61.   "The Late Massacre Near Fort Hall," J. C. Wright to editor, 12 September 1859, *Deseret News*, 21 September 1859, 227; D. R. Eckels to Secretary of the Interior, 23 September 1859, Interior, "Letters, Utah," Roll 899; Madsen, *Shoshoni Frontier*, 105–8.

62.   Amy Timbimboo lists Sagwitch's third wife as Tan-dab-itche and her sons as Botong and Hni-nah-bok-a; Timbimboo, "Genealogy." Parry lists Sagwitch's third wife as Dadabaychee and her sons as Hinnah and Botoe, or variably Botong; Parry, interview. Crum and Dayley translate "the sun" as *tapai*. The most correct spelling for the name is Tan-tapai-cci. Tan means "fire" or "hot," and *cci* is a diminutive ending. Crum and Dayley, *Shoshoni Grammar*, 285.

63.   Peter Maughan to Brigham Young, 1 May 1860, and Ezra T. Benson to Brigham Young, 22 May 1860, Young, "Incoming Correspondence"; Henry Ballard, "Private Journal, 1852–1904," LDS Church Archives, Salt Lake City, 29 April 1860; "Cache Valley," *Deseret News*, 6 June 1860.

64.   Brigham Young to the Settlements in Cache Valley, 18 June 1860, Brigham Young, "Letterpress Copybooks, Brigham Young Papers, 1832–1878," LDS Church Archives, Salt Lake City.

65.   Peter Maughan to Brigham Young, 26 July 1860, Young, "Incoming Correspondence"; "Late Indian Murders in Cache," *Deseret News*, 1 August 1860; A. J. Simmonds, "The Smithfield Bones," *Herald Journal/Cache* (Logan), 30 July 1989.

66.   Ibid.; Brigham Young to Peter Maughan, 26 July 1860, Young, "Letterpress Copybooks"; Peter Maughan to Brigham Young, 29 July 1860, Young,

"Incoming Correspondence"; "From Cache County," *Deseret News*, 5 September 1860; Ballard, "Journal," 23–24 July 1860; Edward Tullidge, "The Cities of Cache Valley and Their Founders," *Tullidge's Quarterly Magazine* 1, no. 4 (July 1881): 536.

67.   "Trading with the Indians," Alvin Nichols to Colonel Benjamin Davies, 11 January 1861, *Deseret News*, 13 March 1861.

68.   "Indians from Cache," *Deseret News*, 3 April 1861.

69.   Seth Millington Blair, "Reminiscences and Journals, 1851–1868," LDS Church Archives, Salt Lake City, 20 July 1861, 56–57; Peter Maughan to Brigham Young, 15 July 1861, and Ezra T. Benson to Brigham Young, 22 July 1861, Young, "Incoming Correspondence"; Ballard, "Journal," 12–24 July 1861.

70.   Peter Maughan to Brigham Young, 18 September 1861, Young, "Incoming Correspondence"; Parry, interview, 12. Beshup comes from the Shoshone noun *pisappíh*, "red oquirrh," meaning a kind of clay used by the Shoshone as face paint; Miller, *Newe Natekwinappeh*, 158, 167. Crum and Dayley list Tempimpooh as the correct grammatical form for spelling Timbimboo, meaning "write on rocks, rockwriting, or petroglyphs"; Crum and Dayley, *Shoshoni Grammar*, 287. Utah State University professor Richley Crapo suggests that a more accurate form is Tímpin-poo, meaning "to mark or write on the rock."

71.   Peter Maughan to Brigham Young, 3 February 1862, Young, "Incoming Correspondence."

72.   Ibid.

73.   Family records say that the infant daughter of Sagwitch and Dadabychee was born in 1863; Parry, interview, 11–12; Timbimboo, "Genealogy." This is unlikely, since the infant was reportedly at least a few months old at the time of the Bear River Massacre, 29 January 1863.

74.   Peter Maughan to Brigham Young, 26 May 1862, Young, "Incoming Correspondence"; "From Cache County," *Deseret News*, 16 July 1862.

75.   "Indian Murders," *Deseret News*, 27 August 1862; "Murder of Emigrants in the Humboldt Country," *Deseret News*, 8 October 1862, quoting *Enterprise*, n.d.

76.   Major Edward McGarry to Col. Patrick Edward Connor, 31 October 1862, U.S. Congress, House, *The War of the Rebellion: A Compilation of the Official Records of the Union and Confederate Armies*, (Washington, D.C., 1897) 55th Congress, 1st session, number 59, series I, volume L, part 1, serial 3583, 178–79; Brigham D. Madsen, *Glory Hunter: A Biography of Patrick Edward Connor* (Salt Lake City: University of Utah Press, 1990), 60–63.

77.   Madsen, *Shoshoni Frontier*, 143, 169.

78.   "Indians Somewhat Troublesome," *Deseret News*, 10 September 1862; Peter Maughan to Brigham Young, 29 September 1862, Young, "Incoming Correspondence"; "Indian Depredations in Cache Valley," *Deseret News*, 8 October 1862; Ballard, "Journal," 23 September–5 October 1862.

79. Peter Maughan to Thomas W. Ellerbeck, 5 October 1862, Young, "Incoming Correspondence."

80. Madsen, *Shoshoni Frontier*, 154; James Duane Doty to C.I.A., 15 April 1862, Interior, "Letters, Utah," Roll 900.

81. Madsen, *Shoshoni Frontier*, 159; James Duane Doty to C.I.A., 26 November 1862, Interior, "Letters, Utah," Roll 900.

82. "Logan General Tithing Office Account Books, 1860–1907," LDS Church Archives, Salt Lake City. Original ledgers were filmed and destroyed in the early 1960s. Microfilms are blurry and difficult to read. Discernible entries seem to show that in 1861, the Logan tithing office dispersed $372.58 to Native Americans and, in 1862, a total of $953.35.

Chapter 2

1. "Expedition for the Recovery of a Captive," *Deseret News*, 26 November 1862. Joel Ricks quotes from writings of Henry Ballard, who described the Van Orman incident, in "Memories of Early Days," 15 March 1924. Madsen, *Shoshoni Frontier*, 172.

2. Major Edward McGarry to Lieut. Thomas S. Harris, 28 November 1862, *War of the Rebellion*, part 1, 182–83; Newell Hart, "Rescue of a Frontier Boy," *Utah Historical Quarterly* 33 (Winter 1965): 51–54.

3. Ibid.; Ballard, "Journal," 23–25 November 1862; James H. Martineau, "The Military History of Cache County," *Tullidge's Quarterly Magazine* 2, no. 1 (April 1882):125; Maughan, "Journal," 388.

4. "New Road North," *Deseret News*, 10 December 1862; A. J. Simmonds, "Indian Troubles on the Montana Road," *Herald Journal/Cache* (Logan), 19 August 1990.

5. "More Indian Murders," *Deseret News*, 14 January 1863.

6. "Another Expedition after Indians," *Deseret News*, 10 December 1862.

7. Ibid.

8. "No Fight with the Indians," *Deseret News*, 17 December 1862.

9. "Indian Difficulties in the Northern Counties—Present and Prospective," *Deseret News*, 31 December 1862.

10. "More Indian Outrages," *Deseret News*, 21 January 1863; "Expedition for the Arrest of Indian Chiefs," *Deseret News*, 28 January 1863.

11. "Expedition for the Arrest of Indian Chiefs," *Deseret News*, 28 January 1863.

12. Col. Patrick Edward Connor to Lt. Col. R. C. Drum, 6 February 1863, "Battle at Bear River, W.T., with Indians 29 January 1863," Records of the Adjutant General's Office, 1780s–1917, RG 94, Old Military Records Division, U.S. National Archives; the letter from Connor to Drum, 6 February 1863, was also published in *War of the Rebellion*, pt. 1, 187. Madsen, *Shoshoni Frontier*, 178–179.

13. Madsen, *Shoshoni Frontier*, 154–55.

14. Ibid., 179–80, 183; Connor to Drum, 6 February 1863, Adjutant General's Office; "The Fight with the Indians," *Deseret News*, 4 February 1863.

15.   Harold Schindler, *Orrin Porter Rockwell: Man of God, Son of Thunder,* rev. ed. (Salt Lake City: University of Utah Press, 1971), 321–22.

16.   Moroni Timbimboo, interview by Collin Sweeten, 9 December 1970, Charles Redd Center for Western Studies Oral History Project, Brigham Young University, Provo, 2.

17.   Daughters of Utah Pioneers, *The Trail Blazer: History of the Development of Southeastern Idaho,* 2d ed. (Preston: Cache Valley Newsletter Publishing Company, 1976), 130.

18.   Connor to Drum, 6 February 1863, Adjutant General's Office; "The Battle of Bear River," *Deseret News,* 11 February 1863; *Letters and Reports Referring to The Battle of Bear River, Utah, January 29, 1863* (Alta California, [1863]), 2.

19.   "The Fight at Battle Creek," *Franklin County Citizen,* 1 February 1917.

20.   Connor to Drum, 6 February 1863, Adjutant General's Office; "The Fight with the Indians," *Deseret News,* 4 February 1863; "The Battle of Bear River," *Deseret News,* 11 February 1863.

21.   Connor to Drum, 6 February 1863, Adjutant General's Office; "The Fight with the Indians," *Franklin County Citizen,* 1 February 1917; Madsen, *Shoshoni Frontier,* 186–87.

22.   Madsen, *Shoshoni Frontier,* 200; "'Sagwitch' Writes The Citizen about New Monument," F. W. Warner (Sagwitch) to editor, 9 June 1918, *Franklin County Citizen,* 11 July 1918.

23.   Alexander Stalker to Peter Maughan, 30 January 1863, "Journal History," 29 January 1863, 1–2; William Goforth Nelson, "Autobiographical Sketch, 1906," LDS Church Archives, Salt Lake City. 29 January 1863.

24.   "Journal History," 7 February 1863, 1; James Henry Martineau, "Map of Bear River Battle, 29 January 1863," LDS Church Archives; Samuel D. Roskelley to Presidents Ezra T. Benson and Peter Maughan, 8 February 1863, "Journal History," 8 February 1863, 1–2.

25.   Peter Maughan to Brigham Young, 4 February 1863, Young, "Incoming Correspondence."

26.   James Martineau, a local settler who viewed the battle ground immediately after the massacre and drew a map showing the site, estimated 160 men and 90 women and children killed for a total of 250; Martineau, "Map of Bear River Battle." Connor, in his official report, claimed 224 confirmed Indian deaths, with the acknowledgement that other dead had been missed in the hurried count; Connor to Drum, 6 February 1863, Adjutant General's Office. Ezra T. Benson estimated 235 Indians had been killed with many other Indian women and children badly wounded; Benson to Brigham Young, 31 January 1863, Brigham Young, "Incoming Correspondence." Peter Maughan estimated Indian casualties of 120 men and 90 women and children; Peter Maughan to Brigham Young, 4 February 1863. Indian superintendent James Doty reported 255 Indian men, women and children as casualties; James Duane Doty to C.I.A., 16 February 1863,

Interior, Letters, "Utah," Roll 901. A *Deseret News* reporter estimated Indian deaths at 250 to 300 people; "The Battle of Bear River," *Deseret News*, 11 February 1863. Mormon apostle Wilford Woodruff recorded on 3 February 1863 that 225 Indians had been killed; Scott G. Kenney, ed., *Wilford Woodruff's Journal, 1833–1898*, vol. 6, *Wilford Woodruff's Journal, 1 January 1862–31 December 1870* (Midvale: Signature Books, 1984), 95–96.

27. "The Fight with the Indians," *Deseret News*, 4 February 1863.

28. Ibid.; Connor to Drum, 6 February 1863, Adjutant General's Office; Ezra T. Benson to Brigham Young, 31 January 1863, Young, Incoming Correspondence."

29. "The Battle of Bear River," *Deseret News*, 11 February 1863.

30. D.U.P., *Trail Blazer*, 132.

31. Ibid., 131–32; Timbimboo, interview, 3; Alexander Stalker to Peter Maughan, 30 January 1863, "Journal History," 29 January 1863, 1–2.

32. D.U.P., *Trail Blazer*, 132–33; Parry, interview, 11–12.

33. "'Sagwitch' Writes The Citizen about New Monument," *Franklin County Citizen*, 11 July 1918.

34. D.U.P., *Trail Blazer*, 132–33; Roskelley to Benson and Maughan, 8 February 1863; J. H. M. to Mr. Editor, 22 March 1863, *Deseret News*, 1 April 1863.

35. Timbimboo, interview, 2; Roskelley to Benson and Maughan, 8 February 1863.

36. Roskelley to Benson and Maughan, 8 February 1863.

37. Verla Allen Comish Harris, "A Brief History of John Comish," 4, in possession of the author, Preston, Idaho.

38. Connor to Drum, 6 February 1863, Adjutant General's Office; James Duane Doty to C.I.A., 16 February 1863, Interior, "Letters, Utah," Roll 901; "The Battle of Bear River," *Deseret News*, 11 February 1863.

39. Ricks, "Memories of Early Days," 2, 9 February 1924. Ricks quotes from the writings of Margaret McNiel Ballard and Sarah Earl Harris.

40. Nelson, "Autobiography"; "The Fight at Battle Creek," *Franklin County Citizen*, 1 February 1917.

41. D.U.P., *Trail Blazer*, 131; Newell Scheib Hart, *The Bear River Massacre: Being a Complete Source Book and Story Book of the Genocidal Action Against the Shoshones in 1863—And of General P. E. Connor and How He Related to and Dealt with Indians and Mormons on the Western Frontier* (Preston: Cache Valley Newsletter Publishing Company, 1983), 125–26.

42. Ibid., 125–29; Parry, interview, 12.

43. Ralph Smith, "Journal," typescript, Special Collections and University Archives, Merrill Library, Utah State University, Logan, 28 January 1863, 4.

44. Ricks, "Memories of Early Days," 29 March 1924.

45. Ballard, "Journal," 29 January 1863.

46. Tullidge, "Cache Valley," 536–37.

47.   Peter Maughan to Brigham Young, 4 February 1863, Young, "Incoming Correspondence."

48.   Connor to Drum, 6 February 1863, Adjutant General's Office.

49.   Ibid.; Madsen, *Shoshoni Frontier*, 196–97.

50.   Alexander Stalker to Presidents Benson and Maughan, 8 February 1863, "Journal History," 8 February 1863, 1.

51.   Roskelley to Benson and Maughan, 8 February 1863.

52.   J. H. M to Mr. Editor, 22 March 1863, *Deseret News*, 1 April 1863.

53.   "Bannock City Express," *Deseret News*, 15 April 1863; "Indian War in Idaho," *Deseret News*, 13 May 1863.

54.   "Establishment of a New Military Post," *Deseret News*, 29 April 1863; "Military Expedition," *Deseret News*, 13 May 1863.

55.   Family traditions state that Sagwitch married Wongosoff's Mother after the 29 January 1863 massacre. It is likely that he married her within a few months of that event. Parry, interview, 12.

56.   Simmonds, "The First Settlements"; Ezra T. Benson and Peter Maughan to Daniel H. Wells, 9 May 1863, Utah Territorial Papers, Utah State Archives, Salt Lake City.

57.   Ibid. Ricks, "Memories of Early Days," 2 February 1924; Ricks quotes from the narrative of John Fish Wright.

58.   Parry, interview, 12-13; Ricks, "Memories of Early Days," 2 February 1924.

59.   Ibid.; Benson and Maughan to Wells, 9 May 1863, Utah Teritorial Papers.

60.   Peter Maughan to Brigham Young, 23 May 1863, Young, "Incoming Correspondence."

61.   Ibid.

62.   Parry, interview, 12–13. Ricks, "Memories of Early Days," 17 May 1924; Ricks quotes from the writings of Joel Ricks, Jr. Glen Fostner Harding and Ruth Johnson, *Barnard White: Convert to the L.D.S Church, 1854. Utah Pioneer, Bishop and Business Leader. Pioneer in Paradise, Cache County, Utah. Prominent in Weber and Box Elder Counties, Utah* (Provo: Brigham Young University Press, 1967), 22–24.

63.   "Indian Depredations in the Northern Counties," J. C. Wright to editor, 12 May 1863, *Deseret News*, 20 May 1863.

64.   Ibid.; "Indian Outrage in Box Elder County," *Deseret News*, 13 May 1863. Forsgren incorrectly states that this incident took place in December 1861. She is probably quite correct in the details of the attack on William Thorp, however. Her source for that information was a conversation with David Rees, a Brigham City resident who removed Thorp's mutilated body from the wagon after settlers brought it to Brigham City. Forsgren, *History of Box Elder*, 157. Maughan and Benson reported the Thorp murder to Wells and added that "the hostile Indians are the remains of the Bands that were in the fight at Bear River last winter and they say they intend having their pay out of the Mormons as they are afraid to tackle the soldiers, these things they have told us for some time past, but we hoped for the best and was unwilling

to believe they would carry their threats into effect untill we are obliged to, and while they are doing these things they are eating the very flour that has been donated to them by the brethern as we have never ceased to be kind to them as well as feed them." Benson and Maughan to Wells, 9 May 1863, Utah Territorial Papers,

65. "Indian Depredations in the Northern Counties," *Deseret News*, 20 May 1863.

66. Ibid.

67. "Recovery of Stolen Stock," *Deseret News*, 20 May 1863.

68. James Duane Doty to C.I.A., 20 June 1863 (two letters), Interior, "Letters, Utah," Roll 901.

69. James Duane Doty to C.I.A., 10 November 1863, Interior, "Letters, Utah," Roll 901.

70. Ibid.; "Murderous and Fiendish Act," *Deseret News*, 5 August 1863.

71. Ibid.; Parry, interview, 18–19.

72. Ibid.

73. James Duane Doty to C.I.A., 10 November 1863, Interior, "Letters, Utah," Roll 901; "Treaty with the Shoshones," *Deseret News*, 5 August 1863; Hugh F. O'Neil, Utah and the Mormons Collection, [n.d.], University of California (Berkeley), Bancroft Library. Within the O'Neil collection is a typescript of a lawsuit filed by Charles H. Merillat and Charles J. Kappler titled "The Northwestern Band or Tribe of Shoshone Indians and the Individual Members Therof, Petitioner, vs. United States of America, Defendant, filed March 28, 1931." These court documents include a typescript of the entire Treaty of Box Elder. Parry, interview, 18.

74. "Treaty with the Shoshones," *Deseret News*, 5 August 1863; Brigham D. Madsen, "The Northwestern Shoshoni in Cache Valley," in *Cache Valley: Essays on Her Past and People*, ed. Douglas D. Alder (Logan: Utah State University Press, 1976), 29; James Duane Doty to C.I.A., 10 November 1863, Interior, "Letters, Utah," Roll 901.

75. "Treaty with the Shoshones," *Deseret News*, 5 August 1863.

76. Robert E. Parson, *A History of Rich County* (Salt Lake City: Utah State Historical Society, 1996), 51; Ezra T. Benson to Brigham Young, 5 September 1863, Young, "Incoming Correspondence."

77. Leonard J. Arrington, "The Mormon Tithing House: A Frontier Business Institution," *The Business History Review* 28 (March 1954): 44–47.

78. Peter Maughan to Brigham Young, 28 July 1864, Young, "Incoming Correspondence."

79. Peter Maughan to editor, 25 July 1869, *Deseret News*, 4 August 1869.

80. Parry, interview, 20; Glen Fostner Harding, *A Record of the Ancestry, Life and Descendants of Amos Warner, Member of a Pioneering L.D.S. Family to Willard, Box Elder County, Utah. Early Settler in Malad, Oneida County, Idaho; Elba, Cassia County, Idaho; and Bear, Adams County, Idaho* (Provo: Brigham Young University Print Service, 1972), 8–9, 12–16.

81. "Indians North," *Deseret News*, 2 November 1865.

82. Parry, interview, 13. "Beahwoachee" comes from *pia*, "big," and *woa* or *wean*, "penis"; Miller, *Newe Natekwinappeh*, 156, 166.

83. Peter Maughan to Brigham Young, 29 May 1866, Ezra T. Benson to Brigham Young, 20 June 1866, Young, "Incoming Correspondence." For a detailed history of the Black Hawk War, see John Alton Peterson, "Mormons, Indians, and Gentiles and Utah's Black Hawk War," (Ph.D. diss., Arizona State University, 1993); and John Alton Peterson, *Utah's Black Hawk War* (Salt Lake City: University of Utah Press, 1998).

84. G. W. Thurston to editor, 12 April 1868, *Deseret News*, 22 April 1868; Peter Maughan to editor, 25 July 1869, *Deseret News*, 4 August 1869. Mary Ann Weston Maughan wrote about the Thurston girl in her autobiography. In part, she said "About 15 years afterwards, a gentleman acquainted with the stealing of little Rosie went to the East and visited some Indian's home and there he found a beautiful white girl dressed nicely and doing beadwork. This he believed to be our long lost Rosie, but she did not remember anything of her people, only her name was Rosie." Maughan, "Journal."

85. Peter Maughan to Daniel H. Wells, 29 March 1870, Young, "Incoming Correspondence."

86. Lewis L. Polmanteer, Affidavit, Paris, Rich Co. 18 June 1870, Young, "Incoming Correspondence."

87. Ibid.

88. Ibid.

89. Madsen, *The Northern Shoshoni*, 48–60.

90. Madsen, *The Northern Shoshoni*, 90–91.

91. J. E. Tourtellotte to C.I.A., 20 September 1869, U.S. Department of the Interior, Annual Report of the Commissioner of Indian Affairs, in Annual Report of the Secretary of the Interior, 1869 (Washington D.C.), 671–72; Laura Williams, "Henry A. Shaw History," v. 31, 43–44, Daughters of Utah Pioneers Museum, Ogden.

92. "Henry A. Shaw History"; Liljenquist, "Experiences."

93. Norval to editor, 13 August 1869, *Deseret News*, 25 August 1869.

94. Liljenquist, "Experiences"; "Henry A. Shaw History," v.31, 43–44.

95. Madsen, *The Northern Shoshoni*, 90–91.

96. M. P. Berry to C.I.A., 13 October, 1 November 1871, U.S. Department of the Interior, "Ft. Hall Letterbook, 1869–1875," Ft. Hall, Idaho, 91–94.

97. M. P. Berry to C.I.A., 24 November 1871, U.S. Department of the Interior, Records of the Bureau of Indian Affairs, Record Group 75, "Letters Received, 1824–1881," Microcopy 234: "Idaho Superintendency, 1864–1875," U.S. National Archives, Washington, D.C., Roll 339.

98. Ibid.

99. J. E. Tourtellotte to C.I.A., 20 September 1870, C.I.A., Annual Report, 1870, 605.

100. Peter Maughan to Daniel H. Wells, 29 March 1870, Young, "Incoming Correspondence"; Peter Maughan to J. J. Critchlow, 7 February 1871, Interior, "Letters, Utah," Roll 903.

101. Peter Maughan to Brigham Young, 14 July 1869, Young, "Incoming Correspondence".

102. Ibid., 28 October 1870.

103. Ibid., 24 May 1870.

104. Peter Maughan to J. J. Critchlow, 7 February 1871, Interior, "Letters, Utah," Roll 903.

105. Lorenzo H. Hatch to J. J. Critchlow, 10 February 1871, Interior, "Letters, Utah," Roll 903.

106. J. J. Critchlow to C.I.A., 17 April 1871, Interior, "Letters, Utah," Roll 903.

107. George W. Dodge to C. Delano, Secretary of the Interior, 10 October 1871, and George W. Dodge to C.I.A., 25 October 1871, Interior, "Letters, Utah," Roll 903.

Chapter 3

1. George W. Dodge to C.I.A., 6 January, 26 January 1872, Interior, "Letters, Utah," Roll 903.

2. George W. Dodge to C.I.A., 30 January 1872, Interior, "Letters, Utah," Roll 903.

3. George W. Dodge to C.I.A., 2 February, 18 March 1872, Interior, "Letters, Utah," Roll 903.

4. George W. Dodge to C.I.A., 18 March 1872, Interior, "Letters, Utah," Roll 903.

5. Ibid.

6. George W. Dodge to C.I.A., 20 April 1872, Interior, "Letters, Utah," Roll 903.

7. George W. Dodge to C.I.A., 26 April 1872, and George W. Dodge to C. Delano, Secretary of the Interior, 24 July 1872, Interior, "Letters, Utah," Roll 903.

8. George W. Dodge to C. Delano, Secretary of the Interior, 24 July 1872, Interior, "Letters, Utah," Roll 903.

9. George W. Dodge to C.I.A., 16, 31 August, 10, 17 September, 10, 28 October 1872, Interior, "Letters, Utah," Roll 903.

10. George W. Dodge to C.I.A., 16 August 1872, Interior, "Letters, Utah," Roll 903.

11. George W. Dodge to C.I.A., 31 August 1872, Interior, "Letters, Utah," Roll 903.

12. M. P. Berry to C.I.A., 5 December 1872, Interior, "Ft. Hall Letterbook," 133–34.

13. George W. Dodge to C.I.A., 3 October 1872, C.I.A., *Annual Report*, 1872, 678–679.

14. George W. Dodge to C.I.A., 7 December 1872, Interior, "Letters, Utah," Roll 903.

15. C. Delano, Secretary of the Interior, to C.I.A., 27 November 1872, and George W. Dodge to C.I.A., 11 December 1872, Interior, "Letters, Utah," Roll 903.

16. "Cache County Court, Record Book A, Census Report, 23 March 1872," Special Collections and University Archives, Merrill Library, Utah State University; "Cache Valley," *Salt Lake Daily Herald,* 11 August 1874.

17. George W. Dodge to C.I.A., 24 July 1872, Interior, "Letters, Utah," Roll 903; Madsen, *The Northern Shoshoni,* 198.

18. George W. Dodge to C.I.A., 24 July 1872, Interior, "Letters, Utah," Roll 903.

19. Charles E. Dibble, "The Mormon Mission to the Shoshoni Indians, Part Two" *Utah Humanities Review* 1 (April 1947): 166.

20. The Book of Mormon (Salt Lake City: Deseret Book Company, 1975), i.

21. Doctrine and Covenants of the Church of Jesus Christ of Latter-day Saints (Salt Lake City: Deseret Book Company, 1958), 32:1–3.

22. Parley P. Pratt, *The Autobiography of Parley Parker Pratt, One of the Twelve Apostles of the Church of Jesus Christ of Latter-day Saints: Embracing His Life, Ministry and Travels, with Extracts, in Prose and Verse, from his Miscellaneous Writings* (New York: Russell Brothers, 1874), 49, 58, 61.

23. Coates, "Indian Education."

24. Dibble, "Mormon Mission to the Shoshoni, Part Three," 288–89; Willard Z. Park, *Shamanism in Western North America* (Evanston and Chicago: Northwestern University Press, 1938), 23.

25. Ibid.

26. George Washington Hill, "An Indian Vision," *Juvenile Instructor* 12 (January 1877): 11.

27. George Washington Hill to C.I.A., Voucher, December 1872; George Washington Hill, Thomas S. Smith, John Knight to C.I.A., Statement concerning distribution of goods to the Northwestern bands on 7 April 1872, Interior, "Letters, Utah," Roll 903; George Washington Hill to C.I.A., 28 August 1874, Interior, "Letters, Utah," Roll 904; Ralph O. Brown, "The Life and Missionary Labors of George Washington Hill" (M.S. thesis, Brigham Young University, 1956), 32–34.

28. Brown, "George Washington Hill," 33–34.

29. Mae Parry related that her people always called George W. Hill Ankapompy; Parry, interview, 6. Hill spelled his Shoshone nickname as Ink-a-pompy; George Washington Hill, "My First Day's Work," *Juvenile Instructor* 10 (December 1875): 309. Dibble also documented the Shoshone nickname for Hill, but spelled it as Engumbambi; Dibble, "Mormon Mission to the Shoshoni, Part Three," 284.

30. Brown, "George Washington Hill," 57.

31. Ibid., 34.

32. George Washington Hill, "Cases of Miraculous Healing," *Juvenile Instructor* 15 (February 1880): 45; George Richard Hill, "Events in the Lives of

George Washington and Cynthia Stewart Hill, Utah Pioneers of 1847, As Recorded by Their Son George Richard Hill," Joel Edward Ricks Collection, Special Collections and University Archives, Merrill Library, Utah State University, Logan, 54.

33. Ibid.; Brown, "George Washington Hill," 35–36.

34. Brown, "George Washington Hill," 36; George Richard Hill, "Events," 54.

35. Brown, "George Washington Hill," 57; Hill, "My First Day's Work," 309.

36. George Washington Hill, "A Brief Acct of the Labors of G W Hill While Engaged on a Mission to the House of Israel, October 1, 1876," LDS Church Archives, Salt Lake City; Hill, "An Indian Vision," 11; Brown, "George Washington Hill," 57.

37. Brown, "George Washington Hill," p. 57, 59.

38. Ibid., 59; Hill, "An Indian Vision," 11.

39. Brown, "George Washington Hill," 59.

40. George Washington Hill, "Account of the Labors and Travels of G. W. Hill While Engaged on a Mission to the Lamanites," n.d. George Washington Hill Papers, LDS Church Archives, Salt Lake City.

41. Brown, "George Washington Hill," 60.

42. Hill, "My First Day's Work," 309; Brown, "George Washington Hill," 60.

43. Hill, "My First Day's Work," 309.

44. Brown, "George Washington Hill," 60.

45. Hill, "My First Day's Work," 309.

46. Brown, "George Washington Hill," 60.

47. Hill, "A Brief Acct"; Hill, "Labors and Travels"; Hill, "My First Day's Work," 309; George Washington Hill to Brigham Young, 6 May 1873, Young, "Incoming Correspondence." In most documents, including the last three cited in this note, Hill reports that he baptized 102 Indians rather than 101.

48. Hill, "A Brief Acct."

49. George Washington Hill to Brigham Young, 6 May 1873, Young, "Incoming Correspondence"; Hill, "My First Day's Work," 309.

50. George Washington Hill to Brigham Young, 6 May 1873, Young, "Incoming Correspondence."

51. Ibid.

52. George Washington Hill to Dimick B. Huntington, 7 May 1873, Young, "Incoming Correspondence."

53. "Journal History," 8 May 1873, 1.

54. Kenney, *Wilford Woodruff's Journal*, vol. 7, *1 January 1871–31 December 1880*, 135, 7 May 1873; "Journal History," 7 May 1873, 2.

55. "Journal History," 8 May 1873, 1.

56. "Shoshones," *Deseret Evening News*, 8 May 1873.

57. "Shoshones," *Deseret News*, 14 May 1873.

58. "Movements of Major Powell & Party," *Deseret News*, 21 May 1873; "Peace Talk," *Corinne Daily Reporter*, 5 November 1873; "Our Country Contemporaries," *Deseret Evening News*, 7 November 1873.

59. C.I.A., *Annual Report*, 1873, 41–42; C.I.A. to John Wesley Powell, 22 April 1873, Interior, "Letters, Utah," Roll 904.

60. H. W. Reed to C.I.A., 31 May 1873, Interior, "Ft. Hall Letterbook," 153–54; C.I.A., *Annual Report*, 1873, 42, 51.

61. G. W. Ingalls telegram to John Wesley Powell, 13 June 1873, Interior, "Letters, Utah," Roll 904; Madsen, *The Northern Shoshoni*, 94.

62. C.I.A., *Annual Report*, 1873, 45–46; John Wesley Powell to C.I.A., [18] June 1873, Interior, "Letters, Utah."

63. C.I.A. to John Wesley Powell, 25 June 1873, Interior, "Letters, Utah."

64. C.I.A., *Annual Report*, 1873, 48.

65. Brigham Young, Jr., to Brigham Young, 19 July 1873, Young, "Incoming Correspondence."

66. C.I.A., *Annual Report*, 1873, 48–49.

67. Ibid., 49.

68. George Washington Hill to Dimick B. Huntington, 27 October 1873, Young, "Incoming Correspondence."

69. *Corinne Daily Reporter*, 8 November 1873; *Deseret Evening News*, 10 November 1873.

70. *Corinne Daily Reporter*, 6, 7, 8, 11 November 1873.

71. "Our Indians," *Corinne Daily Reporter*, 8 November 1873.

72. Ibid.

73. Ibid.; *Deseret Evening News*, 10 November 1873.

74. *Deseret Evening News*, 10 November 1873.

75. George Washington Hill to Dimick B. Huntington, 8 June 1874, "Journal History," 8 June 1874, 5.

76. George Washington Hill to Brigham Young, 5 August 1873, Young, "Incoming Correspondence."

77. Hill, "A Brief Acct."

78. Parry, interview, 2–3.

79. "Shoshone Indians," *Salt Lake Daily Herald*, 9 August 1874; "Journal History," 9 August 1874, 4.

80. Hill to Huntington, 8 June 1874.

81. Ibid.

82. "Shoshone Indians," *Salt Lake Daily Herald*, 9 August 1874.

83. Hill to Huntington, 8 June 1874; Hill, "Labors and Travels."

84. Hill to Huntington, 8 June 1874.

85. "Shoshone Indians," *Salt Lake Daily Herald*, 9 August 1874.

86. Brown, "George Washington Hill," 61.

87. Hill to Huntington, 8 June 1874.

88. Brown, "George Washington Hill," 62.

89. "Shoshone Indians," *Salt Lake Daily Herald*, 9 August 1874.

90. Ibid.

91. Ibid.

92. George Washington Hill to C.I.A., 28 August 1874, Interior, "Letters, Utah," Roll 904.
93. Ibid.
94. Hill, "Labors and Travels."
95. Hill, "A Brief Acct."
96. George Washington Hill to C.I.A., 14 December 1874, Interior, "Letters, Utah," Roll 904.
97. "The Shoshones," *Deseret News*, 18 November 1874.

Chapter 4

1. "Annual General Conference," *Deseret News Weekly*, 14 April 1875.
2. George Washington Hill to Brigham Young, 25 August 1875, Young, "Incoming Correspondence."
3. "Endowment House Endowments Register, Book J," 1; Church of Jesus Christ of Latter-day Saints, "Endowment House Sealings (Living) Register, Book J," Special Collections, Family History Library, Salt Lake City, 193.
4. Kenney, *Wilford Woodruff's Journal*, vol. 7, 218, 22 February 1875.
5. George Washington Hill to Brigham Young, 5 May 1875, Young, "Incoming Correspondence."
6. Hill, "A Brief Acct."
7. George Washington Hill to Brigham Young, 5 May 1875, Young, "Incoming Correspondence."
8. George Washington Hill to Brigham Young, 25 August 1875, Young, "Incoming Correspondence."
9. Hill, "A Brief Acct."
10. George Washington Hill to Brigham Young, 25 August 1875, Young, "Incoming Correspondence."
11. Ibid.; Hill, "Labors and Travels." George Washington Hill, "The Indian Ejectment," *Deseret Evening News*, 27 August 1875; Hill noted that in setting up the new camp near Corinne, "The Indians here did some hundreds of dollars worth of work in clearing out the ditch, making a new dam, repairing the fences of the citizens of Malad City, &c., and here a temporary camp was established and crops were planted."
12. George Washington Hill to Brigham Young, 25 August 1875, Young, "Incoming Correspondence."
13. "Civilization among the Indians," *Deseret Evening News*, 22 July 1875.
14. Ibid.
15. Hill, "A Brief Acct"; "Civilization among the Indians," *Deseret Evening News*, 22 July 1875, identifies the three tribal groups at the camp.
16. George Washington Hill, "Some Items from My Journal," *Juvenile Instructor* 18 (February 1883): 37.
17. Dimick B. Huntington to Joseph F. Smith, 6 June 1875, *Millennial Star*, 5 July 1875, 426–27.

18. "Dixie in and out of the Camera," *Deseret News Weekly*, 28 April 1875; "St. George Items," *Millennial Star*, 19 April 1875, 247.

19. Brigham D. Madsen, *Corinne: The Gentile Capital of Utah* (Salt Lake City: Utah State Historical Society, 1980), 279.

20. Ibid.

21. "Mormonizing Indians: Joe's Band Ask for Baptism," *Salt Lake Daily Herald*, 12 June 1875.

22. "Remarkable Spiritual Movement among the Indians," Newum Bah to editor, *Deseret News*, 16 November 1874, *Ogden Junction*, 18 November 1874.

23. "The Indians," *Deseret Evening News*, 6 July 1875.

24. James Wright to C.I.A., 6 February 1875, Interior, "Ft. Hall Letterbook," 235.

25. Ibid., 237.

26. W. H. Danilson to C.I.A., 31 July 1875, Interior, "Ft. Hall Letterbook," 289–91.

27. James Irwin to C.I.A., 24 September 1875, C.I.A., *Annual Report*, 1875, 877–78.

28. Bannock and Shoshone [pseudo.], Fort Hall Indian Agency, Ross Fork, Idaho Territory, to editor, 16 August 1875, *Corinne Daily Mail*, 20 August 1875, reprinted under "The Corinne Affair: How the Idaho Indians Were Induced to Leave Their Reservations," *Salt Lake Daily Tribune*, 21 August 1875; "The Mormon-Indian Question: War and Extermination of Gentiles in Utah," *Salt Lake Daily Tribune*, 21 August 1875.

29. Dibble, "Mormon Mission to the Shoshoni, Part Three," 284.

30. Hill, "Labors and Travels."

31. George Washington Hill to Brigham Young, 25 August 1875, Young, "Incoming Correspondence."

32. "The Twenty-Fourth in the Country," *Deseret News Weekly*, 4 August 1875; "Pioneer's Day," *Corinne Daily Mail*, 26 July 1875.

33. George Washington Hill, "Cases of Miraculous Healing," *Juvenile Instructor* 15 (15 February 1880): 45–46.

34. George Washington Hill to Brigham Young, 16 July 1875, Young, "Incoming Correspondence." In this letter, Hill discusses the anticipated visit of Washakie and his entire band "comeing for baptism." Chief Washakie apparently did not reach the farm and receive baptism in 1875. He was baptised on 25 September 1880 by Amos R. Wright, in the Wind River Area; Amos R. Wright, "Indians baptized, confirmed, etc.," enclosure with Wright to John Taylor, 18 November 1880, "John Taylor Presidential Papers, 1877–1887," LDS Church Archives, Salt Lake City; Geneva Ensign Wright, *The Adventures of Amos Wright, Mormon Frontiersman* (Provo: Council Press, 1981), 317. Hill, "Papers"; this collection contains a notebook listing several Native American baptisms and ordinations, 1873–1876. An entry in the notebook for 5 May 1875 documents Chief Pocatello's baptism that same day in Salt Lake City. "Another

Indian Scare," *Deseret Evening News,* 16 August 1875, which concerns Pocatello and his entire band who were evicted with the others from the farm and by 16 August had encamped in Cache Valley. It is likely that they had already joined the LDS Church and settled at the farm before the Corinne scare forced them to flee.

35. George Washington Hill, "Some Items from My Journal," *Juvenile Instructor* 18 (1 Feb 1883): 37.

36. James Wright to C.I.A., 10 June 1875, Interior, "Letters, Idaho," Roll 343.

37. James Wright to C.I.A., 30 June 1875, Interior, "Ft. Hall Letterbook," 283–85.

38. W. H. Danilson to C.I.A., 31 July 1875, Interior, "Ft. Hall Letterbook," 289–91

39. "Brigham Battle Axes," *Corinne Daily Mail,* 9 July 1875; "Corinne Items," *Salt Lake Daily Herald,* 11 July 1875.

40. *Corinne Daily Reporter,* 22 August 1872; 20 March, 2 October 1873.

41. *Corinne Daily Reporter,* 25 January, 3 May, 18 September 1872; 7 February, 7 May, 9 May, 13 September, 18 October 1873.

42. "Indian Raid," *Daily Utah Reporter,* 14 February 1871; "Another Indian Raid: The Bench vs. the Tomahawk—Red-skins Attack a Judge—The Ermine Triumphant," *Daily Utah Reporter,* 15 February 1871; *Corinne Daily Reporter,* 4 April 1873; "Indian Raid," *Corinne Daily Reporter,* 14 April 1873; *Corinne Daily Reporter,* 2 October 1873.

43. *Corinne Daily Reporter,* 20 March 1873.

44. *Corinne Daily Reporter,* 18 April 1873. The beheaded Shoshone brave was probably John Indian, a noted friend to Cache Valley settlers who was employed for years by Mormon cattlemen as a stock herder; Ricks, "Memories of Early Days," 61, April 1924.

45. "Leg Off," *Corinne Daily Reporter,* 12 February 1873.

46. *Corinne Daily Reporter,* 18 October 1873.

47. Nat Stein "Corinne: Its Past, Present and Future. Written for, and Read at, the Pioneer Celebration of the Second Anniversary of the Settlement of the City," *Daily Utah Reporter,* 27 March 1871.

48. M. Le Baron de Hubner, *A Ramble Round the World*, 2d ed., trans. Lady Herbert (London: McMillan, 1874), 118; originally published as *Promenade Autor du Monde 1871 par M. Le Baron de Hubner* (Paris: Librairie Hachette et Cie, 1873).

49. *Corinne Daily Reporter,* 6 May 1872.

50. Brigham Young, "Discourse by President Brigham Young, Delivered in the New Tabernacle, Salt Lake City, Oct. 8, 1868," in *Journal of Discourses by President Brigham Young, His Two Counsellors, and The Twelve Apostles* (Liverpool: Albert Carrington, 1869), 287.

51. *Corinne Daily Reporter,* 27 February 1872; *Corinne Daily Mail,* 15 December 1874.

52. Madsen, *Corinne,* 259–67.

53. *Daily Corinne Reporter*, 2 October 1871. A follow-up editorial on 20 October 1871 admitted that such a union was probably not presently formed, but labeled the Indians and Mormons as "treacherous," and warned the reader to "keep a look out for events."

54. John Hanson Beadle, *The History of Mormonism: Its Rise, Progress Present Condition and Mysteries: Being an Expose of Secret Rites and Ceremonies of the Latter-Day Saints; With a Full and Authentic Account of Polygamy and the Mormon Sect from Its Origin to the Present Time* (1870; rpt., Toronto: A. H. Hovey, 1873).

55. *Corinne Daily Reporter*, 4 November 1872; "'Argus' Lecturing," *Corinne Daily Reporter*, 16, 17 January 1873.

56. "War Dance," *Corinne Daily Reporter*, 30 April 1873.

57. *Corinne Daily Mail*, 7, 10, 14, 15 December 1874.

58. *Corinne Daily Mail*, 21 December 1874.

59. "Endowment House Endowments Register, Book J."

60. Ibid.; "Endowment House Sealings (Living) Register, Books J and L"; Timbimboo, "Genealogical Records."

61. "Pocatello and the Garments," *Corinne Daily Mail*, 18 August 1875.

62. James Wright to C.I.A., 10 June 1875, Interior, "Letters, Idaho," Roll 343; W. H. Danilson to C.I.A., 31 July 1875, Interior, "Ft. Hall Letterbook," 289–91.

63. "Read and Remember! Letter from Fort Hall Indian Agency. Destruction and Slaughter Averted by the Prompt Action of Our Citizens. Now Let the Murderous Priesthood Speak! Positive and Reliable Evidence. An Investigation Demanded Immediately," *Corinne Daily Mail*, 20 August 1875.

64. "The Mormon-Indian Question: War and Extermination of Gentiles in Utah," *Salt Lake Daily Tribune*, 21 August 1875.

65. Hill, "Papers," includes a letter of Dimick B. Huntington to George Washington Hill, 9 August 1875. In this letter, Huntington told Hill to make arrangements for "an other company of worthy men and women to go through [the Endowment House]," and asked him to send groups of no more than thirty people, each with a written genealogy of his/her ancestors.

66. "The Verdict," *Salt Lake Daily Tribune*, 8 August 1875; "The Great Crime: The Voice of the Press Still Heard in the Land—Justice Must Be Done," *Salt Lake Daily Tribune*, 8 August 1875; "Blood Atonement: Brigham Young Openly Teaches It—Mountain Meadows Massacre One of the Results," *Salt Lake Daily Tribune*, 8 August 1875; "Bearing Testimony: The Crime of the Leaders of the Latter-day Fraud—Mountain Meadows," *Salt Lake Daily Tribune*, 10 August 1875; "Why Justice Is Delayed," *Salt Lake Daily Tribune*, 11 August 1875.

67. *Idaho Statesman*, 17 August 1875.

68. *Corinne Daily Mail*, 9 August 1875.

69. "Brigham Curses Corinne! Fruitless Attempts at Destruction!! Calls in the Indians, Baptizes Them, and Urges Them to Do His Dirty Work. Mormon Families Counseled to Leave," *Corinne Daily Mail*, 10 August 1875.

70. Ibid; General Cuvier Grover to Assistant Adjutant General, 27 August 1875, Department of the Platte, "Letters Received," 1875, Old Military Records, National Archives, Washington, D.C. (hereafter cited as Department of the Platte, "Letters"); "The Farcical Indian Scare at the Burgh on the Bear . . . ," Rudio, Corinne, Utah Territory, to editor, 12 August 1875, *Deseret Evening News,* 13 August 1875; "The Farce—At the Seat of War—Headquarters on the Banks of the Bear," *Salt Lake Herald,* 13 August 1875.
71. "The Farcical Indian Scare at the Burgh on the Bear . . . ," *Deseret Evening News,* 13 August 1875.
72. "The Farce—At the Seat of War—Headquarters on the Banks of the Bear," *Salt Lake Herald,* 13 August 1875.
73. Ibid.; "The Farcical Indian Scare at the Burgh on the Bear . . . ," *Deseret Evening News,* 13 August 1875.
74. "A Night of Terror!!!" *Corinne Daily Mail,* 11 August 1875.
75. "The Farcical Indian Scare at the Burgh on the Bear . . . ," *Deseret Evening News,* 13 August 1875.
76. Hill, "Labors and Travels"; "The Corinne Fraud: Statement of Geo. W. Hill—Barefaced Falsehood Exposed—Peacable Indians Compelled to Leave Their Ripened Crops," *Ogden Junction,* 14 August 1875; "The Indian Ejectment," *Deseret Evening News,* 27 August 1875.
77. Madsen, *Corinne,* 283; Hill, "Labors and Travels"; "Indian Ejectment," *Deseret Evening News,* 27 August 1875.
78. "An Indian Scare," *Deseret Evening News,* 11 August 1875; "For Shame, Corinne!" *Salt Lake Daily Herald,* 13 August 1875; "Tampering with Indians," *Salt Lake Daily Tribune,* 11 August 1875.
79. Hill, "Labors and Travels."
80. George Washington Hill to Brigham Young, 12 August 1875, Young, "Incoming Correspondence." Hill, "Labors and Travels," says "Sy guitch, John, Jim Brown, and Jack the Indian" accompanied him. "The Indian Ejectment," *Deseret Evening News,* 27 August 1875, says "two chiefs and my informant" accompanied Hill. Sagwitch and Indian Jack were at the meeting. It is possible that either John or Jim Brown was not. "Mormon Indians," *Salt Lake Daily Tribune,* 20 August 1875. In this article, W. H. Clipperton, who accompanied Captain James Kennington, Mayor Johnson, and Corinne businessman Louis Demers to the Indian farm to investigate the purported Indian attack, gives his report of the meeting with Hill and the Indian chiefs.
81. Hill, "Labors and Travels."
82. "The Indian Ejectment," *Deseret Evening News,* 27 August 1875.
83. George Washington Hill, Camp on Bear River, to Brigham Young, 12 August 1875, Young, "Incoming Correspondence"; Hill, "Labors and Travels"; "Our Country Contemporaries," *Ogden Junction,* 14 August 1875; "The Indian Ejectment," *Deseret Evening News,* 27 August 1875.

84. George Washington Hill, Camp on Bear River, to Brigham Young, 12 August 1875, Young, "Incoming Correspondence"; "The Indian Ejectment," *Deseret Evening News,* 27 August 1875.

85. Ibid.; "Our Country Contemporaries," *Ogden Junction,* 14 August 1875; Hill, "Labors and Travels."

86. "An Indian Scare," *Deseret Evening News,* 11 August 1875; *Corinne Daily Mail,* 11 August 1875.

87. "More Troops for Corinne," *Salt Lake Daily Tribune,* 12 August 1875; "The Indian Situation! Arrival of More Troops—Visit to the Indian Camps . . . ," *Corinne Daily Mail,* 12 August 1875. Companies H and K of the 14th Infantry were sent with Captain Carpenter.

88. *Corinne Daily Mail,* 12 August 1875; "The Corinne War!" *Salt Lake Daily Tribune,* 13 August 1875; Captain G. S. Carpenter to Major George D. Ruggles, 14 August 1875, Department of the Platte, "Letters."

89. Hill, "Labors and Travels."

90. "The Indian Ejectment," *Deseret Evening News,* 27 August 1875.

91. Captain G. S. Carpenter to Major George D. Ruggles, 14 August 1875, Department of the Platte, "Letters."

92. Ibid.

93. Ibid; "The Indian Ejectment," *Deseret Evening News,* 27 August 1875.

94. Ibid.

95. Hill, "Labors and Travels."

96. "The Indian Ejectment," *Deseret Evening News,* 27 August 1875.

97. By 1875, Sagwitch was regularly referred to as the "old chief." "The Farcical Indian Scare at the Burgh on the Bear . . . ," *Deseret Evening News,* 13 August 1875.

98. Hill, "Labors and Travels"; Brigham Young to W. C. Staines, 27 August 1875, "Letterpress Copybooks, Brigham Young Papers, 1832–1878," LDS Church Archives, Salt Lake City; "The Indian Ejectment," *Deseret Evening News,* 27 August 1875. An altercation arose when Louis Demers purposely mistranslated Sagwitch's statements, causing the chiefs to get very "excited" and Hill to tell Demers that "he was welcome to interprit but he had got to tell what the Indian [Sagwitch] said or keep his mouth shut." Demers responded to Hill's accusations in a letter published in the *Corinne Daily Mail* on 16 August 1875, where he stated "In reply to the above I will state that any person who says I did not interpret the language of the Indians correctly, or that Hill objected to my interpretation in my presence, is an unmitigated liar." Besides being the government interpreter during the Corinne incident, Demers was a long-time Corinne merchant who hated the Mormons.

99. *Salt Lake Daily Tribune,* 15 August 1875.

100. Madsen, *Corinne,* 285; "The Mormon Indian Trouble. The Appearance of the Military Frighten the Indians and Their Leaders. Citizens Returning to Their Homes. Bishop Hill Flees to Ogden on Foot. The Indians Promise to

Return to Their Reservation," *Corinne Daily Mail,* 13 August 1875; "Last of the Indian-Mormon Raid," *Salt Lake Daily Tribune,* 15 August 1875.

101.   "Telegraphic! . . . The Indians Leave Corinne," *Salt Lake Daily Tribune,* 14 August 1875; "Telegraphic! . . . The Indian Trouble," *Salt Lake Daily Tribune,* 12 August 1875, stated "He [Hill] denies any animosity to the inhabitants of Corinne or the whites generally; claims for the Sangwitch band of Indians staying in this neighborhood, all the land in Bear River Valley, says it was never sold to the Government."

102.   "The Indian Ejectment," *Deseret Evening News,* 27 August 1875.

103.   Ibid.

104.   "Telegraphic! . . . The Indians Leave Corinne," *Salt Lake Daily Tribune,* 14 August 1875.

105.   *Ogden Junction,* 21 August 1875; "Our Country Contemporaries," George Washington Hill, to editor, *Ogden Junction,* 20 August 1875, *Deseret Evening News,* 23 August 1875; "The Indian Ejectment," *Deseret Evening News,* 27 August 1875.

106.   Ibid.

107.   "Telegraphic! . . . .The Indians Leave Corinne," Salt Lake Daily Tribune, 14 August 1875; "The Redskins Depart. They Scatter in All Directions— Brigham's Game Checked. The Troops Return to Camp Douglas," Corinne Daily Mail, 14 August 1875.

108.   Glen Fostner Harding, *A Record of the Ancestry, Life and Descendants of Amos Warner,* 8–9, 12–16.

109.   Hansen Glen, was likely the dairy operation of the Brigham City Mercantile and Manufacturing Association, which was located in a wooded glen above Collinston, Utah, and run for the cooperative by Christian and Elizabeth Hansen; Amos Warner to George Washington Hill, 20 August 1875, George Washington Hill Collection, LDS Church Archives.

110.   "Another Indian Scare," *Deseret Evening News,* 16 August 1875.

111.   "The Battle-axes in Cache Valley," Salt Lake Tribune, 18 August 1875.

112.   Governor George W. Emery to General P. Sheridan, 21 August 1875, Department of the Platte, "Letters"; "Corinne Protected: The Citizens Supported by Government—General Sheridan Orders the Indians Away and Calls for Troops," *Salt Lake Daily Tribune,* 22 August 1875; "Troops for Corinne," *Corinne Daily Mail,* 23 August 1875; "A Guard for Corinne," *Deseret Evening News,* 23 August 1875.

113.   *Corinne Daily Mail,* 25 August 1875.

114.   General Cuvier Grover to Assistant Adjutant General, Department of the Platte, 27 August, 5 September 1875, Department of the Platte, "Letters." By the time these letters were composed, it apparently was no longer the position of senior military officials that the Mormons and Indians had ever intended to attack Corinne. In the August letter, General Grover stated "It does not appear that they [the Indians] committed any hostile acts, but they showed such an unfriendly disposition as to cause alarm." In the September

5 letter, Grover declared, "It is not thought that the Mormons are trying to influence the Indians to active hostilities against the non-mormons, but are trying to keep them off their reservations and away from the influence of the U.S. Authorities, and cause them to become so obnoxious to non-mormons in the way of stealing stock, damaging crops and property and frightening their families, that they, the non-mormons, will be forced to leave the country."

115. George Washington Hill to Brigham Young, 25 August 1875, Young, "Incoming Correspondence."

116. Ralph Owen Brown, "The Life and Missionary Labors of George Washington Hill" (M.S. thesis, Brigham Young University, 1956), 73. The scriptural reference referred to is found in the Book of Mormon, 3 Nephi 20:16.

117. *Corinne Daily Mail*, 27 August 1875.

118. George Washington Hill to Brigham Young, 25 August 1875, Young, "Incoming Correspondence."

119. Ibid.

120. Ibid.

121. Hill, "A Brief Acct."

122. "Poor Scared Corinne's Last Kick," *Deseret Evening News*, 13 August 1875.

123. Madsen, *Corinne*, 284–85.

124. "The Ejected Indians—Should They Not Be Reimbursed?" *Deseret Evening News*, 17 August 1875.

125. "For Shame, Corinne!" *Salt Lake Daily Herald*, 13 August, 1875; *Ogden Junction*, 14 August 1875; "Our Country Contemporaries," *Deseret Evening News*, 16 August 1875.

126. *Record Union* (Sacramento) as reprinted under "The Corinne Farce," *Deseret Evening News*, 16 August 1875; "The Threatened Indian Outbreak in Utah," *Corinne Daily Mail*, 16 August 1875.

127. *New North-West* (Montana), August 1875, as reprinted under "Almost Incredible," *Deseret Evening News*, 25 August 1875; *Helena Independent*, August 1875, as reprinted under "As Big a Hoax," *Deseret Evening News*, 29 September 1875.

128. *Omaha Herald*, 13 August 1875, as reprinted under "The Corinne Conspiracy," *Deseret Evening News*, 16 August 1875; "The Corinne Collapse," *Omaha Herald*, 14 August 1875; "The Corinne Conspiracy and Collapse," *Omaha Herald*, 18 August 1875.

129. Brigham Young to W. C. Staines, 27 August 1875, Young, "Letterpress Copybooks."

130. *Omaha Republican*, 7 September 1875, as reprinted under "Far West Sketches," *Deseret Evening News*, 16 September 1875; *Deseret News Weekly*, 29 September 1875.

131. Ibid.

132. W. H. Danilson to General Cuvier Grover, 20 August 1875, Department of the Platte, "Letters"; W. H. Danilson to C.I.A., 4 October 1875, Interior, Ft. Hall Letterbook, 309–10.

133. W. H. Danilson to C.I.A., 4 October 1875, Interior, Ft. Hall Letterbook, 309–10.
134. Published letter of James Irwin to C.I.A., 24 September 1875, C.I.A., Annual Report, 1875, 877–78.
135. *Ogden Freeman*, 31 August 1875, as republished in *Deseret Evening News*, 1 September 1875; Scott R. Christensen, "Chief Little Soldier: Shoshone Chieftain, Mormon Elder," *Pioneer* 42 (Winter 1995): 16–19.
136. Indian John in behalf of Tsyguitch's band of Sho-sho-nees, 31 August 1875, Young, "Incoming Correspondence," published under "The Indians on the Corinne—Indian Ejectment," *Deseret News Weekly*, 15 September 1875.
137. Ibid.
138. Hill, "A Brief Acct."
139. Ibid.
140. "The Situation," *Corinne Daily Mail*, 26 August 1875.
141. "A Visit to Brigham City," Mac [pseudo.], Salt Lake City, Utah Territory, to editor, *Deseret Evening News*, 31 August 1875.
142. Hill, "A Brief Acct"; Stan Andersen, "Corinne Incident," *Deseret News Magazine*, 16 January 1949.
143. "Correspondence: The Situation—Rabbit Hunt—Shooting Match—Preaching," *Deseret News Weekly*, 22 December 1875.

Chapter 5

1. Brigham Young to Willis Booth, 16 March 1876, Young, "Letterpress Copybooks." Similar letters were sent to W. Davis, Hooperville; Alvin Nichols, Charles Knudsen, John Jones, Brigham City; and George Marsh, Willard.
2. George Reynolds to George Washington Hill, 24 March 1876, Young, "Letterpress Copybooks."
3. Ibid.; Hill, "A Brief Acct."
4. "The Indian Farm in Malad Valley—An Interesting Settlement," A. Milton Musser to editor, 29 September 1876, *Deseret Evening News*, 30 September 1876 (hereafter cited as Musser, "Indian Farm"); *Portrait, Genealogical and Biographical Record of the State of Utah: Containing Biographies of Many Well Known Citizens of the Past and Present* (Chicago: National Historical Record Company, 1902), 72–73.
5. "The Arts of Peace," *Deseret Evening News*, 17 July 1876; George Washington Hill to Brigham Young, 15 August 1876, Young, "Incoming Correspondence"; Hill, "A Brief Acct." These three sources disagree slightly in their descriptions of the amount and types of produce planted at the farm.
6. Hill, "A Brief Acct."
7. Ibid.
8. Kenneth Dean Hunsaker, "Indian Town, Utah: A Pre-Washakie Settlement, 1983," Special Collections and University Archives, Merrill Library, Utah

State University, Logan; Tract Books of Utah, vol. 23, 1–12, microfilm, copy at Special Collections and University Archives, Merrill Library, Utah State University, Logan; *Statutes at Large of the United States*, vol. 18, part 3 (Washington, D.C.: Government Printing Office, 1875); Musser, "Indian Farm." Native American applicants were required to include an affidavit stating that, while formerly a member of a specified Indian tribe, they no longer claimed any connection with it. See homestead applications for Tsyguitch, Soquitch, and Yeager Tsyguitch, U.S. Bureau of Land Management, Homestead Applications and Patent Records for Utah, Record Group 49, National Archives, Washington, D.C.

9.   Donating clerks were Henry Tribe, Lorenzo Richards, Alford Stanford, Robert Watson, Thomas Wallace, F. A. Brown, Cranshaw and his son Ephraim, Orson Badger, Robert Harris, Job Pingree, H. S. Bloncet, and W. Farr, Hill, "A Brief Acct." Tract Books of Utah, vol. 23, 1–12.

10.   Musser, "Indian Farm."

11.   George Washington Hill to Brigham Young, 15 August 1876, Young, "Incoming Correspondence."

12.   Brigham Young to Elder Lot Smith and other Presidents of Companies, Little Colorado River, September 1876, Young, "Letterpress Copybooks."

13.   George Washington Hill to Brigham Young, 15 August 1876, Young, "Incoming Correspondence."

14.   Matthew William Dalton, "Excerpts from Matthew Wm. Dalton's Manuscript History, 1918," LDS Church Archives, Salt Lake City.

15.   Official LDS Church records acknowledge Sagwitch's grandson Moroni Timbimboo, as the first Native American to serve as an ecclesiastical bishop. He served as bishop of the Washakie Ward from 1939–45.

16.   Hill, "A Brief Acct"; Hunsaker, "Indian Town," 7; Tract Books of Utah, vol. 23, 1–12.

17.   Ibid.; Musser, "Indian Farm."

18.   Hill, "A Brief Acct"; "The Arts of Peace," *Deseret Evening News,* 17 July 1876.

19.   Musser, "Indian Farm."

20.   George Washington Hill to Brigham Young, 15 August 1876, Young, "Incoming Correspondence."

21.   Andrew Jenson, *Latter-Day Saint Biographical Encyclopedia: A Compilation of Biographical Sketches of Prominent Men and Women in the Church of Jesus Christ of Latter-day Saints* (Salt Lake City: Andrew Jenson History Company, 1901) vol. 1, 561.

22.   Hill, "A Brief Acct."

23.   George Washington Hill to Brigham Young, 15 August 1876, Young, "Incoming Correspondence."

24.   Brigham Young to George Washington Hill, 18 August 1876, Young, "Letterpress Copybooks."

25.   Ibid.

26. Brigham Young to Lot Smith and other Presidents of Companies, Little Colorado River, September 1876, Young, "Letterpress Copybooks."

27. Brigham Young to Dan W. Jones, 19 September 1876, Young, "Letterpress Copybooks."

28. "Corinne: Prosperity of the Gentile City—Big Crops—Collecting the Reds and Swindling the Government," *Salt Lake Daily Tribune*, 30 June 1876.

29. Ibid; "Corinne Items," Jabez [pseud.] to editor, 21 July 1876, *Salt Lake Daily Tribune*, 22 July 1876.

30. "The Arts of Peace," *Deseret Evening News*, 17 July 1876; Musser, "Indian Farm"; Hill, "A Brief Acct."

31. Dalton, "History."

32. George Washington Hill, Quarterly Report, 1 April 1877, Young, "Incoming Correspondence."

33. Dalton, "History."

34. Hill, "A Brief Acct."

35. "The Lamanites," *Deseret Evening News*, 18 December 1876.

36. Similar letters were sent to Garret Wolverton, Plymouth; Niles Booth, Brigham City; William Davis, Hooperville; and Asa Garner and Albern Allen, Ogden, John W. Young and Daniel H. Wells to Robert Holdroyd, 3 January 1877, Young, "Letterpress Copybooks." "Indians at Malad: Report of the Grand Jury," *Deseret News Weekly*, 3 October 1877; This report includes a copy of the 3 January 1877 letter from the First Presidency to Asa Garner of Ogden.

37. John W. Young and Daniel H. Wells to George B. Marsh, 5 January 1877, Young, "Letterpress Copybooks."

38. John W. Young and Daniel H. Wells to George Washington Hill, 5 January 1877, Young, "Letterpress Copybooks"; George Washington Hill to John W. Young and Daniel H. Wells, 7 January 1877, Young, "Incoming Correspondence."

39. John W. Young and Daniel H. Wells to Bishop William B. Preston, 3 January 1877, and John W. Young and Daniel H. Wells to Bishop Alvin Nichols, 5 January 1877, Young, "Letterpress Copybooks."

40. George Washington Hill, to George Reynolds, 28 January 1877, Young, "Incoming Correspondence."

41. George Washington Hill, Quarterly Report, 1 April 1877, Young, "Incoming Correspondence."

42. Ibid.

43. "Lemuels Garden" is referred to in most of George Washington Hill's 1877 correspondence and in his quarterly reports to the First Presidency.

44. George Washington Hill, Quarterly Report, 1 April 1877, Young, "Incoming Correspondence."

45. George Washington Hill to Brigham Young, 20 May 1877, Young, "Incoming Correspondence."

46. George Washington Hill to George Reynolds, 12 April 1877, Young, "Incoming Correspondence."

47. George Washington Hill, Quarterly Report, 1 July 1877, Young, "Incoming Correspondence."

48. George Washington Hill to Brigham Young, 30 June 1877, Young, "Incoming Correspondence."

49. George Washington Hill to Brigham Young, 15 August 1877, Young, "Incoming Correspondence."

50. George Washington Hill to [Brigham Young?], 15 August 1877, Young, "Incoming Correspondence."

51. "Corinne City Council Minute Book," 9, 11 April, 23 May 1877, microfilm, Utah State Historical Society, Salt Lake City.

52. *Corinne Record*, 22 May 1877, reprinted under "Mormons Peaceful, Indians Peaceful, but Still Send More Troops," *Deseret Evening News*, 23 May 1877.

53. Madsen, *Corinne*, 304–5; "Indians at Malad: Report of the Grand Jury," *Deseret News Weekly*, 3 October 1877; "How Many?" *Salt Lake Daily Herald*, 23 May 1877; "Mormon Land Grab: Using the Fort Hall Indians to Steal Uncle Sam's Real Estate," *Salt Lake Tribune*, 28 September 1877.

54. Ephraim Young to Secretary of the Interior, 9 August 1877, Interior, "Letters, Utah," Roll 905. The District Attorney for Utah Territory, Sumner Howard, seemed to question Ephraim Young's title of "late Secret Service detective" by placing a question mark after that name in a letter written to the United States Attorney General; see Sumner Howard to the United States Attorney General, 11 September 1877, Interior, "Letters, Utah," Roll 905.

55. Sumner Howard to the United States Attorney General, 11 September 1877, Interior, "Letters, Utah," Roll 905.

56. Ibid.

57. J. J. Critchlow to C.I.A., 4 October 1877, Interior, "Letters, Utah," Roll 905.

58. Ibid.

59. Ibid.

60. Governor George M. Emery to Secretary of the Interior, 2 October 1877, Interior, "Letters, Utah," Roll 905; "Troublesome Indians," *Salt Lake Tribune*, 3 October 1877.

61. George Washington Hill and John W. Hess to Hon. George Q. Cannon, 29 October 1877, Interior, "Letters, Utah," Roll 905.

62. J. J. Critchlow to C.I.A., 26 October 1877, Interior, "Letters, Utah," Roll 905.

63. W. H. Danilson to C.I.A., 22 November 1877, Interior, "Letters, Idaho," Roll 345.

64. Ibid.

65. "The Indians," *Deseret News Weekly*, 31 October 1877.

66. Joseph Standing to editor, 6 October 1877, *Deseret News Weekly*, 10 October 1877.

67. Madsen, *Corinne*, 304–5; "The Burg on the Bear," *Salt Lake Daily Herald*, 16 December 1877.

68. George Washington Hill, Quarterly Report, 1 July 1877, Young, "Incoming Correspondence."
69. The volume referred to is George Washington Hill, *Vocabulary of the Shoshone Language* (Salt Lake City: Deseret News Steam Printing Establishment, 1877).
70. *Deseret News, 1995–96 Church Almanac,* (Salt Lake City, Deseret News Press, 1994) 42.
71. George Washington Hill to John Taylor, 22 May 1878, Taylor, Presidential Papers; Brown, "George Washington Hill," 82; Phoebe Zundel Ward, interview by Charles E. Dibble, 31 July 1945, Special Collections, Marriott Library, University of Utah, Salt Lake City.
72. Lt. George M. Wheeler's survey party produced both a map and report; U.S. Army Corps of Engineers, *Geographical Survey West of the 100th Meridian* (Washington, D.C.: Government Printing Office, 1877). An original copy of the Wheeler survey map, including Indiantown, is held at Special Collections and University Archives, Merrill Library, Utah State University, Logan.
73. Box Elder Stake, "General Minutes, 1877–1927," 2 March, 2 June 1878, LDS Church Archives, Salt Lake City.
74. Isaac Zundel and John W. Hess to John Taylor and the brethren of The Twelve, 5 October 1877, Taylor, "Presidential Papers."
75. Isaac Zundel and John W. Hess, to John Taylor, 2 February 1878, Taylor, "Presidential Papers."
76. J. J. Critchlow to C.I.A., 8 May 1878, Interior, "Letters, Utah," Roll 906.
77. Ibid.
78. Ibid.
79. Ibid.
80. Census of the Indians Belonging to the Fort Hall Agency taken 3 November 1878, enclosed with a letter from Captain Augustus H. Bainbridge to the Adjutant General, Department of the Platte, 13 December 1878, Interior, "Letters, Idaho," Roll 351. The census document does not include the place of residence within the reservation. It is assumed that Sagwitch settled at Bannock Creek based on reminiscences of Sagwitch's descendants; see Parry, interview, 15.
81. Homestead applications and patent records for Utah, U.S. Bureau of Land Management, Record Group 49, National Archives, Washington, D.C.
82. Isaac Zundel to John Taylor, 20 August 1878, Taylor, "Presidential Papers."
83. Isaac Zundel and Alexander Hunsaker to John Taylor, 6 November 1879, Taylor, "Presidential Papers."
84. David Zundel, interview, 8–9; Forsgren, *History of Box Elder,* 153.
85. David Zundel, interview, 8.
86. Forsgren, *History of Box Elder,* 153.
87. Dibble, "Mormon Mission to the Shoshoni, Part Three," 287.
88. Forsgren, *History of Box Elder,* 153.

89. Isaac Zundel, Alexander Hunsaker, and Moroni Ward to John Taylor, Salt Lake City, Utah Territory, 23 May 1880, Taylor, "Presidential Papers."
90. Phoebe Zundel Ward, interview, 31 July 1945.
91. Ibid.; Isaac Zundel, Alexander Hunsaker, and Moroni Ward to John Taylor and Brethren of the Apostles, 14 July 1880, Taylor, "Presidential Papers."
92. Jenson, *Encyclopedia*, 561.
93. *Deseret Evening News*, 8 April 1880; Isaac Zundel to John Taylor, 30 November 1886, Taylor, "Presidential Papers."
94. Soquitch applied on 25 May 1881 for 160 acre parcel at Section 28/part of Section 29, Township 14 North, Range 3 West. Yeager applied on 21 February 1883 for 160 acres at Section 10, Township 13 North, Range 3 West; BLM, Record Group 49.
95. Sagwitch's [tsyguitch's] application is filed under Section 29, Township 14 North, Range 3 West, file 4422, application 6206, BLM, Record Group 49.
96. Ibid.
97. Mae Timbimboo Parry, interview by Kathy Bradford, 5 December 1985, collection of the author, Salt Lake City, Utah; Harding, *A Record of the Ancestry, Family and Descendants of Abraham Harding*, 401; Record of Appointment of Postmasters, Utah, Box Elder County, 732, National Archives, Washington, D.C. An entry in this ledger shows that the Washakie school teacher, James J. Chandler, was appointed postmaster at Washakie, Utah, on 7 April 1884
98. Box Elder Stake, "Minutes," 2 July, 1 October 1881.
99. James J. Chandler to John Taylor, 19 April 1885, Taylor, "Presidential Papers."
100. "From Malad," *Ogden Daily Herald*, 10 June 1882.
101. Dibble, "Mormon Mission to the Shoshoni, Part Three," 293.
102. David Zundel, interview, 8, 10–11, 13; Phoebe Zundel Ward, interview, 31 July 1945, 23–24.
103. Ibid.
104. Isaac Zundel to John Taylor, 12 December 1883, Taylor, "Presidential Papers."
105. "Fire at Washakie," *Deseret Evening News*, 7 September 1883.
106. Isaac Zundel to John Taylor, 4 September 1883, Taylor, "Presidential Papers."
107. "Washakie: Description of the Lamanitish City in Malad Valley," *The Utah Journal*, 1 December 1883.
108. Marion Knowles Everton, "Scrapbooks, 1935–36," Special Collections and University Archives, Merrill Library, Utah State University, Logan, clipping for 25 January 1936. The scrapbooks contain clippings from articles written by Everton and published in the *Herald Journal*.
109. "Washakie: Description of the Lamanitish City in Malad Valley," *Utah Journal*, 1 December 1883.
110. Dibble, "Mormon Mission to the Shoshoni, Part Three," 293.

111. Box Elder Stake, "Minutes," LDS Church Archives, Salt Lake City, 1 December 1877.
112. Isaac Zundel to John Taylor, 1 November 1880, Taylor, "Presidential Papers."
113. Dibble, "Mormon Mission to the Shoshoni, Part Three," 290.
114. Ibid; Phoebe Zundel Ward, interview by Charles W. Dibble, 1 August 1945, Special Collections, Marriott Library, University of Utah, Salt Lake City.
115. Box Elder Stake, "Minutes," Logan Temple stake donations financial report from May 1877 to April 1880, 59, LDS Church Archives, Salt Lake City.
116. "Washakie: Description of the Lamanitish City in Malad Valley," *Utah Journal*, 1 December 1883; Melvin Arthur Larkin, "The History of the L.D.S. Temple in Logan, Utah" (M.S. thesis, Utah State Agricultural College, 1954), 124.
117. Isaac Zundel to John Taylor, 20 August 1878, Taylor, "Presidential Papers."
118. Larkin, "History," 124.
119. Everton, "Scrapbooks," 20 December 1935; Larkin, "History," 124, states that the workers came in groups of ten.
120. Charles Ora Card to Isaac Zundel, April 21 1882, 143–44, Logan Temple, "Letterpress Copybooks, 1877–1908," LDS Church Archives, Salt Lake City; Everton, "Scrapbooks," 11 January 1936; Nolan Porter Olsen, *Logan Temple: The First 100 Years* (Logan: Keith W. Watkins and Sons, 1978) 17–20; Alfred E. Crookston, *The Temple Saw Mill* (Logan: n.p, n.d.), 2.
121. Everton, "Scrapbooks," 4 January 1936.
122. Everton, "Scrapbooks," 20 December 1935.
123. Charles O. Card to Isaac Zundel, 21 April 1882, Logan Temple, "Copybooks."
124. Logan Temple, "Indian Ordinances Record, 1885–1886," LDS Church Archives, Salt Lake City.
125. Isaac Zundel and John W. Hess to John Taylor, 18 March 1885, John W. Hess to John Taylor, 15 April 1885, Taylor, "Presidential Papers."
126. Isaac Zundel and Moroni Ward to John Taylor, 12 June 1885, Taylor, "Presidential Papers."
127. Isaac Zundel to John W. Hess, 28 July 1885, Taylor, "Presidential Papers." It is important to note that Zundel did not record in any surviving reports to President Taylor the names of the two Indians with whom he had the altercation at Lemuel's Garden. It seems very clear, however, after comparing Zundel's story with that which has passed down among Sagwitch's direct descendants, that Sagwitch and Yeager were the two men involved.
128. Ibid.
129. John W. Hess to John Taylor, 30 July 1885, Taylor, "Presidential Papers."
130. Parry, interview, 14–15.
131. Ibid; Mae Timbimboo Parry, unrecorded interview by Scott R. Christensen, 7 January 1995.
132. Isaac Zundel and John W. Hess to John Taylor, 23 August 1885, and John W. Hess and Isaac Zundel to John Taylor, 22 September 1885, Taylor, "Presidential Papers."

133. Parry, interview, 15. Isaac Zundel visited Bannock Creek in July 1886 and preached to nearly all of the Native Americans who lived there. He estimated the population to be two hundred people; Isaac Zundel to John Taylor, 17 July 1886, Taylor, "Presidential Papers."

134. Ibid. Family accounts say that Sagwitch and the others remained at Bannock Creek for two years before finally being coaxed to return to the Mormon settlement. Sagwitch was only gone from the settlement after the July 1885 altercation for six months. It is possible that the event has simply been remembered without a precise timeline. It is also possible that family accounts have combined two events: Sagwitch's circa 1879 to 1881 stay at Fort Hall, and the July 1885 altercation with Zundel. There is no way of clarifying the timeline more precisely.

135. John W. Hess to John Taylor, 7 December 1885, Taylor, "Presidential Papers." It should be noted that this letter, like the others concerning the July altercation, does not list by name the Indians involved.

136. John W. Hess to John Taylor, 25 December 1885, Taylor, "Presidential Papers."

137. "The Indian Farm," *Deseret News*, 22 April 1885.

138. John W. Hess to John Taylor, 16 January, 4 September 1886, Taylor, "Presidential Papers."

139. Isaac Zundel to John Taylor, 18 April 1886, Taylor, "Presidential Papers."

140. Ibid.

141. Ibid., 18 May 1886.

142. Ibid., 4 June 1886.

143. John W. Hess to John Taylor, 4 September 1886, Taylor, "Presidential Papers."

144. George Washington Hill to John Taylor, 21 September 1886, Taylor, "Presidential Papers."

145. George Washington Hill to John Taylor, 1 October 1886, 11 October 1886, Taylor, "Presidential Papers."

146. George Washington Hill to John Taylor, 12 October 1886, Taylor, "Presidential Papers."

147. John W. Hess to John Taylor, 14 October 1886, Taylor, "Presidential Papers." The seven men called as carpenters to build houses for the Indians were James Peterson (?), Eli (?) Jenson, John Forsgren, Oscar (?) Forsgren, John McMasters, Peter Baird, all of Brigham City, and John Jenson of Bear River City.

148. Isaac Zundel to John Taylor, 8 November, 3 December 1886, Taylor, "Presidential Papers."

149. John W. Hess, Isaac Zundel, Abraham Zundel, and Moroni Ward to John Taylor, 3 December 1886; John W. Hess to John Taylor, 4 January 1887, Taylor, "Presidential Papers."

150. John W. Hess, Isaac Zundel, Abraham Zundel, Moroni Ward to John Taylor, 3 December 1886, Taylor, "Presidential Papers."

151. Ibid.
152. Isaac Zundel to John Taylor, 10 January 1887, Taylor, "Presidential Papers."
153. Isaac Zundel and John W. Hess to John Taylor, 4 February, 28 February 1887, Taylor, "Presidential Papers."
154. Application by Tsyguitch (Sagwitch), application 6206, final certificate 4422, BLM, Record Group 49.
155. Jenson, "Washakie Ward History."
156. Logan Temple, "Indian Ordinances Record, 1885–1886."
157. Isaac Zundel to John Taylor, 30 November 1886, Taylor, "Presidential Papers."
158. Frank W. Warner to C.I.A., 22 February 1887, Record Group 75, miscellaneous letters, National Archives, Washington, D.C.
159. Mae Timbimboo Parry, unrecorded interview with Scott R. Christensen, 11 June 1998.
160. Isaac Zundel to John Taylor, 23 April 1885, Taylor, "Presidential Papers."
161. Isaac Zundel to John Taylor, 8 November 1886, Taylor, "Presidential Papers."
162. Timbimboo, interview.
163. Zundel was incarcerated on 17 June 1889 for polygamy. He served four months and was released; Jenson, *Encyclopedia*, 561.
164. Parry, interview, 14.
165. Ibid.; Timbimboo, interview, 3–4.

Epilogue

1. "Bishop Zundell's Wards: The Shoshones' Progress toward Civilization," *Deseret Evening News*, 9 September 1884; Parry, interview, 5. Zundel was probably referring to Shoshonitz and John Moemburg (or Moemburger). Moemburg, also known as Ejupitchee (Ica-ppi-cci), "Wolf," was Sagwitch's cousin. He spoke excellent English and was a great friend to many white people. For many years he functioned as Sagwitch's translator.
2. Timbimboo, interview, 8.
3. Jenson, who interviewed Indians at Washakie as he compiled his history, wrote about the leadership structure at the settlement. "Sagwitch became chief after Pahebuahgun was killed in the Bear River Battle. John [Moemburg] was an underchief with Sagwitch, he (Sagwitch) being the leading chief when all the Indians got together. John and others were simply leading men among the Indians"; Jenson, "Washakie Ward History." Parry noted that the leadership structure changed at Sagwitch's death and the position of chief essentially disappeared, making Sagwitch the last true chieftain of his people; Mae Timbimboo Parry, unrecorded interview by Scott R. Christensen, 7 January 1995.
4. "An Interesting Trip," *Deseret News*, 18 June 1883; "Washakie: A Visit to the Indian Settlement on the Malad," *Deseret Evening News*, 25 February

1892; "Washakie: Description of the Lamanitish City in Malad Valley," *Utah Journal*, 1 December 1883.

5. Washakie Ward, "Record of Members, 1885, 1891–1941," LDS Church Archives, Salt Lake City. Moroni, Ammon and Nephi are names of prophets in the Book of Mormon, Joseph Smith was the Mormon church's first prophet. Phoebe Zundel Ward, interview, 31 July 1945, 17; Ward stated in this interview that the white missionaries would "give them [the Shoshone] the [Mormon] names if they wanted them."

6. Dibble, "Mormon Mission to the Shoshoni, Part Three," 293; Jenson, "Washakie Ward History"; "Washakie Ward Elects All Indian Bishopric," *Salt Lake Tribune*, 29 January 1939.

7. *Idaho Enterprise*, 26 April 1923.

8. "Apostle Presides at Rites; Indians Attend," *Salt Lake Tribune*, 22 January 1939.

9. Jenson, "Washakie Ward History."

10. Ibid.; Isaac Zundel to John Taylor, 30 November 1886, Taylor, "Presidential Papers"; Frank W. Warner, "Missionary Journal, 1914 Nov.–1915 Jan.," LDS Church Archives, Salt Lake City; Harding, *Amos Warner*, 8; Glen F. Harding, *A Record of the Ancestry, Massachusetts Relatives and Direct Descendants of Dwight Harding: Convert in 1833 to The Church of Jesus Christ of Latter-day Saints. Pioneer to Utah and Willard (Utah) in 1851. Counselor in the First Willard Branch and Bishopric* (Provo: Brigham Young University Press, 1968), 495; Parry, interview, 21.

11. Jenson, "Washakie Ward History"; Parry, interview, 21.

12. Jenson, "Washakie Ward History"; "Washakie: A Visit to the Indian Settlement on the Malad," *Deseret Evening News*, 25 February 1892.

13. "Lamanite Testifies to Mormon People at Annual Conference: Address by Aborigine Dramatic Episode of Meeting; General Authorities Sustained and Session Ends," *Salt Lake Tribune*, 7 April 1926.

14. Ibid.; "Indians Quit Reservation; Come to City; Carry on Church Work; Farm Carefully," *Deseret News*, 6 April 1926; "Indian Conference Visitors," *Deseret News*, 10 April 1926; *Church of Jesus Christ of Latter-day Saints, Ninety-Sixth Annual Conference* (Salt Lake City: Church of Jesus Christ of Latter-day Saints, 1926) 136–138.

15. "Indian Conference Visitors," *Deseret News*, 10 April 1926. The photograph by George Edward Anderson is published in this paper. The location of the original is unknown.

16. Moroni Timbimboo served as bishop of the Washakie Ward for six years, and was released on 11 March 1945."Washakie Ward Elects All Indian Bishopric," *Salt Lake Tribune*, 29 January 1939; Church, "Journal History," 11 March 1945, 5.

17. "Journal History," 29 June 1935, 10.

18. Brian Parry (born 1945) served in the Central States Mission, 1965–67. Darren Bruce Parry (born 1960) served in the England, Manchester

Mission, 1979–81. Jeffery Brian Parry (born 1966) served in the Virginia, Roanoke Mission, 1986–88. Sherri Kay Warner served in the Dominican Republic, Santo Domingo East Mission.

19. Warner began his mission in January 1990, initially serving in the Austria Vienna East mission and working in Yugoslavia. Church leaders then asked him to proselytize in newly opened Bulgaria, where he served from November 1990 until February 1992. Jon Trent Warner, "Papers, 1989–1992," LDS Church Archives, Salt Lake City.

20. "Bishop Zundell's Wards: The Shoshones' Progress toward Civilization," *Deseret Evening News*, 9 September 1884; "The Indian Farm," *Deseret News*, 22 April 1885.

21. "From the Indian Farm: Sickness among the Children, Appearance of Crickets," *Ogden Daily Herald*, 27 June 1882; "Crickets," *Salt Lake Daily Herald*, 28 June 1882; Jenson, "Washakie Ward History." Parry noted that some Indians at Washakie felt that the fires which destroyed the two Washakie stores might have been purposefully set in order to destroy incriminating evidence concerning the misuse or theft of communal property; Parry, unrecorded interview.

22. Lawrence G. Coates, "Mormons and Social Change among the Shoshoni, 1853–1900," *Idaho Yesterdays* 15 (Winter 1972): 9.

23. Ibid.; Lorena Washines, untitled history of her father Lee A. Neaman, 1979, 9, 11, Special Collections and University Archives, Merrill Library, Utah State University, Logan.

24. "Bishop Zundell's Wards: The Shoshones' Progress toward Civilization," *Deseret Evening News*, 9 September 1884; "The Indian Farm," *Deseret News*, 22 April 1885; "Washakie: The Indians Have Raised Over 7,000 Bushels of Grain This Year," *Utah Journal*, 7 November 1885; "Washakie: A Visit to the Indian Settlement on the Malad," *Deseret Evening News*, 25 February 1892; "Prosperous Indian Settlement," Salop, Washakie, Utah, to editor, 24 May 1898, *Deseret Evening News*, 26 May 1898.

25. "The Indians Industrious: Working in the Beet Fields and Man and Wife Earn $3 Per Day," *Box Elder News*, 9 April 1903; "Washakie: An Indian Village," *Idaho Enterprise*, 26 April 1923.

26. "Indian Settlers," *Utah Journal*, 9 February 1883. Indians whose homestead applications had been approved were Wos Pitch, Que di gidge, Gaots Owa (widow of Pooe Owa), Tope Sanpitch, Charles Ahbuck, Shosho nits, Py-Numboo, Ashimbo Pitsy, John Mowberg (Moemburg), Que-endo-gitz, James Brown, and Mary Ticker (widow of Tigwe Ticker).

27. BLM, Record Group 49. Sagwitch filed homestead application 6206. His widow, Anna Tsyguitch, received homestead patent 4422 for his property. Anna Tsyguitch is probably Beawoachee, or Mogogah, generally acknowledged as Sagwitch's last wife. Parry feels that Anna Tsyguitch must have been an Anglo name given to Beawoachee, since, she says, it was Beawoachee, with her son from a previous marriage to Chief Bear Hunter,

who sold Sagwitch's 160-acre parcel several years after the patent had been awarded. Parry, unrecorded interview.

28. Sagwitch's son, Soquitch, filed homestead application 5249 and was awarded homestead patent 4329; BLM, Record Group 49.

29. O'Neil, Utah and the Mormons Collection; this collection contains a complete typescript of the 1931 lawsuit. "Indians Seek Compensation," *Deseret News,* 30 June 1931; "Indian Tribe Presses Claim at Washington," *Salt Lake Tribune,* 16 October 1931.

30. Henry A. Smith, "Visit with Indians at Washakie: Project to Aid Members Is Underway," *Deseret News Weekly Church Edition,* 8 August 1942; Washines, "History," 8–9.

31. "Over the Battle Creek Battle Ground with an Eye Witness," *Deseret Evening News,* 2 June 1917; Franklin County Historical Society and Monument Committee, "The Passing of the Redman: Being a Succinct Account of the Last Battle That Wrested Idaho from the Bondage of the Indians," (Preston: Franklin County Historical Society and Monument Committee, 1917).

32. "'Sagwitch' Writes the Citizen about New Monument," F. W. Warner (Sagwitch), Ashton, Idaho, to editor, 9 June 1918, *Franklin County Citizen,* 11 July 1918.

33. Washines, "History," 5.

34. Robert Merrill, "Site of Bear River Massacre to Be Dedicated Oct. 18," *Herald Journal,* 11 September 1990; John J. Wise, "Landmark Upgrade Not Imminent," *Herald Journal,* 11 June 1991.

35. The granite tablet marking Sagwitch's grave still stands where it was placed 25 May 1963 in the Washakie cemetary in northern Box Elder County. The text of the marker is as follows:

> SAGWITCH TIMBIMBOO PROMINENT SHOSHONI CHIEF. BORN 1822 NEAR PRESENT SITE OF BEAR RIVER CITY, BOX ELDER COUNTY, UTAH. DIED MARCH 20, 1884 WASHAKIE, UTAH. SON OF BEANEANEAR WOOMETADSEGIH. BAPTIZED INTO L.D.S. CHURCH AUG. 1875. GRANDFATHER OF MORONI TIMBIMBOO, BISHOP OF WASHAKIE WARD 1939–1945. ONE OF FEW SURVIVORS OF THE "BATTLE OF THE BEAR RIVER" JANUARY 1863. FIRST BURIAL IN WASHAKIE CEMETERY. ERECTED BY OGDEN PIONEER LUNCHEON CLUB CHAPTER OF SONS OF UTAH PIONEERS, MAY 25, 1963.

36. "Bishop Zundell's Wards: The Shoshones' Progress toward Civilization," *Deseret Evening News,* 9 September 1884; "Washakie: A Visit to the Indian Settlement on the Malad," *Deseret Evening News,* 25 February 1892.

37. Jenson, "Washakie Ward History."

38. "Impressed by Service of Washakie Indians," *Deseret Evening News,* 1 February 1915.

39. Jenson, "Washakie Ward History."

40. Timbimboo, interview, 9; Washines, "History," 9.

41. Lee A. Neaman to Nolan Porter Olsen, 31 January 1981, Nolan Porter Olsen papers, 1950–1979, LDS Church Archives, Salt Lake City.

42. "Journal History," 20 November 1960, 7.

43. Jenson, "Washakie Ward History."

44. Ibid.

45. "Journal History," 2 January 1966, 4.

46. Henry A. Smith, "Visit with Indians at Washakie: Project to Aid Members Is Underway," *Deseret News Weekly*, 8 August 1942; Washines, "History," 9–10; Timbimboo, interview, 8; Parry, unrecorded interview; Mae T. Parry, "Record of Meeting Held at the Church Office Bldg., Salt Lake City, Utah, 26 March 1973," copy courtesy Mae T. Parry, Clearfield, Utah.

47. "Constitution of the Northwestern Band of the Shoshoni Nation, 24 July 1988," copy of typescript in possession of the author; Jennifer Paul, "Shoshone Adopt New Constitution," *Standard Examiner*, 2 January 1988.

48. Cindy Yurth, "Shoshoni Awarded $1.8 Million Grant," *Herald Journal*, 28 June 1996; "Testimony of Mae Parry, Tribal Council Member, Northwestern Band of th Shoshoni Nation, before the Subcommittee on Interior and Related Agencies of the House Committee on Appropriations, March 3, 1992," copy in possession of the author.

Index

by nearby Shoshone population, 113,
114; anti-Mormonism of, 115, 117,
120; as freighting center for
Montana, 116, 117; opposes
Mormon-Shoshone alliance, 118,
120, 142, 147, 157, 158; residents
prepare for war, 121–25, 129, 130;
federal troops in, 122–28, 130;
Brigham Young responds to, 132,
133, 135; economic decline of, 147;
second "Indian scare" in, 153, 154
Cousins, Samuel, 31
Cowan, James, 31
Creel, Lorenzo D., 204
Critchlow, J. J., 75, 79, 154, 155, 156,
161, 162
Cub River Canyon, 60
Cumming, Alfred, 28
Cummings, B. F., 87
Cutler, Sheldon B., 30

D

Dadabaychee, 30, 34, 37, 54, 67
Dalton, Matthew, 135, 143, 147
Danilson, W. H.: replaces Wright as
Fort Hall agent, 71, 110; opposes
Mormon-Shoshone alliance, 113,
119, 152; questions how to feed
Indians after Corinne scare, 133;
denies G. W. Hill's request to visit
Fort Hall, 151–52; assigned to eval-
uate Bear River farm Shoshone,
156, 157
Danites, 115, 117
Davis, Benjamin, 33
Davis, William, 135
Dawes Act, 185
Delano, C., 76
Demers, Louis, 122, 125, 127
Devil's Gate, Utah, 29, 30, 37
Deweyville, Utah, 157, 174
Dodge, George W., 76, 77–82, 85, 92,
100
Doty, James Duane, 39, 40, 57, 64, 65,
66

Downey, John G., 38
Duabowjanapumpychee, 11

E

Eastern Shoshone, 2, 4, 64, 164
Ech-up-wy, 84
Egan Canyon, Nevada, 94
Eggleston, William, 140
Egyptitcheeadaday, 14, 30
Ejah, 91
Ejupitchee. See Moemberg, John
Elkhorn Ranch, Utah, 24
Elko, Nevada, 69
Emery, George W., 122, 124, 125, 130,
153, 155, 157
Empey's Ferry, 44
Endowment Ceremony (LDS), 104, 113,
118–19, 154, 177

F

Fairview, Utah, 147
Farrell, George L., 58
Ferguson-Shepherd Emigrant Train, 28,
29
Ferris, Warren Angus, 12
Fielding, Utah, 199
Flatheads, 21, 27, 28
Floyd-Hall, De Lancey, 71
Forney, Jacob, 25, 27, 28
Fort Bridger, 64, 65, 71
Fort Connor, Idaho, 64
Fort Hall, Idaho: uses Cache Valley as
herding ground, 24; emigrant train
attacked near, 30; Pine threatens to
drive Cache cattle to, 34; Shoshone
plan to attack Cache settlements,
69; Shoshone-Bannock Reservation
established at, 71; Shoshone
encouraged to settle at, 72, 80, 94,
131, 157; Indian population at, 73,
74, 112, 113, 155, 204; annuity distribution at, 74, 95, 101, 109, 110,
204; G. W. Ingalls visits, 93, 94;
Northwestern bands refuse to settle
at, 96, 133, 156, 162; agents oppose